Sometimes Rhythm

Sometimes Blues

Young African Americans
on Love,
Relationships,
Sex, and the
Search for Mr. Right

Sometimes Rhythm

Sometimes Blues

Young African Americans
on Love,
Relationships,
Sex, and the
Search for Mr. Right

Edited by Taigi Smith

SEAL PRESS

Sometimes Rhythm, Sometimes Blues:
Young African Americans on Love, Relationships, Sex,
and the Search for Mr. Right

© 2003 by Taigi Smith

Published by
Seal Press
An Imprint of Avalon Publishing Group Incorporated
1400 65th Street, Suite 250
Emeryville, CA 94608

"Love Letters" was excerpted from *Keepin' It Real,* published by Ballentine Books, © 1997 by Kevin Powell. Reprinted with permission of the author.

A version of Shawn E. Rhea's "Black, White, and Seeing Red All Over" appeared in *When Race Becomes Real: Black and White Writers Confront Their Personal Histories,* edited by Bernestine Singley and published by Chicago Review Press, © 2002. Reprinted with permission of the author.

Kristal Brent Zook's essay "Love Down Under" first appeared as a feature article in the July 2002 issue of *Essence* magazine. Reprinted with permission of the author.

asha bandele's essay is reprinted with the permission of Scribner, an imprint of Simon & Schuster Adult Publishing Group, from *The Prisoner's Wife: A Memoir* by asha bandele. © 2000 by asha bandele.

A version of Cheo Tyehimba's essay "I Don't Need No Man" first appeared in the March 2003 issue of *Honey* magazine. Reprinted with permission of the author.

Victor LaValle's essay "Big Time" first appeared on Nerve.com. Reprinted with permission of the author

Portions of "Security" by Leon Patillo reprinted with permission of Word Music Group, Inc., a division of Warner/Chappell Music, Inc.

Library of Congress Cataloging-in-Publication Data

ISBN 1-58005-096-4

9 8 7 6 5 4 3 2 1

Cover design by David Riedy
Interior design by Amber Pirker
Printed in the United States of America by Malloy
Distributed by Publishers Group West

I dedicate this book to those fearless enough to sing love songs while walking down the street alone: It is for those who dance to their own beats and love in a way that is soulful and real. These true stories are dedicated to those who love despite the odds, and most importantly, for anyone who recognizes that Black people loving other Black people is truly a revolutionary act.

Contents

Interview with Audrey B. Chapman

 The debate about the state of relationships between Black men and women is raging—Black men are dating White women, Black women expect too much and are driving away Black men, Black men won't commit . . . Opinions on what's really going on, especially amongst African Americans, vary widely, so in an effort to contextualize exactly what is happening with African-American twenty- and thirty-somethings, I consulted nationally recognized relationship expert and therapist Audrey B. Chapman, who has studied intimate relationships within the Black community for over twenty years. Here is what she had to say.

Smith: All of the writers in this book have heard about the difficulties that Black men and women have finding eligible marital partners. Is there a problem? Please set the record straight.

Chapman: There are two things we have to look at. There has always been a shortage of men period. Black or White. But then, when you look specifically at the African-American community, there are several factors that contribute to our marital decline, including economics and the fact that some men are choosing to relate to women outside of their ethnic group. Also, Black men are choosing different sexual orientations and there is a large group of men that Black women don't consider "quality men,"—meaning they're on drugs, alcohol, or in jail. When looking at all these factors, it narrows the numbers down to almost one man to every four women. And then, when you look at who's desirable to African-American women, the ratio of eligible men for Black women becomes even less—to one man for every *six* women. She wants him to look and be a certain way. She wants a certain stature, a certain physique, a certain complexion, a certain income, a certain worldly experience, a certain education, a certain family background—when you start doing all of that, the pool of eligible men narrows even more. Two generations ago, the woman didn't care what the man's background was. He needed to come from a good family, he needed to be churchgoing, and he needed to be a part of a community that was upstanding and if he worked for the railroad, and she was a schoolteacher or a nurse, than that was fine. He was chosen more for the content of his character rather than how he looked and how deep his pockets were. All of these superficial criteria are creating the marriage gap for Black women. And then, Black women tend to almost eliminate the small pool of men that are left. They're not interested in men in the military. That's one large, available pool of men. They're not interested in working-class men. That's another pool. They're not interested in a man who may be a little younger and they're not interested in Third-World men. That's another large pool. So, there are men there, but by the time Black women narrow down their prototype, and there is a prototype with African-American women, the number of eligible men diminishes substantially.

Smith: Is it wrong to have a prototype? Obviously it's limiting, but what's wrong with having a clear idea of what we're looking for?

Chapman: A strange thing has happened over the last few years. Somehow, people are more image conscious. They are more worried about what the person looks like and what their friends are going to think. That seems to be more of a big deal than "Is this a decent person?" Often Black women eliminate potential partners before getting to know them. The man gets eliminated before you can even find out who he is. A lot of

women tell me that it is not that they don't meet men—
they meet men. But many of them almost discard the guy
after the first meeting. If he doesn't come up to snuff on
the first meeting, or vice versa, he's gone. I think you have to
take more time to get to know a person. You have to go out
with him much, much longer before you figure out what's really there. And I'm not sure what the urgency is and what the
intolerance is. I'm still trying to understand that. Why is it
such a horrible thing to meet someone and explore a little bit
more of who he or she really is. At the very minimum, maybe
that person just ends up being a friend.

I think that in the last twenty to twenty-five years, Black
women have become more liberated and more financially
comfortable, but the thing that they've lost is their sense of
feeling safe, secure, and protected. There is this guardedness
with some Black women and it makes it difficult, symboli-
cally, for anyone to enter a room when all doors are locked.
As Black women, we want people to break the doors down
and fight to get in. Because of the supply and demand, men
don't have to do that! Frequently, I hear Black women discussing the double bind that they are in. Because of the
shortage of Black men, Black women are less likely to recognize when they are not compatible with their partners. In
fact, they hold on to that man and rarely release him,
thereby, making him to unavailable to other women. If it
isn't working with a particular man, release him!

Smith: Are we bringing baggage into our relationships as African
Americans—baggage that hurts our relationships?

Chapman: Everybody's got baggage—Black, White, Asian, Latino—it
doesn't matter who they are. Our baggage comes from our history, our family experiences, and the society we live in. We automatically have baggage, but some people are more aware of
their baggage than others. They work on their baggage differently. Then there are those who dump their baggage on
other people and decide that it's not them, but it is the other
person who has the baggage. These men and women refuse to
examine their emotional issues and won't look at how they're
baggage affects the other person they are trying to relate to.

Smith: What issues are you seeing in your private therapy practice
and in your workshops with African-American couples?

Chapman: There is an enormous amount of fear and need for control. No one wants to be vulnerable, when, in fact, the essence of loving someone is to render yourself vulnerable. No one wants to be in position where they feel that they are at risk of being hurt by another individual. Yet, to love someone is to open yourself up to the risk. That is the possibility when you love someone. No one wants to go through any changes anymore. No hassles, no challenges. Love is supposed to be the cure-all and it's supposed to take you to a level where you're almost on cloud nine—but that's just not the case. Love does not keep relationships together without the basic relationship tools. I see people in my private practice who give up on their marriages after a year. That was not the case many years ago. People struggled. They may have given it up, but it was after a long struggle. But, not now. Today, there is no tolerance and there is no patience. People don't realize the difference between sacrificing and being victimized and there's a great difference between the two. And, somehow, there's been such a emphasis placed on the material stuff—having credentials, having a title, having money—that there's been very little emphasis on the development of self.

Smith: Talk to me about the effects of materialism on African-American relationships. How does the "sense of entitlement" play itself out in our romantic relationships?

Chapman: Black women tell me that they feel entitled to have all of what they've worked very hard for. They are not settling. How dare anyone expect them to have to settle! And that attitude comes out, not just in words, but also in behavior. And the guy feels like he's not valued and that he's not good enough. These days, women want everything in place when the guy shows up. You can't always determine where a man will be five, six, or seven years from now. A woman is not entitled to have a man come into her life in a perfect package—especially when she doesn't have herself together.

Smith: Talk to me about interracial dating. How does the influx of Black men dating White women affect our relationships? Also, the new research indicates that Black women are dating White men now more than ever before. What are your thoughts on this?

Chapman: I have always said that Black women should have a rainbow coalition and I have advocated that for many years. I think Black men have always been ahead of the game in dating women outside of their ethnic group. During the Korean War and Vietnam War, Black men got involved with Asian women. Through the years, Black men have become comfortable marrying Latina women and certainly White women. Black men have always been ahead of the game on giving themselves options. Some Black women tell me they would not date the men who are dating women of other races anyways because they deem the non-Black women that Black men are dating physically and intellectually unacceptable. But, as time goes by, I think that Black women are starting to realize that if they don't start branching out and selecting men of other ethnic groups, they are going to be without men—period.

Smith: Do Black men and women have a difficult time communicating?

Chapman: Well, I think men and women of all ethnicities have a hard time communicating. I do think there's probably not enough emphasis on Black men and women getting training in basic skills needed to maintain healthy relationships.

Smith: What are the basic skills?

Chapman: It's communication. It's problem-solving skills. It's healthy conflict-resolution skills. It's being able to tolerate someone else's pain through the indulgence of empathy. In my workshops, I try to teach participants to be more empathetic of other people's experiences. The experiences that they are having in that moment with the other person should be validated by them, and as a partner, you need to try to understand it. Instead, what happens is people get very defensive, and when you get defensive, the arguments begin. I think Black men can be very macho, like many other men of color. The moment a woman tries to make a point and places emphasis on that point, the man starts to feel like he's being proven wrong. And because he can't be wrong, everything goes crazy. I spend a lot of time in private therapy practice asking men, "What do you think you heard her say?" Sometimes Black women can be very aggressive and intolerant which creates an argumentative atmosphere. We were raised to be independent, aggressive, and outspoken by our families. We were told not to depend on men and not to hang on their every word. We were taught to be the driving force. While those strengths are important, they are not the best strengths to have when you are in a relationship. When you are in a relationship, you have to have mutual balance and both people involved should know how to compliment the weaknesses and strengths of the other.

Smith: You've coined the term "gender blending." What does that mean?

Chapman: You've got women who have more masculine energy than feminine energy. If the woman has all the masculine energy and the man is feeling threatened by being forced to have the feminine energy, than the relationship doesn't work. She needs to strive for balance. When is the last time you let a man just open a door? Or pull out a chair? Or even help you with something? I think men should also work on gender blending.

Smith: Do men want to be needed?

Chapman: Yes. I just conducted a workshop called, "What Men Really Want That They Want Women to Know." We had a men's panel and the men kept saying that they wanted to feel needed. The man wants to hold that door for you and open the jar.

Smith: Do Black women walk around with obvious defense mechanisms?

Chapman: There's this chip, this air, this intensity. That edge is a turn-off—it's not a turn-on. Women have to become so conscious of their stuff and take responsibility. They're not likely to be approached because they're wearing this frown on their face and showing so much intensity. One guy told me, "I've given sisters up. They're too much work." He told me, " I can take a White woman out and she'll usually think about where we're gonna go. She'll come up with some ideas and bounce them off of me. She might even suggest that we go dutch. She pretty much goes with the flow. It's easy to talk to her. I'm not fighting with her." He told me, "I've got to fight with the man downtown everyday. I don't want to come home everyday to a partner that's harassing me." I also hear Black women say the same thing about the men.

Smith: Are Black men afraid to commit?

Chapman: Well, I've talked to an awful lot of Black women who've been used and abused, and now, they seem just as afraid of commitment. The men are avoiding commitment because they don't have to make the decision anymore and some of the women are avoiding it because they're not sure they want to pay the price.

Smith: What are the challenges that present themselves to Black people in marriages?

Chapman: Money is a big challenge. The person who makes the money has the power in the relationship. Racism also plays a big role—not allowing Black men to make as much money as White men make. Men need to feel like they're in control and that they're in charge and that they're breadwinners, but in today's world, often the woman is making more money than the man and that creates problems. There is a term called "marriage fit," and the belief is that most African Americans are not a good fit for each other because of the economic piece and the education piece. The average African-American man and woman have different concepts of what marriage is. I think expectations need to be explored in pre-marital therapy. I believe that if more people went to pre-marital therapy and did a twelve-week course or even a one-year course, and really prepared well, more people would stay together. They would have the tools required to make a marriage work.

Smith: Can a relationship between a blue-collar man and a white-collar woman be successful?

Chapman: It can work if you deal with the person for who he really is and not for what you really want him to be. If you marry a blue-collar man but you're constantly pushing college applications on him and trying to clean him up, then he's not going to like that. But if you can accept that you've married a blue-collar man who works for the telephone company and makes great money, then the marriage might work. The marriage can work if he doesn't run around, is a family man, plays with his children, and is church-attending. If the woman can accept him as he is, then it works.

Smith: What about him? Can he deal with it?

Chapman: The man can accept it if the woman doesn't cram it down his throat. It comes back to the one line that I say every week on my radio talk show: "How's your relationship with yourself?" If that's not in good shape, you aren't going to be able to have a good relationship with anybody else.

Smith: What kinds of Black women are finding partners?

Chapman: Women who are realistic, flexible, open-minded, broad-minded and emotionally healthy and secure are finding mates. These are women who have good relationships with themselves and their families. Women who find partners have strong supports systems and solid spiritual foundations—those are the ones.

Smith: Is there hope for single, Black women?

Chapman: There is hope if Black women work on being conscious of who they are and what gets in their way. You have to work on the hurts and the wounds that you will experience if you're out there trying to meet someone—if you work it out so that you don't take it out on the next person, than I do think you stand a chance. And Black women have to be more open-minded. Practice that rainbow coalition with zest!

Audrey B. Chapman is the author of several relationship books, including Seven Attitude Adjustments for Finding a Loving Man, *and* Getting Good Loving: How Black Men and Women Can Make Relationships Work. *Ms. Chapman is currently a therapist in private practice and has appeared on numerous television shows including* 20/20 *and* Good Morning America. *Chapman also conducts monthly relationship seminars and is the weekly host of a relationship-based radio show in Washington, D.C. She has been featured in the* Washington Post, Essence *Magazine,* Honey *Magazine, the* New York Times, *the* Los Angeles Times, *and several other publications.*

Introduction

Sometimes Rhythm, Sometimes Blues was born a few months after I turned twenty-nine, somewhere between the time I purchased my first piece of real estate, *alone*, and broke up with a boyfriend who couldn't get his life together even though he was pushing forty. It was then I ran down my roster of girlfriends and realized that each of us was college educated, financially stable, highly intelligent, sexy, goal-oriented, and—*single*. I looked at Michelle, the Ericas, Apryl, Rene, Melissa, Nateena, Lorna, Katrina, Valerie, Nikki, Tracy, Jill, Rochelle, Octavia, Donna, and, of course, me, and realized that while the White girls were comparing carats and planning weddings, the Black girls were sitting at home on Saturday nights watching movies, eating microwave popcorn, and talking on the telephone late into the night about—*brothers*. These late night conversations, which focused on the complex and the mundane, always led us back to one basic question: Why?

Why were we alone? Why weren't we getting married? Why couldn't Black men just "act right"? Why weren't our relationships working out? Why were brothers dating White girls? And why were we constantly feeling overlooked and under-appreciated by the men who should love us the most? We spent hours at the gym, the hair salon, the nail salon, in church, and at Victoria's Secret, and no matter how good we looked or how sweet we smelled, it just never seemed to be enough. We crammed our feet into stiletto heels and spent money on clothes we couldn't afford, all in the hopes of attracting our own, personal Mr. Right, but still, our efforts seemed useless. Through these talks I realized that many of my girls, myself included, were just plain fed-up with the drama and disappointment. It was in the midst of trying to understand this thing called love that *Sometimes Rhythm, Sometimes Blues* was born.

Some of us were afraid of becoming childless and had begun to consider the unthinkable: Perhaps we could freeze our eggs or convince our closest gay male friend to contribute a bit of sperm to our cause. We were reconfiguring our daily schedules and thinking about how to balance careers with single motherhood. Many of us had become sick and tired of hearing Black men make fun of the "biological clock," and quite frankly, I had personally become a bit irritated at the arrogance of many of the brothers I came across in social situations, of an attitude that said, "I'm single, educated, have no children, live alone, and am emotionally unavailable."

As Black women, we discuss brothas every chance we get: on the subway, at the gym, at the hair salon, and especially, over drinks with our girlfriends on Friday nights. We analyze Black men when we're riding the high of a new relationship and when we're feeling the rug of romance being snatched from under our feet. We're constantly trying to get to the bottom of the "issues" that plague our relationships with Black men, and all the while, we hold out hope, and pray, that perhaps in time, the complications that overtake and often times destroy our relationships will somehow smooth themselves out. As heterosexual, female twenty- and thirty-somethings we have found ourselves in an awkward predicament: Recent research shows that the heated conversations we've been having amongst ourselves for the past several years may actually be a part of a national trend. The startling research, documented in places like *Newsweek* magazine and by the U.S. Census Bureau, is telling the Black women of my generation something we've known all along: The number of eligible marriage partners for our generation has dwindled. More Black men are marrying White women, and more often than not, brothers are making the conscious decision to remain single for as long as possible. Many of these Black men are not incarcerated or uneducated, but instead, a good number of them are hardworking, college educated, professional members of the Black middle class.

According to a report released in 2002 by the Centers for Disease Control, Black women are least likely to marry and most likely to divorce, with more than half splitting within fifteen years. The explanation for this trend has to do, partially, with high levels of incarceration and un-employment among Black males. Recent census reports show that Black women are significantly less likely to marry than White women. By age thirty, 81 percent of White women have married compared to only 52 per-cent of Black women. The current federal population survey reported that the number of Black women who married White men more than tripled from 1980–2000, which is surprising, considering that histori-cally, Black women have always been resistant to marrying members outside of their ethnic group. During this same time period, the number of Black men who married White women more than doubled, going from 94,000 in 1980 to 227,000 by the year 2000.[1]

After obsessing over these statistics for months, both alone and in the company of my girlfriends, I realized that a dialogue was needed to help redirect the relationship path amongst members of my peer group. I re-alized that my generation was facing some serious relationship road-blocks and we needed to act quickly. It was time we started talking *to* one another instead of *about* each other. In a word, we needed to start a na-tional dialogue amongst ourselves about intimacy, love, relationships, and the pursuit of marriage. And, so, I contacted African-American writers na-tionwide in hopes of documenting this very pivotal moment in African-American history.

Writers write to make sense of those things that often have no rhyme or reason. We write so that our personal histories will not be forgotten, to immortalize ourselves in a world where loyalty to memory or oral history is scarce. We write in response to those thoughts that lurk in the deep crevices of our hearts and minds because we are unable to ignore those in-ternal voices that demand answers about who we are, what we stand for, and what our lives are all about. We write so that we will not forget about our joys and disappointments, past lovers, and old friends. On crowded trains, in tattered notebooks, on laptop computers, and on empty buses—we write. We write poems, e-mails, and letters without addresses. We rant and rave, get angry, write polemics with words that don't make sense and essays we pray no one will read until we've left this place. And sometimes, when we've sunk to the bottom of the well, with our shoulders hunched and our hearts hardened, we write towards a place of understanding, hoping to reach a comfort zone. So, in a sense, when it all gets too much to handle, when our life experience embit-ters us or makes us sad, we write in search of solace—with hopes that at some point love and life, and all things worth loving, will eventually converge. We write to live. We write to breathe. And most importantly, we write to heal. With nothing to lose, I contacted writers across the country, instinctively knowing that they, like me, would have something to say. I was hoping to start a national conversation about love and relationships using the first-person essay as a vehicle toward understanding.

Sometimes Rhythm, Sometimes Blues is the result, a compilation of first-person responses by women, both single and married, that work to make sense of the statistics. A special section of this book, "Talking Back," features five essays by Black men that speak directly to the issues of love and relationships. (It should be noted that two of the male essayists are married to Black women.) I started this project because I refused to believe that an entire group of young, Black women would have to give up their dreams of marriage and family. At just twenty-nine years old, these statistics were basically telling me that my dreams for a happy, stable marital relationship might go up in smoke.

I had and still have a hard time believing that Black men in this country don't want healthy relationships, companionship, and families with Black women. The essays in this book were written by writers who also refused to take the statistics sitting down. Even more importantly, every contributor was courageous enough to tackle the "issues" head on, addressing the effects of racism, economic inequality, infidelity, "broken" families, single-parenting, socioeconomics, materialism, incarceration, hip-hop, and yes, White women, on African-American relationships. But the search for truth only begins there.

Each of these essays is a personal glimpse into one person's experience with love, marriage, or intimacy. As writers, we have allowed you, the reader, to journey, if only for a moment, into our bedrooms, our relationships, and our minds. At times, as writers, we become naked, baring our souls and bodies to any and all who will listen. I often equate the process of writing the first-person narrative to stepping outside without one's clothes, in front of hundreds of people. Through these essays, we've let it all hang out by telling stories about our relationships, both positive and negative, that will help us, and hopefully our readers, reach a place of clarity, hope, and, most importantly, understanding.

I started this project expecting to receive hundreds of essays from women with bruised hearts and broken egos, but instead, I received tales full of strength, passion, wisdom, and wit. What surprised me most was that more Black women were actually married than I ever imagined, and not only were they married, but they were also willing to put their relationships under the microscope in hopes of helping other Black people understand just how challenging, beautiful, and complex the institution of marriage actually is. The essays in this book are uplifting, spellbinding, sometimes sad, and brutally honest. There are stories of love and stories of loss, tales of pain and tales of commitment. Some of these essays were written by women who refused to give up on love, and some by women who threw in the towel, not because they were weak, but because they were strong enough to make difficult decisions in order to preserve their souls and their beings. I see these essays as distinct musical notes that together construct a rocky orchestra of truth.

These stories not only give life to the statistics, they also smash the figures into a million tiny pieces, illustrating that, contrary to popular belief, African Americans are getting married, having children, and working furiously to construct "normal" families. As a group, Black women are working towards healthy relationships, and most importantly, those of us who are single are moving forward, achieving personal goals, developing tight relationships with our sistergirls, and maintaining hope. We're taking the stereotype of the "old maid" and stomping on it, opting to travel, start businesses, pursue careers, pamper ourselves, and develop our spirituality, instead of waiting for Mr. Right to show up on the doorstep. The statistics may show that a large number of us are single, but they also shout loud and clear that Black women are educating ourselves, pursuing careers, heading companies, buying homes, and making their own money. Considering the damaging legacy of slavery from whence we came, that's saying *a lot*.

Many women in my generation grew up witnessing our grandparents' stable, loving relationships. For many of us, our grandparents have become the relationship models that guide us. At the same time, there is an entire generation of young African Americans (myself included) who were raised by single mothers. It is my opinion that the male and female members of my generation have reacted differently to growing up under the watchful eyes of single women. During the conversations I've had over the years, I've learned that many of my peers, the female members of the new middle class, want nothing more than to have "normal," healthy relationships. We want to replicate the relationships we saw our grandmothers have with our grandfathers. Many of us don't want to be single parents, but instead have made the conscious decision to raise our children in two-parent households. And then there are those of us who have chosen to have children without significant others because we are in economic positions to support our offspring single-handedly. We have decided to "go it alone" instead of waiting around for Mr. Right—wherever he might be.

On the other side of this coin is a generation of Black men who have grown up without strong male role models, and oftentimes have no idea how to maintain lasting, healthy relationships. Many of them have decided to replicate the behavior they see on television, music videos, and movies, and the end result is an entire generation of African Americans in their twenties and thirties who see heterosexual relationships from totally disparate points of view, and have no idea how to conduct adult relationships. Thankfully, each of the writers in this book has owned up to his or her role in the breakdown of relationships, and simultaneously, every contributor has worked furiously to move forward. Each of us, in one way or another, is working toward relationship balance.

In each of us lives a cooling salve, a balm of healing that lies somewhere deep inside of us in spaces that often go untouched and unnoticed. It is this inner balm that allows us to look at the truth as it presents itself instead of how we see it, and it is this balm that helps us grow. While it would be unfair to place the burden of proof on the shoulders of one group—Black men or Black women—it is indeed fair to see that we have a lot of work to do if we are to move forward and make some serious changes in the ways we relate to one another as lovers, friends, spouses, and individuals. Personally, editing this anthology has been my healing balm. The stories of these writers have given me hope, helped me heal, and restored my faith in the institution of Black love. *Sometimes Rhythm, Sometimes Blues* represents my personal march toward stability, and ultimately, the beginning of a journey that will leave me whole.

Taigi Smith
Brooklyn, 2003

[1] Material gathered from *New York Newsday,* "The Decline in Black Marriage," March 19, 2003 and *Newsweek* Magazine, "The Black Gender Gap," March 3, 2003.

A Tangled Web We've Weaved

Exploring the Complexities of African-American Relationships

When Conception Equals Confusion: The Battle Between Mothers and Would-be Fathers

by Kiini Ibura Salaam

It happens in silence. A man—young, tall, hooded—sits in a waiting room. All the chairs are taken except the one diagonally across from him. A woman comes in carrying a child. She sits in the only seat available and busies herself removing the child's coat and hat. The man's eyes cut to the corner checking out mother and daughter. The woman pretends not to notice his stare. Someone vacates the seat next to mother and child. The man moves to the seat quickly and sits, eyes still on the child. He leans forward. The child tips toward him. She raises her little hands and reaches out. He opens his arms to embrace her. They fall into each other. He lifts the little girl onto his lap. The woman looks away.

I am watching this scene unfold while dressing my own daughter for the cold, wet outdoors. I am touched by the man's tender interest and love. I see his bond with the little girl and I wonder, what are they doing here? Here, being the DNA testing office. Here, being the place where we baby-mamas bring our offspring to prove that we're not lying or mistaken about who the father is. It is a task best done with a light heart. Better not to delve into the nastiness that wafts from the demand for a DNA test. The test itself is not overly demeaning or embarrassing, yet when I walk out of the testing office, I am changed. I wonder how the process affects the middle-aged woman and her two round-headed boys who were being tested when I arrived. Unlike my daughter, these two boys are far from infancy. How does a mother explain to eight- and ten-year-old boys why they had to have a large Q-tip rubbed inside their mouths by a White man listening to country music and calling their mother "mama"?

Everyone in the waiting room is Black and Latino, but I am not fooled. These battles are not the sole domain of people of color. I read about supermodel Elizabeth Hurley's billion-dollar baby-daddy drama in a glossy fashion magazine. This ugliness I'm tied up in is not bound by class or color. Paternity fights are a woman-man thing.

"Fatherhood," James Joyce writes, "in the sense of conscious begetting, is unknown to man." The physiological reality of gestation unfolding *inside* the female body creates an irrefutable certainty about a woman's relationship to her child. Women learn about a child's presence through internal notices: a missed period, tender breasts, morning sickness. Men, however, find out about their offspring's impending arrival from an external source, from the lips of a woman. The vast difference in the physical proximity of women and men to a growing fetus is one of life's confounding complexities. Babies grow outside of men's bodies. This simple biological fact breeds questions and doubts in the minds of men that pregnant women never experience. "Maternal love," Joyce concludes, "may be the only true thing in life, [while] paternity may be a legal fiction."

Due to biology's immutable rules and formulas, the stage is set for the disputes that lead women and men into family courtrooms and DNA testing labs. Procreation is—in its nature—an unbalanced event. While conception demands material from two bodies—female and male—to create a child, only one body—female—is required to gestate and birth a child. Through the unchangeable laws of the universe, the "we" that creates a child disappears when the embryo attaches itself to the uterus. From the moment of conception, women are physically, physiologically, and chemically altered to a drastic degree while men are not. The female body is literally the field upon which the dance of life plays out.

Is reproduction fair?

Some say it's not worth the breath it takes to ponder this question for no amount of mulling or meditation can change reality. It simply is. The best we can do is live our lives cognizant of the facts of life. For women, being cognizant means approaching sexual intercourse from the stark truth that the cards are stacked against us. My friend Jana believes, "Given the terrain of today, when it comes to consensual sex, contraception is a power women cannot give away. And when they do give it away, they cannot then turn around and say to men, we had an equal choice." The assertion that women and men have equal choice "may be true in theory, but it operates as a fiction in real life. In this instance, sharing the buck feels like an attempt to pass the buck."

In other words, women be warned: Should you conceive a child, you bear the burden of pregnancy, childbirth, and childrearing. You cannot afford to have sex under the pretense that you and the man will share the consequences of unprotected sex equally. Whether married, partnered, or single, mother and father are different animals.

This is a tough pill to swallow, and it is still stuck in my throat. When single women rage at baby-daddy's absence, society's response is, "You should not have had unprotected sex." It is almost as if, in deciding to have a child alone, women are expected to remain silent about reproductive and childrearing injustices. It is a classic catch-22. Certainly without unprotected sex, I would not have baby-daddy drama. But it is also true that without unprotected sex, I wouldn't have my daughter. The erasure of my daughter is no more a solution to the problem of parental inequality than the disappearance of Black people is an answer to hostile race relations. Sure, not having a child would disappear *my* baby-daddy drama, but it would not alter the societal issue of reluctant fathers. It is tempting to blame unreliable and absentee fathers on irresponsibility, casual sex, and unplanned offspring. However, mothers raising children alone after failed marriages and dissolved unions are among the voices vocalizing this bitter chorus of complaint. Even women sanctioned by marriage or cohabitation get the raw end of the deal when a man refuses fatherhood.

Parenthood is a demanding, sometimes debilitating, duty. Perhaps more women would flee from parenting if they could. But as it stands, men—the beneficiaries of patriarchy—are entitled to absolve themselves of parenting, while women, as my friend Radha declares, "are left in the default position of childrearing, with all the physical, psychological, emotional, spiritual, and financial duties that come with it, with baby-daddy or without." Many disinterested men ward off fatherhood by asserting that a pregnancy ascribed to them is not the result of *their* sexual activity, but rather someone else's indiscretion. Even without proof of a woman's infidelity, these reluctant fathers imagine themselves as one of many men on a firing squad. In this imaginary firing squad, only one man has the bullet, everyone else is "shooting blanks". When they are ordered to shoot, each man aims and fires, banking on his belief that his gun is loaded with blanks. It is a comfort, a psychological cover that allows would-be fathers to sleep at night after they have denied their children. Patriarchy grants men this refuge. In some male minds, the hypothetical possibility that any man's sperm *could have* reached the woman's egg is justification for negation. It doesn't seem to matter how many hours, days, or months a reluctant father may have spent engaging in unprotected, baby-making sex. If he does not desire fatherhood, denial is a reflex and a right. In a society where men get to choose whether or not they want to be fathers, a man can always convince himself that he was shooting blanks.

Simply by questioning the child's paternity, a potential father redirects the focus of the conversation from his accountability to the woman's credibility. For men, uncertainty is a biological reality of pregnancy. The universe—it seems—is not concerned about fathers knowing which children are their biological offspring. Stories of men being fooled into fathering the wrong child abound. Until the invention of DNA tests, no man could be certain his child was his own. Which leads me back to the scene I witnessed at the DNA testing office. The love between the father and daughter was obvious. Perhaps he was not there to deny paternity and responsibility. Perhaps he was there to quell all doubts that this child was not biologically his. For a moment, I caught a glimmer of the man's vulnerability in the situation. In a bizarre way, it seems that he needed external permission to love his daughter. Perhaps his pride, as well as his wallet, balked at the prospect of fathering a child that wasn't his.

While some men have legitimate reasons to doubt a woman's claims of paternity, many men wield the DNA test as if it were a get-out-of-fatherhood-free card. My friend's brother pretends not to know if his five-year-old is his child. He plays the father when he feels like it. When he's done, he quits, saying, "Well, I don't know if she's mine or not." Without the test, he can pretend his absences from his daughter's life are legitimate. My daughter's father takes this madness to another level. He refuses to even discuss his possible participation in our daughter's life without a DNA test. Yet, he finds the cost of the test prohibitive. This tangled logic allows him to abandon his child and continue viewing himself as a human being. I don't buy the subterfuge. Ghost fathers don't miraculously transform into model parents when they read a few scientifically sanctioned numbers that match the child's genes to theirs. Ultimately, with or without the results from a DNA test, a man has to choose whether or not to be (and to act as) a father.

The question of choice looms large in women's and men's power struggles over unborn children. As my friend Dan describes it, his first pregnancy scare brought home the shocking realization that he would not have the last word in the birth of his child. Should his girlfriend become pregnant, the choice would be up to her whether she would birth or abort the child. He said there was no way to put into words the deep, dark sensations of powerlessness that swept through him. Though he thinks it is unquestionable that it is a woman's choice whether she wants to have a child or not, he also believes that by having a child when the father doesn't want it, a woman takes away a man's choice in one of life's major decisions. My daughter's father agrees with Dan. Despite the fact that he willingly sent his sperm into my body, once he spoke the words, "I am not mentally, physically, or psychologically prepared to become a father," he expected me to abort. By not aborting, he argues, I forced a life change on him. I became the enemy the day I decided to have the child we both conceived.

The delusion of Dan's argument is that it equates conception and abortion. Though it's easy to blame a child's existence on a woman's decision not to abort, conception does not start when a woman chooses to allow a child to continue growing in her body. Conception starts with unprotected sex. Yet, many angry fathers-to-be act as if a woman's refusal to abort is the crux of the problem. Because women make choices at two points in the reproductive process (once at conception and once after the baby is conceived), many men feel women have all the power. As my friend Michael argues, "It is one of the characteristics of entitlement to expect power as a prerequisite for responsibility." Women know, however, that power and responsibility don't always go hand in hand. Upon the first twinges of monthly menstrual cramps, we are responsible for managing the pain although we have no power over the presence of cramps in our lives. From puberty (and sometimes before), we are made responsible for men's reactions to our bodies, though we do not control men's behavior. While women are fluent in responsibility without power, patriarchy teaches men that they are not bound to take responsibility in situations where they have none. In my brother's words, "Women are socialized to recognize their own powerlessness. Men are socialized to resist it. When a man is put in a [powerless] position, particularly when he is put in that position 'by' a woman, he finds himself in a bizarre and deeply unsatisfactory place." Michael takes the discussion even further by pointing out, "Even though men have controlled the laws governing choice, the social welfare system, the health-care system, and even public perception regarding pregnancy, sexuality, and morality—this one small point in the process where the woman's voice is more powerful than the man's—make men feel justified in absolving themselves of responsibility."

Ironically, men's absences protect them from censure. Single mothers are the visible symbol of paternity issues and absentee-father conflicts. Society not only grants men considerable flexibility in the realm of fatherhood, it also gives men's parenting choices so much weight that the father's level of involvement decides how the mother will be perceived. Patriarchy labels the single mother depraved and misdirected due to the man's choice not to parent. Before I became a baby-mama, I made all kinds of assumptions about women raising children alone. Rather than focusing on the men who abandoned their duties, I doubted the women's abilities to resolve conflict and their willingness to make peace. When we don't challenge sexism and patriarchy, women are easy targets. Mothers are always on stage.

Mother's bodies stretch to contain and birth new life. In addition to handling the constant shifting and internal distortion of pregnancy, many women are called upon to physically shelter a new life without receiving any emotional shelter or physical attention themselves. Today I look at young mothers differently. Even the youngest baby-mother must locate prenatal care, find a place to birth her child, and secure clothing and food for her infant. We mothers dress our babies, change their diapers, and feed them every two hours for the first few months of life.

Whether we are fifteen years old or fifty, mothers consistently engage in the toughest work in the world, often alone and sometimes in the face of animosity from both society and the fathers of our children. The stereotype of baby-mamas is of bitchy, controlling drama queens who are always yelling and demanding money. Yet, in reality, we are often justifiably angry, seeking ways to succeed at an undervalued, belittled task that contributes to the planet's future.

Once the violent shock that you are alone in the rearing of a child wears off—once you digest that the person you created a new life with won't return your calls, let alone sit down and discuss the future of the child you conceived together—it is time to face the quandary that breeds baby-mama drama. Do you bitterly shoulder the responsibility and go at it alone? Or do you put on your battle gear and go to court demanding, at least, financial assistance? Once you realize there is no negotiating, no common ground to speak of, do you embrace your inner bitch or suffer in silence? How do you take the high road when someone has stooped so low?

I was not prepared to be a player in baby-daddy drama. I never expected to be questioned, nor did I anticipate that my child would be negated. Perhaps it's because the men in my circle are fathers. Regardless of whether it was a one-night stand, the end of a relationship, or a strictly sexual affair that produced their children, the men I know create and maintain relationships with their offspring. Maybe I wasn't prepared for the drama because my mother created a different scenario for my brothers. "If your girlfriend is pregnant," she told them, "you're pregnant." I've heard other mothers criminalizing single mothers in a ruthless fashion. I once overheard one mother telling another, "I told my son: If my daughter comes home pregnant I know it's hers, but if his girlfriend's pregnant, I don't know whose child that is." The other mother said, "Yeah, I told my boy to watch out for women with kids. They just want to trap him and take his stuff. He's got a woman with three kids now, but I don't mind because she buys him diamond earrings and leather jackets."

From mothers' lips falls the rationale for the pathology that leaves baby-mothers stranded and alone. The casual, joking manner of these mothers' anti–baby-mama conversation reveals our society's willingness to paint baby-mothers as immoral wildcards who are prone to promiscuity, lying, and cunning. It is accepted communal lore that unattached, unowned women are liable to be "out there" doing "anything" with anybody while no one's looking. Society's profile of single mothers eases the way for men to remain untouched by pregnancy. There is little social retribution for men who walk out on their children. Yet, a woman who dares to have a child unsanctioned by a man is held accountable not only for her child, but also for choosing to procreate with a man who didn't stick around. Patriarchy means that women's choices and credibility are always being questioned.

As the gender that is bound to take the biggest role in childrearing, women are encouraged to "choose right." Single mothers bear the shame of reproducing alone and the stigma of choosing a "bad" father. Women are not only responsible for the children they create, we are also accountable for the men who become our children's fathers. "What did you expect?" one well-meaning friend asked me in reference to my baby-father's absence. "You two weren't in a real relationship." My friend's question is socially accepted as rational. Wild, immature, irresponsible women are expected to develop and mature in the face of motherhood. Yet, women who expect wild, immature, irresponsible men to participate in fatherhood are told they are fooling themselves. More often than not, when a man decides not to become a father, society expects women to examine the relationship to find clues that prove she made a bad choice. We are told to accept that because we chose unsuitable men, we must walk the path of parenthood alone. A man's responsibility to his offspring, it seems, is not determined by the fact that he is the father, but by the degree of closeness he shares with the mother. In a sexist world, motherhood is unquestionable, while shirking fatherhood is considered understandable, justifiable, reasonable.

Becoming a mother is like joining a sisterhood. Mothers, both married and single, reached out to me as my pregnancy progressed. They opened their histories and hearts to me. One-night stands that turned into loving relationships. Marriages that became strained under the weight of childrearing. But mostly, varied versions of my own story. Tales of support disappeared, expectations unmet, shock and disappointment. One friend's husband woke up one morning and decided their marriage and their three-month-old child were a mistake. He left, making her a single mother. Another friend's baby-father tired of her being a stay-at-home mother. When the baby was just a few months old, he stopped buying groceries, leaving the refrigerator empty for weeks at a time. The woman was forced to move home. Then there's the boyfriend who heard that his girlfriend was pregnant and disappeared, leaving neither address nor telephone number. He periodically broke the silence of his absence with threatening phone calls and harassing visits.

Without conscious resistance, many baby-mothers succumb to waves of anger and acrimony. One divorced mother reached out to me during my emotional turmoil by sharing her own rage. She writes:

> the taste is so bitter in my mouth
> so bitter I can't swallow it
> it is thrown up before it touches my tongue
> [he] left me with a girl-woman to guide
> through stormy hours
> all by myself
> the bitter has reached my heart
> my bitter can not reach her heart

The battle of the baby-mama is to beat down the compulsion to be bitter as we struggle to embrace our moral, social, and legal responsibility to rear our children without pointing the finger at the absent party. Some of us have found balance as we work in partnership with our baby-fathers. Those of us who have not must not allow our animosity to taint our children's love for their fathers, nor can we allow that animosity to shade our children's opinions of themselves. We are charged with conjuring up peace from hostility, offering cordiality despite anger, and subverting our need to rage in favor of harmony. We surf stereotypes and employ radical means to care for and celebrate our children while disassociating from the ugly reality of their fathers' attitudes and actions. We are forced to accept the reality that, as my baby-father says, "In this country, men have a choice of whether they want to be fathers or not."

As I lay in the hospital bed, exhausted from my daughter's birth, I was appalled to read the warning attached to the front of the birth certificate form. The notice advised fathers: When you sign this birth certificate, you are taking legal and financial responsibility for this child. There in the hospital, hours after the rigors of childbirth, I was introduced to the gender-based realities that were to color my future as a parent. I was not asked to sign a single piece of paper stating I would take legal and financial responsibility for our daughter. This society does not require it. My contract is etched on every inch of stretched-out skin and altered body tissue. It is written in blood.

The Edge: Topography of a First Date in Prison

by asha bandele

When I went to see Rashid, we arrived for the six-hour visit at almost nine in the morning. Now, after these eight years of going up and back, the ride can feel endless, those four drawn-out hours from door to door. But my first time I was so excited and nervous, I thought we got there, to the prison, almost before I even found a seat in the van.

We pulled into the parking lot of the prison, the one I was so familiar with, the one that looked like a castle, the one I had been volunteering in for almost two years, the one which held Rashid. I followed the more experienced visitors up a long ramp, through two sets of unbelievably thick, heavy metal doors. It was not an entrance I had ever used before. But that was not the only thing which was different about this visit.

How I got treated by police had also changed; I was no longer a volunteer. I was a prisoner's lover now, his woman, his partner. Being a volunteer afforded me a tiny measure of courtesy, but being a lover, a girlfriend, afforded me mostly hostility and suspicion. Mothers, sisters, friends, fathers, cousins, and wives, all of us were treated with hostility and suspicion.

I entered a room with gray lockers and black plastic chairs, two bathrooms, a metal detector, and two police positioned behind a desk with no chairs. As instructed, I filled out a form, and when the police called my name, not my name, but Rashid's number, I walked over to the desk. I had put all of my things into a locker, except a change purse, a lipstick, a comb, and a pen. As a volunteer, I could always bring in my bag. As a visitor, the same bag became contraband. I handed over my change purse, form, and ID to an officer who did not look at me.

Remove your shoes, coat, and jewelry. Place them on the desk.

I did as I was told, and then began to walk through the metal detector.

Not yet! I was admonished. *Go back to the other side of the machine and wait until I'm ready.*

Pen and lipstick ain't allowed. I'll hold onto them until you come out or you can put them back in your locker. He said this, and then told me, *Now, go through the metal detector.*

I stepped through and it beeped.

Do it again and don't touch the sides.

I did as I was told, and went through once more without making a sound.

The officer motioned me through two electronically locked doors. The first one opened, and I stepped through. It closed, and then the second one opened, and I entered another large room with rows and rows of orange and black chairs, vending machines, and tables. I handed my entry form to an officer who was sitting at a desk in the front of the room. I took a seat at a table which was in the furthest corner of the room. I waited, nervous, feeling discomforted by the search process.

There would come a time a few years later when that search would seem like child's play, friendly almost. That time came after I married Rashid, and it would remind me of a story, a piece of history that had been trapped in my throat since I learned of it. It had been trapped there and it had been rotting.

It was the story of Venus Hottentot, the eighteenth-century Black South African woman who had been tricked into migrating to England, who had been stripped and forced into a British circus cage, who had been gawked at, talked about, trampled by a thousand hard, White eyes. I had never been inside a prison. What did I know then about cages, humiliation, and forced exposure?

Getting processed into visiting rooms across New York State means police have the right to scan even my tampons and hold them up to the light. It is almost always men who do these searches. Almost every single time.

After we were married and granted conjugal visits, before I enter the trailer site where Rashid and I will spend our time, it will be my panties, diaphragm, and K-Y Jelly that male officers hold out in public often as a company of inmates is walking past five, maybe eight feet, from us. They have fingered my black silk panties, the ones I bought only for Rashid to see. They've shaken down my bra, my nightgown, even though it is sheer.

The first two or three times that happened to me, I felt immodest. I felt shame and embarrassment. Now I feel camaraderie with women who work the peep shows or who lap dance for a living. Except, of course, that I don't get paid. But you know, I think I should. For every glance that gets held too long, for each time one of those police runs his fingers across my underwear, those motherfuckers owe me, in the very least, cash money.

And then there was the morning when the wire in my bra set off the metal detector. The sergeant looked at my chest and then told me that,

Of course you don't have to go through this kind of search. But if you want to get this visit, you're going to have to open your shirt and let the female officer scan you. In the bathroom, of course. It's a normal security procedure and the directive's posted over there if you want to read it.

What choice did I have? I followed the female officer, a Puerto Rican woman who looked as though she could have been my mother, into the women's restroom. She did not want to search me any more than I wanted to be searched. She knew like I knew that it was completely unnecessary. A hand scanner could have been used over the top of my denim blouse. But in prison, those who have any modicum of power need neither logic nor decency to guide them through their decisions. Had I chosen to argue the point, even if I won, visiting hours would have been over.

Because she could not be hostile to the man who was her ranking officer, this female police officer was hostile to me. So much for sisterhood being global. It wasn't even local. In any case, as nasty as she got, barking orders as though I had offended her, her attitude had little impact on me.

Before I had even walked into that bathroom, I was gone, the soul of me was gone. It had disappeared out of my body. I was functioning but not present, split off and detached. It was a trick I had learned to do while having sex. It was an ancient trick. I could not remember a time when I did not know how to live this way.

My hands undid the first few buttons of my blouse, as my mind drew pictures on the walls, orange and green strokes dipped in screams. I saw myself dancing between the colors on the wall, uninhibited and unburdened. My body was see-through blue, a Caribbean ocean wave. I was rising in slow motion, all strength and untouchable, roaring skybound, winged.

Lower, the officer said, *open your shirt up all the way. You're still beeping. And the jeans, take them down past your thighs.*

I unbuttoned, pulled down, turned forward and back. I outstretched my arms, shook out my bra, all the while, all inside myself. I was chanting and singing, visualizing and meditating.

In the end I was left standing there with my shirt and bra open and my pants pulled down. And for all of that, contraband was never found, nor was it ever really expected to be found. The reality is that if they truly feared that I had some weapon stashed on me which was making the metal detector go off, why would they send me into a locked room with one of their unarmed officers, who was a woman twice my age and half my size?

All right, she growled, *get dressed and next time don't wear no underwire bra.*

I haven't worn anything but underwire bras since I was fifteen, maybe fourteen years old. In all the years I have been going into prisons and through metal detectors, I have never worn anything but underwire bras.

But those machines can be adjusted to varying degrees of sensitivity, which always makes us, the visitors, wonder if the metal detector has as much to do with the harassment and power as with security. *If this was about security,* I complained once to another woman who had just gone through the metal detector drama, *the machine would always register that I was wearing an underwire bra.*

Yup, she said. She nodded and poked out her lip, frustrated. *You right about that.*

I mean the thing would always be hypersensitive, unless of course, the police felt it was okay to sneak knives or guns in one day, but not the next. You know what I'm saying, I continued, and she agreed.

Given this, it has, therefore, been no surprise to me that in the years since the incident, the years where all of my bras have had underwire in them, not once has the metal detector ever gone off again. Not once.

When I told Rashid what happened to me, I expected him to be outraged about it, but he wasn't. Disturbed, maybe. Sorry that I went through the search. But not livid, rushing to his word processor to pound out memorandums and complaints to officials in Albany.

At some point I realized why my ordeal must have seemed so small in his eyes. After every visit he has with me or anyone else, my baby gets strip-searched, often by men who openly despise him. In a small cubicle, he is told to remove all of his clothes and shake them out. He is made to run his hands through his hair, to open his mouth wide, lift his tongue, lift his balls, turn around, and squat, then stand again, display the bottom of his feet, and then turn back around and face the police. Once, while waiting to be processed, a female officer bragged to me and two other women about how she could strip-search a male inmate if she had to. *It's in the rules*, she said to us, grinning and confident.

When I learned about strip searches, what they entailed, I was shocked. My stomach knotted up. Whatever I had imagined did not live up to the description Rashid gave me, and I knew that despite the arguments that explained why such a process was necessary, I could never, ever do such a job. No matter what. I couldn't participate in that sort of humiliation. Not of anyone. Not at any time. I wondered about the police who did it, day in and day out, especially the ones who could brag about it to wives and girlfriends. What did they go home and tell their children? *Daddy looks up men's assholes for a living.*

I realized that Rashid was not outraged by what happened to me because searches were something he was nearly desensitized to; humiliation is the daily fabric worn to fray in the life he leads and the life I was choosing to live along with him.

Both of us knew, we said this to each other, that we had a responsibility to fight some of the battles the prison system instigated, but if we fought every single one that was thrown our way, what time would be left to laugh or to dream, to hope or to just be at peace? And then who would be the real winners?

We take the experience and shove it deep down inside ourselves. We crush it like trash to be bagged, compacted, taken out, and eventually, incinerated.

Dance Like Nobody's Watching

by shani jamila

Our breathing beat in unison. Tap one two three, tap one two three . . . Smoke swiveled in between our bodies flexing and stretching like something out of a series of Ernie Barnes stills. It was almost cartoonish, our joy was so tangible. His hand sat securely in the small of my back, and every time the music swelled I would have to consciously remind myself to step away from my natural impulse and let him lead. I remember how he laughed softly and leaned in closer, velvet whispers touching his tongue as he lightly licked my ear. "Baby, I know you're independent, but just let me do this . . . "

"Shiiit," I sighed to myself, "this is why I be checking for these international-type brothers . . . "

We were working out a particular combination this night. One that made me feel like I was just a few rehearsals away from putting on a little silver shimmery something and spinning gracefully while appreciative judges held up 9.9s from their sideline booth. And I could see us standing proud, bowing to the cheering crowd as they scattered petals and poems that I would use later to make collages . . .

✂ ✂ ✂

Salsa lessons in Trinidad. The romance of the rainy season. Afternoons spent looking forward to graying skies, when I'd open all the doors and windows so that the wet wind could swirl through the house. Put on Carl Thomas's "Summer Rain" and let it filter through the billowing curtains that exposed palm fronds whipping like a frilly fan in front of smoky seductive eyes . . . Inside I'd have my hips going, salsa dancing around my house in time with the tropical breeze. Tap one two three, tap one two three . . .

I was so caught up in my little private lessons that I'd mess around sometimes and practice my steps to hip-hop. Hands up, back straight . . . you know, like *Dirty Dancing* except to DMX. The rhythms aren't all that far apart, but the style of dancing is miles away. Swaying sinuously to music you ordinarily bob your head to made me realize too many of my peers in the States don't know nothin' 'bout this. The closest our generation's come to the art of partner dancing is Kid N' Play! With our music you don't even really have to have someone else there in order to do your thing . . . to hear Goodie MoB tell it, we just don't dance no more.

In fact, I think it could be argued that this conception of partnership is a parallel of the way we relate to each other as men and women. In contemporary hip-hop, even when we do dance with someone it's possible to make it through a whole song without touching once. Someone who's *really* feeling it might even keep their eyes all closed as they move in their own groove! And when you reach that space, it's a beautiful thing. But it's also nice to not always have to do for self, to be able to rely on someone else to guide you in a way that you know is beautiful.

Inside the comfort of my classes I learned a lot about what being a couple is. We'd joined together to work on a routine that we both loved. In our pursuit of perfecting it, we could anticipate each other's movements because we'd spent time learning each other's strengths and practicing against our weaknesses. At the same time, we had to be flexible enough to adjust without appearing to when the other one threw in a little unexpected something. We also had to have the trust to be able to let go when we needed to, understanding that the other person wouldn't let us fall. For example, if I pulled against him to bring myself up from a deep dip it would literally throw his back out. I had to trust him to pull me back to my feet. He had to trust that he could risk his well-being for me, knowing that if he held back at all, we would both get hurt.

But I was just temporarily in Trini, and new to the salsa and soca soundtrack that backed up my semester at the University of the West Indies. There were life lessons I'd already learned growing up on hip-hop that were reinforced in this space as well. Like in salsa, the dance is nearly completely defined by the abilities of your partner. If you get stuck with someone who doesn't move well with you, someone who's sweaty or stank (don't act like y'all don't know), or a brother who won't experiment outside of his one signature step, it will completely limit your ability to fully express yourself. I can't be with someone whose direction leads me to trip, and I value myself enough to know when to step out and do my own thing. Hip-hop has given me that. I know I can have a damn good time tearing up the dance floor by myself and I find no stigma in it. A benefit of the individual nature of our dancing is that women no longer have to sit on the sidelines waiting for someone to ask us to dance.

It hasn't always been like that. In just the past fifty years, the shape of African-American dance music has morphed from bebop to rock 'n' roll, doo wop, Motown, disco, and now hip-hop. All of this music was characterized by some sort of partner-dancing for our parents and their predecessors. It wasn't until the death of disco that this genre of dancing began to phase out while hip-hop took root, but the change didn't happen in a vacuum. By the early '80s when hip-hop was beginning to sweep the country, the second wave of the women's movement had just wet up the world. It was also the era that witnessed the birth of the AIDS epidemic, the war on drugs, Reaganomics, and the first music videos. All of these factors may have contributed to the shifting behavioral patterns and cultural customs that were played out in part on the dance floor.

Of course, hip-hop has transformed with time. As mainstream corporate culture discovered its earning power, the influx of major money began to figure in the creation and commercialization of this culture in a way never before paralleled. With that, the look of success in hip-hop changed. Misogyny-saturated videos became the venue of choice to showcase the flaunting of newfound wealth and the commodification of the female body. The pimp/ho ideology that was the mantra of early songs like Slick Rick's "Treat Her like a Prostitute" blew up in the overwhelmingly male-defined realm of hip-hop, and women started to be depicted as things to be bought, collected, and displayed as status symbols. Now we are at the point where you have 50 Cent and Snoop draping themselves in diamonds and writing odes in praise of pimpdom, while Lil' Kim's new enterprise is manufacturing life-size anatomically correct blow-up dolls in her likeness.

The void left by the majority of lyrical and visual depictions of male/female relationships makes many hip-hoppians, myself included, long for models of balanced and healthy partnership in our generation. However tempting it may be to salsa off into the sunset, our problems cannot be solved by escapism, or by glorifying other people's practices while vilifying our own. We should draw from the best ways of others, but it's both silly and unrealistic to superimpose perceived beliefs of one culture on another. There is no place completely free from oppression. And anyway, it's one thing to shimmy around your house and quite another to be in a hip-hop club looking like the Lord of the Dance on crack because you think someone else got it right.

Conversely there is no sole place to lay blame for our complicated gender dynamics, like the nigga/bitch syndrome which is typically the immediate culprit. This factor tends to snatch the spotlight when we examine how men and women of our generation relate, often at the expense of other reasons. For example, there ain't a sister alive who can't relate to this one occasion when I found myself squeezing down the stairway of a popular D.C. club. Midstep, some dude reached out from behind to caress my waistline. I didn't even turn around before I instinctively snatched his overly familiar hand up off my body and froze it midair as I gave the cat responsible the nastiest look I could conjure up. His boy watching the exchange chuckled and leaned in as he said confidingly to me, "Don't trip. It's because you're pretty. If you were ugly he wouldn't *want* to touch you!" Still smiling he walked away shaking his head muttering, "I'm glad I don't have a sister . . . " My stunned response reverberated off his retreating back. *"Brother, you do."*

Now aside from the sitcom-ready nature of this situation, let's just take a second and look at the underlying premise of his statement. This brother called himself doing his good deed for the night when he stepped in to smooth shit out. But his argument, taken to its logical conclusion, asserts that if you are a woman fortunate enough to be considered fly when you walk up in the club your *reward* is getting felt up by strange men?

It's a trip—women are so used to being accosted like this that many of us have become numb to it. We pick our battles, understanding that defending yourself against the wrong mothafucka could get you called out by your name or even physically hurt. This phenomenon, which the damage wrought by the nigga/bitch paradigm functions inside of, is about the definitions of masculinity and femininity that we've adopted. It's a "yeah I did it what you gonna do about it" assertion of power from men, and the tangible objectification and devaluation of women. In order to truly understand our issues, we need to be able to deconstruct the larger raced, classed, and gendered realm in which they operate.

Some people take measures to contest these oppressive structures by seeking antidotes to specific issues, like purposefully naming each other "king" and "queen." But even this well-meaning demonstration of respect can be flawed. Mos Def spoke to it on the *Black Star* album when he rhymed, "I find it distressin' there's never no in between, we either niggas or kings, we either bitches or queens" ("Thieves in the Night"). It's definitely tempting to grasp on to any nomenclature that seems like it's assigning value, especially when you feel caught out there without any positive characterizations, but it's also essential to acknowledge that either extreme is a categorization that comes with its own restrictive social norms. What we need to figure out is what's in between these pendulum swings. How do we emancipate ourselves from stereotypes and determine what we truly value in each other as men and women?

He looked me straight in the face and told me that if he were to propose to a sister right now, more than likely she would say yes. He could say this with complete confidence—not because he was sweating himself, but because he could look at the situation realistically. He'd done his undergraduate work at a nationally known school and was in the process of finishing up his law degree. He was fairly attractive, goal-oriented, educated, and a good brother. He knew that the pickings for similarly situated sisters were slim. And he was right.

The stats always sound so fatalistic, and the countless articles they've spawned bemoaning the new single woman in her thirties is enough to make a sista consider shit she know she shouldn't. And truthfully, while I would never advocate settling, I understand the rationale. The fact is that our injustice system has Black men making up 7 percent of the general population and nearly half of the prison population. The fact is that many of them are in there for killing other Black men. The fact is that there are more brothers in prison than there are in college, and now that this country is at war, we are dying on the front lines in disproportionate numbers as well. The fact is that single mothers are already raising a huge percentage of our children, and the impact of all these factors on the Black family structure is yet to be fully felt.

But in spite of all the numbers to the contrary, I remain convinced that the problem is not finding a "good man." The struggle is to find a good man that you are compatible with. Now what compatibility means is a wholly subjective thing. Some people measure it by achievement, status, or if both of y'all cry at made-for-TV movies. Some people figure if you're lucky enough to find a good one you better work with what you got. Me, I'm looking for that brother who understands that intelligence without analysis, consciousness without commitment, may as well not be. The brother who surprises me with bouquets of lilies, orchids, and gardenias because he knows that roses are beautiful, but trite. The brother that will hold my hand when I stand on a foreign beach watching the sun, the moon, and two rainbows in the sky all at once. The brother whose embrace carries me to the place where time's spent standing still. Idealistic?

Maybe. But the examples of my elders have taught me to ask one central question in this quest: Who do you want next to you when you can no longer do for self?

When Russell died of cancer ten years ago, his whole family gathered around him. His daughter moved her entire family from D.C. to Illinois to take care of him, and they lived there for a year. His wife stayed by his side, caring for him and holding his hand. He was able to call each of his descendants back into his room where he lay there and told them last things he wanted them to hear from his lips. He'd been an honorable man who raised his family well. Everyone was there when he transitioned. And they were there in love. It was beautiful.

Chris got his girlfriend pregnant and left her to raise the child. Their baby girl was raised by her mother's side, and didn't get to know her biological father until she sought him out at age thirty. She was married and pregnant when they re-established a relationship, and he became a peripheral figure in her new family's lives. When he died last year he felt alone. His children were there, and had made their peace with him, but in the end they did not have close relationships. His new wife made him cry when she yelled at him for soiling the death bed. He couldn't help it anymore. It was sad.

Marlon was an evil, abusive man who talked down to his wife his entire life and was still popping shit from his death bed. Talking dirty to the nurses in front of her, demanding cigarettes and liquor when he couldn't even walk, bathe, or use the bathroom on his own. In spite of it all she loved him, and near 'bout wore herself out to care for him. She'd forget to take her own medicine because she was fussing about whether or not he'd taken his. She wouldn't eat because she was trying to cook something he would accept. She couldn't sleep because he would stay up at nights hollering so that she wouldn't leave him by himself. When he finally died most folks were glad to see him go.

I use these examples because in death lies a commentary on how you live life. In some eyes, even the worst of these examples would be considered a success because they'd lasted "until death did they part," two of them for over fifty years. But I ask this: Are you surrounded by love or duty? Are your relationships based on reciprocation or abuse? Desire or obligation? And if you are lucky enough to have people there to hold your hand when you pass on, who will be there and why?

My parents' marriage has shown me that, like a good dance partner, a life partner should be someone who constantly has your back but allows you your own space to shine. I've learned from their example that a companion should be a complement—not completion. Both of them have maintained their individual identities, even as they represent one of the most solid couples I've ever seen. Over thirty years into their marriage they still make "family time" every night, cooking together and sharing cleaning responsibilities. Since time they've treasured each other, always prioritized their union, and never allowed one to be played against the other. They exemplify the old adage that you should never marry the person you can see yourself spending the rest of your life with, you should marry the person you can't see yourself spending the rest of your life without.

When you choose a partner it should be someone who responds to your rhythm, whether you're hearing hip-hop, salsa, zaico, or zouk. And in the meantime, give thanks for the moments you have to enjoy all the songs in between. Hands in position, one eye out for the cutie prepared to shimmy through with you like tap, one two three . . . mic check, one two . . . dip, break, cut.

Marriage:
The Unfulfilled Prophecy

by Tracy LaRae Ruffin

On many occasions, I've gone to family functions only to be asked that nagging question, "So, when are you going to get married?" Although I know my relatives mean no harm, the question implies that marriage is something that can just be decided on a whim, almost as if it's something I could just wake up one morning and decide to do. After numerous venting sessions with many of my thirty-something and still single girlfriends, one thing became clear to me: African-American women, myself included, still believe that a husband is guaranteed us.

I feel as though I was groomed and prepared for marriage and motherhood from childhood. My mother made sure I knew how to cook, sew, and maintain a household because according to some invisible "life rule book," if I didn't, I would never find a husband. My fate would be sealed in becoming the dreaded "old maid." In addition to becoming a skilled cook and mastering many of the great recipes of my mother and grandmother, I carried myself as a young lady should. I was even reluctant to participate in sports that would be considered unladylike to avoid the infamous label of "tomboy" or any permanent scarring that my potential future husband may not find attractive.

Growing up, marriage was always referred to as a given. Repeatedly, I've heard my elders speak in the future tense, using phrases like, "when you get married," or "your husband will want," and even that old saying, "a woman needs to be a cook in the kitchen, a whore in the bedroom, and a diplomat in all arguments." Listening to my elders speak this way instilled an unintentional arrogance within me regarding marriage. I grew to assume that marriage was a part of life, something that would just automatically happen to me. In retrospect, what I should have been raised to believe was that marriage would be Plan B and not Plan A. Twenty years ago, if Dionne Warwick, Miss Cleo, or Nostradamus himself would have told tell me that at the age of thirty-four, I would be single and childless, I never would have believed it. Nothing or no one could have convinced me of that fact.

My primary goal should have been vested in Plan A, which simply put, is merely the pursuit of my education and a career. The problem with Plan A for me is that I was never really interested in chasing degrees and establishing some lucrative career. My "career" was going to be that of homemaker. It may sound like a fairy tale to some, but I wanted the husband, the house, and the children to match. This was, I'm sure, the result of growing up as an only child. And since society, and to a certain degree my family, had instilled in me the fact that marriage was a foregone conclusion, I didn't see anything unrealistic about my utopian dream.

By the age of sixteen I had my future pretty much all mapped out. After graduating from high school, I did go away to college, where I assumed that while furthering my education, I would also meet my husband. When I left college just as single as when I had arrived, I wasn't discouraged. Most of us were too busy partying and having too much fun to be thinking of marriage anyhow. It also made sense that being a die-hard New Yorker I would meet Mr. Right in my hometown. By my twenty-fifth birthday I began to wonder, "Where the hell is this guy?" My schedule was being thrown off course and the six children that I wanted to have just didn't seem very realistic, so I revised the blueprint down to four.

Four children would still provide me with the large immediate family of my own that I never had growing up as an only child. I wanted the family my grandmother had. My greatest joy, my utopia in my middle-aged years, would come from observing all of my children and grandchildren, anxiously awaiting that hearty "Amen" at the end of the blessing of the food, so they could pillage the dinner table, like we do at my grandmother's house on Christmas. At the end of the evening, I'd sit back in my favorite chair to open all my gifts and count all the money I'd received. Although the construction of the life and family I wanted to build wasn't too far behind schedule, I decided it was time to go over the blueprint once more. The actual layout looked fine, and I didn't seem to be taking short-cuts. The most crucial part of the carefully drawn-up plans at this point was dating, and I was definitely doing that. But I realized that I was encountering some structural problems with dating. On the outside, the brothers appeared strong, solid, and sound, but it turned out to be just a shell, like one of those old brownstones in Harlem that had been completely gutted out. I thought the older I became, the easier dating would become, but no one told me it would be just the opposite.

My precious time was being wasted on guys who were afflicted with various issues. There was the guy that couldn't show up anywhere on time; the guy who just wouldn't show up; the guy with the baby-mama drama; the guy who hated his mama; the guy that was a wimp; the guy that seemed to have some form of agoraphobia (he would freak out anytime I suggested we actually go out); the guy with so many garnishments, he couldn't go out; the guy with no job; the guy with the drug problem; the guy with the erection problem; and one of my all-time favorites, the guy who asked me out on a date and decided to wait until the bill arrived to tell me that he didn't have enough money to pay.

I wondered then and I still wonder now, where have all the "real" men gone? I'm at a point in my life where I'm really sick and tired of having to teach thirty-something-year-old men how to date me. And while I understand that many men may lack knowledge of certain things due to the lack of a positive male figure in their home, I just assumed that dating fell into one of those commonsense categories. The Learning Annex should offer workshops for men on "The Art of Dating." Many of the brothers out here apparently need someone to teach them things like if you don't believe in Valentine's Day, this is something you should bring up in the early stages of dating and not seven months into the relationship. The irony of situations like this is, the mere fact that there are thirty-something-year-old men still pulling stunts like this tells me that desperate women from their past have been letting them get away with that kind of crap! Why else would they feel that I would even submit to such a lack of consideration and respect?

The type of man that I want isn't just some stud who can lay the pipe on me right, night after night. Don't get it twisted, either, because I have great respect and appreciation for a good "pipe-layer." But I'm also looking for a partner, or what the Bible refers to as a "helpmeet." My ideal partner is a strong Black man who understands that although I'm an independent Black woman, I still want doors opened for me, I still want flowers sent to my job, I still want to be escorted to a taxi or walked to the train station. My ideal partner is a man who wants to get married because he wants a woman to love, raise a family, and grow old with, not because his mother is getting too old to continue doing his laundry and cooking his meals every night. My future husband is supportive and encouraging of all my endeavors, even if they mean reaching a financial level that will exceed his.

No one is perfect and we all have issues, but one of the mistakes I found myself making with men is that I thought "association would beget assimilation." I assumed, if I were strong for him, if I stroked his ego and if I did all I could to make him feel like a man, he'd reciprocate and become the strong man I needed him to be for me. In theory, it's a great strategy but it never works because unlike women, most men refuse to admit that they have issues of any kind and, therefore, their various issues never get resolved. After being drained emotionally, I finally woke up and realized that it sure would be nice if my ego was stroked occasionally. And it sure would be nice to spend the night at a man's apartment and be beckoned by the mouth-watering aroma of bacon and scrambled eggs in the morning, instead of being offered an effortless bowl of Captain Crunch with borderline spoiled milk (when I'm lactose intolerant).

Before I knew what hit me, *bam!* I turned the big 3-0. It's as though it just snuck up on me. It was at this point when I officially started to worry. Here I was, now thirty years old and never married and some of my friends were already on their second marriage. I wanted to know: What am I doing wrong? Is there something wrong with me? Should I switch deodorants? I have, however, been offered the esteemed honor, on more than one occasion, to bear a man's child, or "carry his seed," as some of them put it. But none of them could understand my taking offense to the invitation because marriage was never proposed. Being raised by a single mother, I am all too familiar with the trials and tribulations of being a single parent, and that, as a lifestyle choice, just does not appeal to me. I no longer ask the "what's wrong with me" questions because I realized that although I am far from perfect, there really isn't anything "wrong" with me except for the fact that I refuse to settle for less than I deserve.

One thing that always would remain constant in my carefully designed plan would be that I did not want children out of wedlock and I did not want to start a family immediately after getting married. Children too early in a marriage, in my opinion, is a relationship killer. I want an adequate amount of time to devote exclusively to my husband and vice versa. I want my husband and me to be able to enjoy just being married for at least the first three years. I want to enjoy as much time as possible, greeting him at the door wearing butt-naked and a smile. We should be free to do whatever we want, without being burdened with the task of trying to find someone to watch our bad-ass kids while we try to have a romantic weekend somewhere. A three-year waiting period would still afford me the necessary time to have at least three children to stroke my ego and shower me with love in my golden years, provided my biological clock co-operates with the schedule.

Unfortunately, because of that invisible little ticking clock, most women do not have the luxury and ability to have children as long as men do. And sadly, in my family, the women seem to go through menopause much earlier than what is considered the norm. It must have been about three years ago when I discovered that this seemed to be a trend in my family. I was at a family gathering and I listened (like I always do) while my mother, aunts, and grandmother discussed "going through the change," and the age they were when it happened. In health education class, I remember being taught that menopause was something to be expected somewhere around the age of fifty or beyond. The women in my family were citing age thirty-nine and forty-two, which is far from the norm. What is unnerving to me is that this is an issue that does not affect men. They tend to have more of a go-with-the-flow attitude toward dating; an attitude that, as a woman in my thirties who wants to someday get married and have children, I cannot afford to have. Recently, I realized that many men are unaware that a woman is born with all her eggs and that the biological clock is, in fact, real. At the same time, I don't view every man that comes across my path as a potential husband, like some women. I'm not thrusting some man at my family after only the second date, but my past experience has taught me that asking the right questions—sooner as opposed to later and watching to see if the gentlemen's actions coincide with said answers—helps to eliminate a broken heart and a lot of wasted time and energy.

I must admit that in the past, just like many other women, I have blamed men for some of the unnecessary heartache and drama that I have gone through in relationships. I finally had to admit to myself that it was just as much my fault because I invited it into my life. As a woman, I believe that I'm both blessed and cursed with the bequest of compassion. On numerous occasions, I've given someone the benefit of the doubt, knowing in my heart this brother's particular situation may have sounded shady. But I went ahead and took a chance because I thought maybe I was being too picky or too hard on this person, or maybe stereotyping them. I took chances, hoping that the obvious foreseeable problems would not arise in these particular cases, and then when those problems did arise, I blamed the guys. I had to be accountable for the role that I played in these failed relationships. Once I was able to take a step back and look at the situation with both eyes wide open, I was finally able to stop being so angry and bitter toward men because they were not entirely to blame.

Intuition is a very powerful gift and I think many of us, especially women, tend to underestimate it or not take it seriously. Nine times out of ten, when we look back on our relationships, there were all sorts of red flags that we chose to ignore. Someone once said that repeating the same mistakes over and over is called insanity. I thank God that my age has wrought wisdom and discernment.

Now that I'm thirty-four, I no longer repeat the mistakes that I made at thirty, or at twenty-five. On my own, I've finally come to the realization that marriage is promised to no one and that I love myself enough to accept being alone. There's a big difference between loneliness and being alone. And most important, *it's okay to be alone.* Our families and society have attached all sorts of negative connotations to being a single woman, which has, in turn, given many women complexes once they reach a certain age and find themselves still single. Why is it, a man can remain single forever and be considered an "eligible bachelor," but a single woman past a certain age is branded an "old maid" or a "spinster"? It's because of these derogatory comments and stigmas that some women find themselves at the age of thirty-something sitting in therapists' offices twice a month, trying to work through their depression because they can't understand why they're not married. After all, it was *prophesied*—it was something that everyone said would come to pass. The reason is quite simple; society has sent women a subliminal message that says a husband is what validates you as a woman.

Our validation, if there is such a thing, should come from loving ourselves, furthering our education, and pursuing our own personal dreams like starting our own businesses or devoting time to our favorite charities. Women should teach their future daughters that spending quality time with oneself is just as important as a healthy social life with others. If Mr. Right should just so happen to come along while en route, at least mother has already prepared you and there's no rule that says Plan A and Plan B can't coexist. Most importantly, Mr. Right should be not just a mate, but a partner.

I'm glad that I've learned to cook very well and yes, I have that recipe for macaroni and cheese down pat. I learned how to make a bathroom sparkle and balance a checkbook. However, these are skills that I'm glad I learned for my own benefit. I should not have been raised to believe that marriage was somehow promised or guaranteed to me. And, although I was encouraged to go to college and further my education, I still did so with the belief that somewhere along the way, I'd meet Mr. Right, become Mrs. So and So, and start a family. In essence, the prophecy would have been fulfilled.

Let me be clear in expressing that I am in no way bitter or angry because I'm not married (as of yet). On the contrary, I'm actually grateful for the experiences that I've had up to this point and will continue to have, because they've helped me to learn more about who I am and what I know I deserve. I've come to know that there's nothing wrong with being single. I now know there's a difference between being alone and being lonely. If I didn't love myself, I could have been married a long time ago, willing to settle for some of the men in my past who were mentally abusive, already had several children out of wedlock, or in the past have been referred to as "the defendant."

I'm perfectly aware that some of my girlfriends have boyfriends who see me as that female that "can't get a man" or "can't keep a man," and I'm okay with that. I guess they're clueless to the fact that I'm not one of those women that would rather have a dirty pair of pants to wash than no pants at all. Why do I have to be called all types of lonely bitches because I won't let some guy move in, eat up all my food without contributing a dime to my household, run up my phone bill and not pay it, and ruin my credit? How could I possibly be lonely, when I have *your* girlfriend, constantly calling me at all hours of the night because she needs to vent her frustration, because she's sick and tired of being sick and tired of her trifling man! I'm an attractive young woman who's in pretty good shape and I don't have any children out of wedlock. By being gainfully employed, I'm afforded the luxury of being able to support myself, and I'm a homeowner.

Believe it or not, I came to find out that these things are a tad bit of a turn-off to a lot of men. Black men nowadays act as if there is something wrong with an independent Black woman. Of course I'm independent; I don't have a choice. Being an independent Black woman is the only thing that many Black women know how to be because it's all we've ever seen growing up. In most households, mother was the head of the household, mother was the breadwinner, mother was the authority figure, and it was mother who was the strong disciplinarian. Recognizing that pattern is what helped me to understand what men mean when they say, "Some women don't know how to let a man be a man." And, because of the lack of men that were fathers to their children, we now have a society of Black men who don't know how to be husbands, or even fathers. Sometimes the male/female relationship becomes somewhat of a catch-22 situation. Black men claim they want a woman who can bring something to the table, but on the other hand, if I'm bringing more to the table than he is, he doesn't want me because he feels like less than a man. He claims he wants a woman who is smart, but if I have more education than he does, then I must think I'm better than he. If I contradict him or correct him in any way, then I'm "puttin' a brother down." And, because I'm still single and childless by a certain age, I must have "issues."

Why must there be something "wrong" with me, as some men put it, because I'm a thirty-something woman who isn't married and doesn't have any children? Once upon a time, a woman who had children out of wedlock was shunned not just by her community, but by her family as well. Unfortunately, in the African-American community, it has now become the status quo to be a single parent. African Americans are the only race of people who have it backwards, and the rest of society knows it. I remember once, a White female coworker (knowing that I was not married) asked me if I had any children and I told her that I didn't. When I in turn asked her the same question (also knowing that she was not married), she immediately responded, "Oh no, I'm not married." This woman was totally aware that I was not married, but because having children out of wedlock is so prevalent in the Black community, I guess she figured she wouldn't be too far off in assuming that I already had a child or two.

I remember once running into an old friend and she asked me why I didn't have any children. I told her that I was waiting for marriage, and she actually told me that I was living in a fantasy world. I thought that was one of the saddest things I had ever heard. This cycle of broken homes needs to be broken.

I haven't given up hope on the idea of someday getting married and I am not at all on some kind of "I'm a strong Black woman who doesn't need a man" campaign. It's just that my overall experience has taught me that while I still have the desire to get married, I can still enjoy being single, until the prophecy is fulfilled.

Retracing Our Steps

An Examination of the Personal Histories That Shape Us

The Trial

by Danielle K. Little

I notice all the yellow as the judge takes the bench. I once read somewhere that the color of enclosed spaces affects mood. Black, they say, is gloomy and depressing; red elevates blood pressure and induces anxiety. Orange is harsh and makes people nauseous, which is why the interiors of airplanes, at least ones that travel long distances, are never so painted. I think that certain types of yellow, like the bright shade glaring inside this courtroom, can also be upsetting: too indifferent, making one feel as if she is under an unrelenting spotlight. The color blue, though, is a different matter. Blue comforts, invoking trust and fostering a sense of safety. This courtroom should have been painted blue.

I wonder how I must look, seated at the prosecutor's table amid a pile of folders and legal pads, trying my best to look serious with my braids pulled back in an uncomfortable bun, big-girl blue suit, immaculate French manicure, and unassuming loafers. Such is the classic ensemble for a professional, modern woman, though my homegirl's man not so affectionately describes it another way, "the can't-even-*smell*-the-pussy look." I think about my ex and how excited he acted when I told him about the new case that I had been assigned to work on.

"Really?" Marc cried. "Congratulations, D, I'm so proud of you."

Marc *was* genuinely happy for me, though I suspected that his excitement had more to do with relief that we were discussing something other than the reconciliation that I had so desperately wanted. I didn't even bring it up. Marc had assured me that he would come back one day—maybe within the year; the next month, perhaps; or who knew, the next day. All he needed was space. And time. I was not going to push and force him to close the cracked door that he promised had been waiting for me.

"D," he rattled on, "this is the opportunity you've been working so hard for. Who deserves it more than you!"

Marc was only partially right. I had deserved it, the chance to second-seat a high profile case, so-called because the crime had been reported in the news. I certainly deserved it more than those cretins with whom I worked. Brooklyn and Fordham Law School yahoos who began each morning with cream cheese and grape jelly bagels, "kawfee-black-two shoogas" and cigarettes. Public officials who plastered the mug shots of the mostly Black and brown defendants on the office walls, sprawling obnoxious one-liners beneath the faces. Before transferring to Appeals, where I was given the chance to work on this trial, I spent several months cutting my teeth in the Criminal Court Bureau, handling misdemeanors and being routinely abused by my colleagues *(Why you set up files so early in the morning? You tryin' to make us look bad?)*, court personnel *(What the hell are you smiling at this early in the morning?)*, and manic judges *(Counsel, where in God's name are those files? Is this your incompetence or that of your office? Don't bother responding, I'm sure it is one and the same)*. So while the opportunity afforded me was well earned, I also knew that my struggle through law school, relocation across the country, and first job at the bottom of the food chain was not what I had worked for, whatever that might have been.

And, the trial could not have come at a better time. Marc had finally left me, ostensibly because I asked him to reimburse me for the fourteen-dollar cab fare I fronted after a less than ideal night out in Manhattan. He was disgusted. His cinnamon-brown eyes stabbed me with a glare of such palpable contempt that I knew. The breakups never happen over the big things, the things that truly define your values. Whether or not he believes in abortion. The section of the country where you will spend the rest of your lives. Your beliefs in the existence (or not) of White folks' humanity. No. The breakups always take you off guard and are triggered by the most trivial events. Like when he goes to get the orange juice and there is only a swallow left. When she hears him loudly crunching on his cereal. When he rents, then has the nerve to enjoy, Demi Moore's naked ass in *Striptease* or when she casually corrects a mispronounced word, those are the moments that become the proverbial final straw. The assault that confirms for the one you love more than earth that they cannot take it, or you, anymore. So after a night of lovemaking that lasted well into the morning, a night in which he whispered "Always" with every entry and promised that we had the rest of our lives for shared sunsets and moonlit walks through Prospect Park, Marc walked out of my brownstone. Forever.

I sit here at this prosecutor's table, a coiffed but unmistakable mess. I have deteriorated from a sistah-twelve to a White-girl six, a difference so noticeable that the cute Korean guy (and one of only two men of color in my bureau) who only talks to the Jewish girls is beginning to sweat me. Even my mother, a woman who has kept a birthing-bed promise to never inquire about my life, recently wondered aloud if I was "sick," that is, if I had AIDS. I did not of course, though I dared not confess that her suspicion was not so far off the mark, as I was suffering from something else just as devastating. Like countless others before me, I had taken an inventory of my life and realized that I had nothing beyond my résumé-impressive achievements. So I packed up my books and other possessions and relocated to New York City. Doing so had little to do with the oft-stated (though fatuous cliché) of wanting to make it here, and depending on which Nina Simone ballad I cried myself to sleep to, I was forced to accept that my being here was not attributable to one easily recognizable event—the girlfriends no longer spoken to for reasons that one will no longer remember, the left-behind lover whose cowardice and cruelty knew no bottom, a mother who chose to save the world but not me. I came here like so many others, an orphan of the circumstances of my life, settling in this place because I had nowhere else to go.

But upon arrival, I, like many others, quickly and brutally realized the real reason why I was destined to be here. Sometimes, the reality hits you as soon as the moving van pulls off, leaving you in your new world consisting of one block, several if you are lucky. A strange land overwhelmed with unrelenting mechanical and human noise, debris (mechanical and human as well), and endless rows of indifferent buildings that block out the sun and, at night, because of all the bright lights, the stars. What kind of place is it where one cannot see the stars? One arrives here and discovers that this is not a place where anyone can truly live, not with the pushing and yelling and spitting that stands in for normal human interaction. This place where survival itself is a nonstop series of hustles *(This is where you can buy fresh meat and vegetables—even though the forty-minute subway ride is a hassle. White folks shop here so the quality is assured; This is the number to call when your landlord fails to turn on the heat, and do not doubt it for a moment, he will; This is how you look into space while riding on the subway because to make eye contact means you asked for whatever you are likely to get).* One ends up here, like all motherless children, only to discover one's true reason for coming in the first place—that you have come here to die. I recognize this now, but thinking about it too much pushes me further into the abyss. So yeah, this trial is right on time and the facts are horrific enough to distract me from myself.

On December 12, 1996, Anthony and five other young brothas lured Chante and Mariah to a Brooklyn brownstone under the pretense that they were going to attend a party.[1] But the girls, lifelong friends and teenage mothers, had been set up to exact a ghetto's revenge. Anthony's cousin, Borne, had been shot several months earlier and the defendants believed that Chante's boyfriend (who was actually her ex) was responsible. Anthony, who had met Chante the previous day, asked her out on a date and Mariah, knowing that a young woman should never go anywhere alone with a man she had just met, tagged along with her friend.

The girls entered the house and were led to a basement where music was blaring. They were immediately surrounded by the defendants, all of whom had their faces covered with ski masks and several of whom pointed weapons at them, including a gun, a large tree branch, and an antique sword. Both girls were ordered to strip: Chante, down to her socks and Mariah, down to her underwear because she was menstruating. One of the defendants told Chante that "this was a message from Borne."

> **Q:** What happened then?
> **A:** And one of them had asked would I do anything to live.
> **Q:** What did you say when they asked if there was—if you would do anything to live?
> **A:** I said, yes.[2]

Chante was then repeatedly and simultaneously raped and forced to engage in oral sex.

---

[1] The names of the victims, though not the defendants, have been changed. The trial involves the six cases of *The People of the State of New York* versus Anthony Gibson (age 18 when the crimes took place), brothers Elliot Johnson (20) and Christopher Johnson (24), their roommate, Timothy Butler (24), and brothers Alonzo Reed (18) and Dashaun Reed (20).

[2] All cited testimony is from the trial of *People v. Elliot Johnson.*

Q: Now, when that first started, it was just this one individual?

A: It was one after another.

Q: And after this first man had his penis in your vagina, did anyone else come in?

A: Yes.

Q: How many other people came in?

A: Four.

Q: And what did you do with those other individuals?

A: They made me suck their penis.

Q: Now, how many men, in total, do you believe you had to suck their penises?

A: Four.

Q: Was there any point in time that both of those things were happening at the same time, that is, you were having vaginal sex with one man from behind at the same time that you were sucking another man's penis?

A: Yes.

Q: How often did that happen during the course of this?

A: How often?

Q: Yes, how many? I mean, did it happen once that that happened or was there a couple times that it happened; how many times did that happen that there were two men at the same time?

A: Couple of times.

While Chante was being assaulted, Mariah was in the other room, crying for her life. The defendants were loath to rape her because she was on her period. When Anthony asked some of the others why "nobody was try[ing] to fuck Shorty" and was told that she was on her period, he said "her mouth ain't" and she too, was forced to engage in oral sex.[3] Chante was later doused with a bottle of Ivory Liquid soap and sprayed down with a garden hose. Both girls' hands were placed behind their backs; they were then bound with duct tape and plastic garbage bags about their eyes, mouths, and hands. The defendants drove the girls to a notorious housing project several blocks away and led them to the rooftop, whereupon Anthony told them to "have a seat."

Q: What happened then?

A: I heard the shots.

Q: How many shots did you hear?

[3] Videotaped confession of Elliot Johnson, dated December 14, 1996.

A: Two shots.

Q: What happened after you heard the two shots?

A: I blacked out.

Q: When you came to, after blacking out, tell the jury what was happening with you?

A: I woke up and I couldn't really see, but I was bleeding. When I looked—

Defense Counsel: Would she like a recess?

Prosecutor: I think we're okay.

Court: If she does, we'll take one. Feel okay?

A: Mariah's head was on my sneaker.

Q: Now, when you told us before that there was a binding around your face, how were you able to see, at that time?

A: Because I was bleeding and it had fell.

Q: When you saw Mariah's head on your sneakers, what did you do?

A: I couldn't help her. I tried to wake her up, but she didn't wake up.

Anthony had shot both Chante and Mariah once in the head, killing Mariah instantly. However, divine providence, as the trial judge noted, must have intervened to save Chante: the wetness of the blood, the moist night air combined with the manner in which her head had been bound with plastic, all of which combined to make the bullet merely graze her back and scalp. Chante survived, later lamenting in my dusty, sixth-floor office that one of the injustices she endured that night was the doctors having to cut off her "good hair" in order to remove the bullet fragments that remained lodged in her skull. I looked at her for a moment, then continued prepping her for the next day's testimony. How could I respond to that, really?

Marc's building was known as the Black Melrose Place. At least that's what the folks were murmuring at the Tyson-Holyfield party that he co-hosted with his first-floor neighbors. After everyone recovered from the infamous ear-biting fiasco and cleared out, I focused my attention on Marc, who frantically cleaned up the apartment and rejected my offers to help. He finally shooed me into the bedroom, promising that he'd be in soon.

I closed the bedroom door behind me and felt my way over to the stereo. I carefully lit a single Donna Karan candle and watched the growth of the flame, waiting until the match reached my fingertips before shaking it out. I sat on the edge of welcoming forest green sheets, a green so deep it looked black in this light. The room was free and uncluttered. Just the simple elegance of hardwood floors, a wooden bed frame with matching bookcase, and a stereo. Everything had a place.

I fingered Marc's music collection, which had been neatly arranged along the windowsill and tried to select the perfect music to complement the moment. I excitedly picked up Fourplay's *Between the Sheets* and thought about how my homegirl routinely scoffs at such music and the cooljazz radio station that plays it. In loving defiance of my friend, I played the CD anyway: The music sounded like love and loss, so it was jazz to me, and I allowed myself to be carried away by instrumental genius.

I noticed the only picture frame in the room and picked it up. There was no picture inside. A beautiful silver frame with an intricate floral pattern, the lone piece of glass stared back at me in haunting resignation. What was it to keep such a thing by one's bed? A few nights before, on one of our moonlit walks through Prospect Park, Marc had told me stories of lovers past, the ones who had tried, unsuccessfully, to break through his wall. "Some gave up and the others," he explained, "just crashed. That's just me. Can you deal?" he added, more to himself than to me.

But a wall is different than a world, and it was Marc's world that I wanted to enter. A world of restaurants with names like Mekka and The Soul Cafe, havens where beautiful Black folks gathered after a midtown/Wall Street workday and feasted on turkey-seasoned collard greens, sweet potato French fries, and grilled catfish. A world where sistahs and brothas wore their sense of entitlement to this city's treasures as smugly as they wore their designer suits and smiled, constantly, as if the real world of hardships was long, long behind them. Marc had a lifetime pass to a world of brick walls as a backdrop to our candlelit dinners and Ralph Lauren umbrellas to shield us from the harsh, New York elements. When I was with him, I found myself slowly, much too slowly I would later learn, finding a home.

I took mental note that the song playing was called "Chant," pushed repeat-hold and walked toward the mirror. I rejoiced in God's love as She enabled me to feel it: the soft flicker of the candlelight, the enchanting melodies of love, the cool and serenity of the color black. I looked into the mirror and saw Marc sitting on the edge of the bed, watching me. I smiled at him and soon felt the warmth of Marc's hands on my waist. I inhaled as ripples of firm muscle enveloped me and absorbed the heated chill that overcame me as I felt the moisture between my legs rise. We captured our image in the mirror and marveled at the contrast of perfectly complementary shades of mahogany and hazelnut upon the other. I felt him growing harder against me as we danced, so I continued, trying to hide the fact that the waters inside of me were tattle-telling along my inner thighs. Marc's tongue made a perfect line down the small of my back. We kissed, our tongues searching and loving what was found. This is what love is, I think, after coming up for air.

"Yes," Marc answered, "this is exactly what love is." He nudged aside several braids that snuck forward to get a closer look. "Beautiful," he whispered. "D, you are so beautiful."

Between kisses, I noticed Marc's eyes. They were the color of cinnamon, even in the candlelight. But they didn't fit. They were the eyes of a wise old man, someone who had known truth and pain and was now awaiting the eternal Footman. I traced my tongue along Marc's lips and kissed both of his eyelids, which were closed and waiting just for that.

"Danielle," he said, "I love you." The earth opened and I placed one of Marc's fingers inside of me. "And I have always loved you," I confessed.

Marc was now inside of me and I was overcome with a passion and wet so intense, I could do nothing but weep. We walked into our lives at that moment, making love every day, beginning with our mornings, when I would wake up to the Brooklyn sun on my face and Marc deep inside of me. I was in love.

Since a standard defense table is only designed to accommodate several people, there is not enough room for all six defendants and their attorneys to sit, so they must all be seated in the jury box. The spectacle of these much-too-young brothas seated in the first row with their somewhat dispassionate, often disgusted, White attorneys seated behind them was appalling. The prosecutor's table is nearest the jury box, so I am but several feet from the defendants.[4] Anthony's attorney, a wiry and nice-enough Jewish guy, tells me that I am sitting too close to his client, then proceeds to regale me with stories of witnessing "these guys" going off throughout his career. I accept his warning in a womanish way: I smile, but do not move my chair.

All of us—the attorneys, judge, court personnel, and the victims' and defendants' loved ones—eventually become a sort of regular, if not dysfunctional, family. I learn whose mama is whose, which girlfriend is paired up with whom and who that adorable, afro-puffed child who keeps interrupting the proceedings by yelling "hi, Daddy" from the back of the courtroom belongs to. Her little voice vexes all of us, so much so that the judge threatens to expel all children from the courtroom if he hears another. And perhaps, because of time and revelation, or simply because looking evil every day wears one down, the hate-filled glares that the lead prosecutor and I initially get from the defendants' families' subside, then disappear altogether.

[4] Because prosecutors theoretically represent "the People" or "the State," they are always seated closest to the jury.

The pre-trial hearings last the longest since their purpose is to determine what, of all the evidence collected—the weapons used, the gruesome photographs of Mariah's brain splattered across the rooftop, the self-serving videotaped confessions—will be admitted at the defendants' individual trials. I speak so quickly as I argue the search warrant issues that the court reporter attempts to pace me by creative eye gestures (assistance that will prove to be of no help as the transcript of my performance reads like garbled nonsense). My ease in rattling off relevant case law in between stutters, however, catches the attention of the court, who busily takes notes and asks me a series of pointed questions when I am done: *Counsel, was the scope of the search warrant sufficiently narrow?* (yes); *if the evidence shows that the officers moved anything during the search, would I be wrong in suppressing the evidence?* (no). When it is finally over, the lead prosecutor is beaming and slides me a note that reads "Great job!!!"; during the break, several of the defendants' lawyers congratulate me. I sit down smiling profusely, then suddenly feel overwhelmed and fight the urge to collapse, having just realized that I too am a part of the machine.

Marc was in love too. I was the woman with whom he would spend the rest of his life, but I was supposed to enter it *after* he had turned thirty, closed on his Long Island home, and opened his own brokerage firm. I was premature and Marc, a self-professed regular guy, just a Brooklyn College boy, as he loved to say, a man who had his trademark bow ties custom made, was not accustomed to glitches.

But he could not resist this new woman in his life, the one who made him stop at every vendor's book table and gave money to homeless people before they even asked. The woman who recited poetry at any moment and for whatever reason. The girl who loved everything Disney. When they watched *The Little Mermaid* at her urging, he marveled at how she sounded so much like Princess Ariel as she sang a simple enough tune about wishing that one could leave the bottom of the sea, if only for a day. It was only later that he realized that she was singing for her very life.

And so it began. He noticed that she only spoke of friends when directly asked and then, only in past tense. While he admired that she was very much in love with her niece and nephew and constantly bragged about them, he wondered why she never spoke of anyone else in her family and why she never called her mother. Marc had always been loved. Children wanted to go to his birthday parties, old friends made sure to look him up when they came to town, and his parents kept his old room in order for him. How was it possible for another human being to be all alone? How could it be possible for someone not to be loved?

One morning, after he had gotten out of the shower and stood before his closet trying to decide which shirt to wear, a strange feeling overcame him. He tiptoed into the bathroom and stood paralyzed by the door, horrified by what he saw. There she was, seated in the tub, her face buried in her hands as she sobbed quietly, though uncontrollably, as the shower rained mercilessly upon her head. She was the love of his life, this he knew, but she was broken. And he, who had experienced disappointment and at times, even sadness in his life, had never known despair. He knew that he could not fix her, but he also knew that he would never want to do such a thing, even for this woman, who was his very earth.

We decide to try Anthony's case first, a logical choice since he was the shooter and perhaps morally, the most heinous defendant. If he were convicted there would hopefully be a domino effect such that the other defendants would be more willing to accept a plea offer, or at the very least, make it easier for us to "flip" them against each other. The day before Anthony's trial, the judge suggests that we offer Anthony a plea deal of fifty-seven years to life. Secret bench conferences are rarely secret in these mainly empty, hollow rooms and Anthony, who sits merely several feet away, utters an audible smirk and shakes his head in disbelief. The smirk does not go over well with the judge, who demands that Anthony's attorney bring the offer to his client.

I can't blame him. Even though in my legalmind I knew that such a plea was most reasonable given the facts, I also knew in my realmind that the offer was utterly ridiculous. How can you tell a boy who has not even reached his twenty-first birthday that spending the next fifty-seven years of his life—*at the very least*—in a prison upstate is somehow a bargain? I am but twenty-eight years old and the previous three years of my life have been, to put it mildly, protracted and tumultuous. I cannot even imagine being *alive* in fifty-seven more years and I'm sure, neither can Anthony.

Anthony is convicted in the space of a few weeks and we urge the court to impose the maximum allowable sentence. He does, and sentences Anthony to one hundred years to life. Even though I know that his sentence is well deserved, the exposure nevertheless seems obscene and I struggle to fight back tears as the court methodically renders its ruling. The judge says that not even Anthony's youth and relatively innocuous prior criminal history (he had been arrested for a subway slashing when he was fourteen) were mitigating circumstances sufficient to weigh in his favor and reduce his prison exposure. The court points out that while the goals of the criminal justice system are not merely to punish but to have a rehabilitative and redemptive quality, Anthony's crimes demonstrate that he is far beyond any hope of either.

Then I remember. Of all the defendants, Anthony was the only one who did not have a regular visitor (one girl came to court twice during the pre-trial hearings, but never showed up again). Anthony's mother never came and her absence was as palpable as it was stinging. The day before his trial, I overheard Anthony's attorney ask him if his mother would be attending. I'll never forget the look of irritation (and pain) on Anthony's face as he smacked his teeth and threw up his hands to dismiss such an obviously ludicrous question.

Anthony's attorney would have liked to wash his hands of him too, I noticed, as the man rarely sat with Anthony during the breaks. It felt weird, sitting in that dilapidated courtroom, knowing that Anthony was handcuffed in a holding cell several feet away from us, while his attorney bought the lead prosecutor and me coffee and bullshitted with us. His attorney did not even know how far Anthony had gotten in school, information that seemed so essential to me, nor did he know whether Anthony had a nice shirt and tie to wear to his trial (Anthony and the other defendants often came to court sporting Tommy Hilfiger and FUBU, attire not likely to sit well with a jury), or much, if anything, about Anthony's mother. After I prodded, the attorney finally took a break from our vapid coffee banter, spoke with his client, and dutifully reported back to me that yes, Anthony had graduated from high school and received a diploma and *not* a GED (a distinction Anthony was quite proud of); he was going to borrow a shirt and tie from a fellow inmate; and his mother had long before washed her hands of her eldest son to focus her energies on her husband (not Anthony's father) and other son.

As I look at these boys during each of their individual trials, I will be forced to face a sobering truth every time: God must bless the children who have their own because no one else will. I will look at the defendants and think about fate, whether or not it is preordained or whether we create our own. I write furiously in my legal pad in a vain attempt to determine if this clichéd question is even a relevant inquiry for Black people, especially those of us who live in this country where the legacy of racist oppression has circumscribed our lives. I will look at each defendant and wonder which, of all the historically Black colleges or any other college for that matter, one of them would have attended had the stars been fairly aligned. I pick out the Alphas, the Kappas, and which one of the six would have been a "Q." I even see one of them, the one that I still worry about, at one of my own alma maters—U.C. Berkeley—and fancy him campus president.

And, the case will continue to haunt me. The defendants took turns raping Chante from behind while forcing her to orally copulate their condomless dicks. They breathed. They hosed her down as if she were a dog. They had people out there who loved them. They scoffed at the women's tearful pleas to let them go because they had babies at home. They were children once. They tied Chante and Mariah up so tightly that the bindings cut into their wrists. They had being. They casually deliberated about whether or not they should kill Chante and Mariah or simply take them to a park and have one of their ghetto whores "beat 'em up or cut 'em up." They loved women. They hated women. My heart will continue to break.

In Ana Castillo's epistolary novel, *The Mixquiahuala Letters*, the narrator poses life's penultimate question, "How long does death take?" Anthony's mother had not been to the court at all and I supposed, given the nature of her son's crimes, such was understandable. Here was this embarrassingly handsome young man who the lead prosecutor and I both agree is painfully cute. In fact, I might have dated him had I been Chante's age and remained connected with a community with a similar aesthetic (Anthony was identified, in part, because of his distinctive, initialed gold fronts). But I cannot stop wondering where his mother had been all his life: where she had been before he slashed an unsuspecting person on the subway or before her son wound up with a universe consisting of a Riker's Island transport bus, a rat-infested courthouse and, ultimately, an obscene life sentence in Attica.[5] Where was she when Anthony was developing his thought processes, the notions that coalesced in his brain that made it possible for him to annihilate two lives, two Black female lives, women who were virtual strangers to him? Where in the hell was his mother? Where was mine?

I wondered then (and still do) what Anthony and the other boys think about. Do they remember Chante and Mariah and feel anything for them? And if by some chance they don't think of them directly, I can't help wondering if they remember their own mothers, the laying on of hands that I am sure they always wanted but never received. I assume a lot, I know. But I also know even more that death takes as long as childhood. It is the blanket of empty that surrounds a child by the absence of hugs, kisses, and any other indication that they matter. Death is that thing that made it possible for the defendants to do what they did, that thing that exists inside all of us that makes us insanely cruel, oblivious, unloving.

This is indeed a bitter pill, knowing that God gave you something and you threw it away. As if Jesus himself descended into your midst and

---

[5] Anthony will be eligible for parole on December 11, 2096. Elliot Johnson pled guilty and received fifteen years to life; his brother, Christopher Johnson, was convicted after a jury trial and received thirty years to life. Their roommate, Timothy Butler, was convicted after a jury trial and received thirty years to life. Alonzo Reed pled guilty before trial and received seventeen years to life; his brother, Dashaun Reed, was finally convicted after three trials (his first two ended in a mistrial when both cases had one hold-out juror) and was sentenced to fifty years to life.

was not recognized in time. Eternity: what one must endure knowing that one was wrong. If I had known, really, that this moment would be here, I would have done things differently. But I did not envision today. And now, all I have, all we ever have, is eternity. The entire universe existed inside that jury box. Life really was not fair; justice, whatever that was, could not make it right. My boyfriend was never going to come back. Nothing could be changed. Ever.

Black, White, and Seeing Red All Over

by Shawn E. Rhea

It is spring, 1995 in New York City. I descend the steps of my brownstone apartment in Ft. Greene, Brooklyn, and before I even hit the last one I am caught up in the glow. The sky is a bright, azure blue, kids are playing in the park across the street, people are actually smiling at one another, and I can feel the warmth of the sun hitting my shoulders. It is the kind of day that renews my love affair with New York. It is the kind of day when I like to walk the streets of my neighborhood—an area that has been dubbed the Black Arts Mecca.

I have an affinity for Black men, particularly artistic, culturally aware brothas—poets, musicians, and artists who sport dreadlocks or untamed afros, and wear baggy, casual clothes that may even be splattered with paint. For the past decade this neighborhood has been the place to find them in abundance. It is not unusual to step into a café and see table after table of Black couples huddled together, looking as if they're sharing a wicked secret, or walking down the street hand in hand, appearing to hold the strength of creation between their palms. But recently the neighborhood has become more multicultural. There are signs of gentrification everywhere: from the new massive Pathmark grocery store, to the rising rents, to White homeowners and tenants becoming regular faces at local haunts. As I turn the corner, I am confronted with another sure-fire sign of urban gentrification: I see an interracial couple coming in my direction, walking hand in hand.

The brotha is dreadlocked, brown, and beautiful. The woman is attractive, shapely, and sporting a head wrap. I have seen Black men with White women in my neighborhood so often recently that I no longer have to have that embarrassing internal conversation with myself: the one that says I am being racist, petty, and insecure when I become upset over a brotha's choice to be with a White woman; the conversation that I would never repeat out loud because my parents didn't raise me to have such feelings. I am consciously struggling to be more accepting of each person's right to choose whom they love. I am trying not to take a brotha's decision to sleep with, date, or marry a White woman personally, so I keep walking, and force myself not to throw any glances their way that may be interpreted as disrespectful. I do not want to pass judgment on this couple, these individuals whom I have never met. But then, as we pass each other, the woman's eyes meet mine, and in hers I believe I see a look of defiance, boastfulness almost. The brotha shifts his head so that he can avoid our making eye contact. Suddenly I am angry. There are no words, no internal dialogue that can quell my feeling of betrayal. My feeling is that, like the Trojan Horse, an enemy has been welcomed into our homeland and it is only a matter of time before it gleefully and irreparably destroys the very binds of our nation.

I do not want to be diagnosed with Angry Black Woman Syndrome, so I constantly check and question myself. I wonder what is truly at the root of my feelings. Is it my own fear of ending up alone, without a mate who truly appreciates and understands me? Is my own sense of worth and beauty threatened by the thought that Black men who date White women have opted for a physicality that is impossible for me to realize, and, in doing so, have rejected me at my core, my very essence? Do I simply need someone to blame for the fact that I haven't been in a serious relationship for several years now? I toss these questions around, vacillate between answering "yes" and "no" to each, check to see which response feels more like the truth and gets me closer to understanding. But whenever I reflect, I only find more questions. I ask myself why my ill feelings are specific to Black men with White women. I do not feel the same uneasiness when I encounter brothas with Latinas, or Asian or East Indian women. Then again, the history between our people is different. Their ancestors were not stolen, raped, beaten, killed, and permanently enslaved by their forefathers and foremothers. No matter how much we want to disregard it, the legacy of slavery perpetuated by early European Americans is still reaping a stunted harvest. But I'm determined not to be a slave to this history, so I tell myself that this hostility which I have over Black men dating White women is irrational, unfounded.

The truth is, every important man in my life, from my father to my oldest brother to both of my deceased grandfathers, has devoted his life to building a strong, enduring, supportive relationship with the Black woman who is or was his wife. I remind myself that most of the brothas whom I've known to date White women at one time or another have ultimately ended up building their lives with sistas. I develop a list of affirmations that I employ whenever I feel myself falling prey to the ugly, hurtful, unexplained belief that Black women have been abandoned by the men who should protect and cherish us. My invocations go something like this:

- I will not let someone else's choice define how I feel about myself.
- I will judge people based on their actions, not their appearances.
- White women are not my enemy; oppression, racism, sexism, and classism are.
- Happiness does not always come in a convenient package.
- There are good brothas, kind brothas, culturally aware brothas, loving brothas in abundance, who cherish Black women and could never imagine their lives without us by their sides.

I am at home one evening right before the Labor Day weekend when a friend phones. He is upset over a recent breakup with his girlfriend. This man and I dated at one point, but have long since become platonic. He is thirty-two and the sista who has broken his heart is several years younger. In fact, she is only twenty-four, relatively new to the city, a struggling model/waitress, and a bit of a wild child who enjoys, among other things, large quantities of liquor, cocaine, and multiple sex partners. I have felt almost from the very beginning that their relationship was doomed. He is looking for love, she for someone to take care of her. Whenever he calls me complaining about something she has done, I ask him why he is attracted to her. "She's a little crazy, and I've always liked women who are slightly touched," he tells me time and again. "Yeah, but she sounds certifiable," I always respond.

When we speak, he is livid and railing over her most recent behavior. His pain becomes an indictment of Black women. "You see," he says to me, "sistas just don't know when they gotta a good brotha. Y'all are too hard to please; that's why I'ma have to open up my options. I'm through dating Black women." His tone is joking, but I feel on some level he actually believes what he has just said. "Crazy is crazy," I snap, no longer sympathetic to my friend's pain. I feel that he has unjustly turned it on me. "If you date crazy women that's how they'll treat you. It doesn't matter what color they are. I have a ton of single girlfriends who are attractive, smart, successful, loving, and sane, so that's utter bullshit," I offer.

"Yeah, well why are they by themselves? Probably because they're high maintenance."

"Do you call wanting respect and commitment high maintenance?"

We begin arguing and end the call by hanging up on one another. Later that weekend, I break down in tears telling a girlfriend how hurt I was by his comment and our ensuing fight. He and I don't speak again until he calls to wish me a happy birthday almost three months later. I muster up the nerve to ask him about the argument and whether he has truly sworn off Black women. He tells me no, and says he only meant what he said as a joke, that I had blown it totally out of proportion and taken it way too personally. He wants to know why I was so offended, but I am only able to discern bits and pieces of a rational reason, and I know that any attempt to explain my feelings would only cause another argument, so I simply say, "It didn't feel like a joke at the time, but maybe I did misread you."

My cousin Jamie is the absolute closest thing that I have to a sister, and in many ways we are closer than most sisters. She is also my best friend, and she knows every secret that I would ever draw breath to repeat. As children we were inseparable. Our bond was sealed as babies, when she came to live with my parents and me shortly after I was born. Her parents were drug addicts and unable to care for her. She was only with us for a year, but my mother says that after her parents came and took her away, I cried for weeks asking when she would be coming home.

Jamie's father was an amazing singer, who even recorded a hit record in the 1950s. Her mother, I am told, was very attractive as a young woman. She is also White. Jamie received her father's face and beautiful singing voice, but she got her straight, light-brown hair, fair skin, and hazel-green eyes from her mother. When we were little, people never believed Jamie and I were related. "Are y'all jus' play cousins?" or "How come y'all don't look nothin' alike?" were the questions that newly acquainted friends and even their parents felt compelled to ask us, but Jamie and I were family, and we were determined to honor that bond, so we became fiercely protective of our kinship. "No! We're real cousins," both of us would vehemently declare to whomever dared question our shared bloodline.

We became even more protective of that bond as teenagers. Jamie was easygoing and popular, while I was sharp-tongued and tended to take longer to warm up to people. New acquaintances, men in particular, always gravitated more readily towards Jamie and that was a painful reality for me. A large part of their attraction had to do with her personality; she is one of the most endearing people I have ever known. But there was another reason, an unspoken reason that neither of us knew how to name as children or teenagers. There was a high value placed on Jamie's long hair, fair skin, and light eyes, and there were people who wanted to be close to her for no other reason. Still, there were others who disliked her for the same reasons.

We didn't realize it then, but I made it my job to be a buffer between Jamie and those who I felt were disingenuous towards her, while she made it her job to defend me against folks who thought me too acerbic, bossy, and aloof. At times she and I found ourselves at odds over people who I felt were phony, but she was unprepared to write off as such. The arguments sometimes strained, but eventually strengthened, our friendship. Years later, when she moved to Los Angeles and I moved to New York, our loyalty to one another was hardly tested by distance. I remember clearly her desire to seek an ugly revenge on a Los Angeles–based brotha who broke my heart, and I recall seething when she told me about a particular brotha who would not date her because he thought her skin too light and hair too straight. Then there was the White female coworker who had wondered out loud why Jamie "admitted" to being Black when no one would ever have guessed. On another occasion that same coworker told Jamie she was "slipping" when the tone of her voice became a little too Black for the coworker's tastes.

Experiences like those have become so commonplace for Jamie that, though they are painful, she has developed a serious ability to check folks and leave them holding their own crap. When we were younger, however, I was just beginning to understand that being close to my cousin often gave me an uncomfortable view of racial dynamics that most folks only speak of in the abstract. It would take years for me to realize that our friendship and kinship were the genesis of my internal battle against Black folks' coveting of "the other."

Jamie has come to New York to celebrate New Year's, 1998. One evening during her stay we are visiting Charles, a man I've been dating. Tony, a mutual friend of ours, is also there. The four of us are having a wonderful time listening to music and drinking wine when Charles starts teasing me about a guy who, at a club the night before, was determined to talk to me despite the fact that I was obviously with someone. The brotha planted himself in a seat at our table when Charles went to the bathroom and all but refused to get up when he came back.

I remind him that that was not the first time something like that had happened to us. "Remember that time we were at that club and that White woman came and stood in front of our table? She started dancing by herself and throwing kisses at you. She saw me sitting right there; she saw me looking at her like she was crazy and like I was 'bout to kick her ass, but she just kept on going."

We all laugh and shake our heads in disbelief. But I am not content to just compare notes with Charles about whose admirer was craziest. I begin making blanket commentary about White women. "They are a trip," I continue. "Why are they so blatantly sleazy when they're going after men?"

I do not notice it at first, but Jamie has become quiet. I go on to make some other less-than-complimentary remarks. When my cousin can no longer bear my comments she blurts out a command that silences me in midsentence. "Shawn, stop dogging White women!" she snaps angrily. "You know, my mother just happens to be White."

My eyes fall upon her face, and, despite her venomous tone, I see only hurt. "Sorry," I say, knowing that my apology can in no way compensate for the pain that I've caused. Charles quickly changes the subject, and I realize that I have hurt my cousin in a way that I would not have intended even at my angriest moment.

At home later, I remember an essay that Lisa Jones, daughter of Amiri Baraka, wrote in *Bulletproof Diva*, her book of personal and political essays on race and culture in America. Jones, whose mother is also White, has struggled for years to come to terms with her own multi-ethnic background. In one piece she tells of her own less-than-stellar feelings about brothas who pass over sistas in favor of White women. But she also writes that she fiercely loves her own White, Jewish mother, and that if one particular Black man had not lain down with one particular White woman she herself would never have been born. I think long and hard on that statement, and I realize how much it rings true in the case of my own cousin and best friend—someone who I could never imagine not having in my life.

That night I begin doing some serious soul searching. I am disappointed that I have let defensive feelings that initially were a means of protecting someone I love fester into ugly pain and rhetoric. Before Jamie leaves New York, I give her my copy of Jones's book, hoping that she, like I, will find something familiar and helpful in it.

It is July 1999 and I am preparing to move to New Orleans. The unyielding pace and expense of New York City, coupled with a severe case of writer's block and restlessness are causing me to flee southward. I am looking for a more nurturing and productive environment. Also, I am convinced that I am never going to meet a man with whom to share my life in New York. Over the last year I have seldom dated. Then again, my days have been so crammed with story deadlines and moving arrangements that I've rarely had time to think about men.

While packing for my move, I stop to browse through some photos and I come across one of me with a former boyfriend on vacation in London. I keep flipping and find more of me with other exes in Jamaica, in D.C., and at parties. Usually these pictures fill me with a small sense of regret and longing, but this day it dawns on me that my fear of being perpetually single has subsided. Though I definitely still want a partner, a husband, a man with whom to raise a family, I no longer wonder what I will do with my life if this scenario does not manifest. I know that I will build a fulfilling existence. I find peace in this awareness.

I keep looking through the pictures, and eventually come across one of Jamie at her graduation dinner. She is obviously tipsy, her eyes narrowed into small slits. It is a telltale trait of inebriation that we both inherited from our fathers. I think about how often Jamie and I have visited each other in L.A. and New York, and I realize that a chapter in my life is closing. I also remember how much I hurt her the last time she was here. But like everything else, our bond survived, and I have grown at least a little. I rarely have a visceral reaction when I see Black men with White women, and that is something for which I can thank my cousin, but I also know that, even though I no longer feel like marriage is the ultimate prize and I can accept relationships beyond the color boundary, I want to be someplace where I can possibly meet a brotha with whom I can build a life.

I move to New Orleans in August and, as fate would have it, my first week there I meet Franklin. He and I have an immediate attraction. We are both writers, both new to the city, and we each have eclectic taste in music. Neither one of us is anxious to acknowledge an interest beyond friendship, however. He is a bit cautious, and I sense that it is probably because there is someone in his life. My suspicions are confirmed when, at a party one evening, I meet his girlfriend, who is visiting from out of town. I am somewhat surprised to discover she is White, but I am relieved when my feelings do not linger past our initial introduction. While I had never considered the possibility that Franklin's significant other might not be Black, I find that I do not have to struggle to suppress territorial or angry feelings when I learn she is White.

Over the next few weeks Franklin and I meet for coffee, go to poetry readings, play pool, and take in movies. We talk late into the night, sharing our struggles to find our voices as writers, and our concerns that we probably don't devote enough time to the act of writing. We talk about our personal lives and relationships. I tell him about the challenges of being a single, thirty-something woman. I reveal that I am used to living by myself and that my family believes I'm becoming too intolerant of other people's idiosyncrasies. They hint that I may not be fit to share a home. I say I fear they may be right. He divulges that having made the choice to date a White woman, there have been uneasy moments: moments when people's judgments and assumptions have intruded upon the sanctity and peace of their relationship; moments when he has felt the stress of their obvious cultural differences. But he says that he learned long ago not to let other people's expectations dictate his own choices.

Over drinks one night, it becomes obvious that neither Franklin nor I really want to remain strictly platonic. We talk about the complications of our getting involved.

"Long distance monogamy is just not very realistic," he tells me in a confessional tone.

"Yeah, I hear you, but I don't want to be the thing that you do until the real thing gets here," I say. What I don't tell him is that more than being concerned with whether I might be entering a relationship with a man who may eventually have to choose between me and another woman, I am concerned about the fact that this other woman is White.

I silently ask myself if he is dating a White woman because he has issues with Black women, or because he just happens to be attracted to this particular woman? I want to make sure that he is not—as my cousin so aptly describes Black men who are infatuated with her looks—"O.J.-icized." But the proper words for posing such a sensitive question never come to me. I feel that it is impossible to respectfully ask someone, especially a man with whom I ultimately wish to be intimate, whether he has racial identity issues. I also wonder whether asking him directly will get me an honest answer. I am clear that few folks struggling with identity issues are willing to give voice to that fact, and I know that race identity and allegiance are particularly insidious issues. So I bite my tongue and force my uneasy feelings back down into my stomach.

I watch his actions instead, convinced that they will provide a more truthful answer to the question I can't ask. I tell myself that any successful relationship requires a leap of faith in its early stages, and that this is the point at which I must make mine if I am going to truly find out if Franklin and I have a future. He and I agree not to put any limitations on the relationship and to see where it takes us. We officially begin dating, but our romantic endeavor is short-lived. One morning, several weeks into our involvement, Franklin tells me that the guilt and emotions of trying to juggle two relationships is becoming overwhelming and complicated.

"I didn't expect to develop such strong feelings for you so quickly, and I can't let myself go there because I already have someone in my life."

I am disappointed and upset. While I shoulder much of the blame for getting involved with a man who is already in a committed relationship, I can't help but feel betrayed. A big part of me is angry that he has chosen being with a White woman over being with me, but I never speak this out loud. How can I reveal such an ugly, antiquated insecurity? Instead, I put on my best game face and confront him about everything but the one insult clawing hardest at my gut. I say we discussed the possibility that we might develop serious feelings for one another and that he knew it was a risk. He says he didn't realize how big of a risk it was and that he still wants to be friends. I say friendship is not a subject that I care to discuss now, but that I do want to know why this guilt has come upon him so suddenly. Angry tears well up in my eyes, and I realize that he has mistaken my anger for a desire to be placated when he says hurting me is something he never intended to do. I say it's time for him to leave.

It is spring 2000, and I am riding down Interstate 10 enjoying the breeze blowing through my windows. The wind is turning the intense Louisiana sun into a stream of sensuous warm air flowing over my still winter-pale brown skin. The radio is blasting tunes from my 1970s childhood and I become particularly enraptured when the deejay spins a seldom-played track, the Stories' "Brother Louie." I croon along, belting out the lyrics about love across racial lines.

The song's whining guitar immediately takes me back to the summer when I was an eight-year-old riding my bike through the streets of Detroit. Several girlfriends and I are swinging from monkey bars as we sing the tune. Back then, I liked the track not only for Ian Lloyd's gritty vocals, but also because, even at that young age, I appreciated the defiant image that it painted: two people refusing to let a societal taboo regulate their capacity to love, nurture, and claim one another. I remember feeling hope and a powerful subversion in that image. Why is it that I now have difficulty embracing similar feelings whenever I come across a Black man who has chosen to break the taboo, I ask myself? I wish that I could be that little girl again—the one who saw power in the type of relationship that I now struggle not to resent.

I can never be her again. My feelings about interracial dating, specifically Black men with White women, are forever colored by a racial and sexual caste system that often views Black women as ball breakers, while White women are seen as easygoing, sexually accommodating, and physically desirable.

Of course, these are only stereotypes. Women, Black or White, cannot be reduced to or explained by such derogatory definitions. Nor can we be held accountable for any man's physical, cultural, and emotional preferences. But these still powerful stereotypes are bandied about so often that people have embraced them as truths. For some, they provide easy excuses for complex choices, while for others, like me, they trigger feelings of rejection and low self-esteem.

It is this epiphany that strikes me at my center: the acknowledgment that—despite the self-love and acceptance gospel preached by modern-day therapists, the consistent encouragement and esteem-building dialogue of loving parents, and the support of a community of friends and extended family—at least part of my self-worth is inextricably linked to a need to be loved, desired, and cherished by Black men. It is an innate want that I feel as strongly as instinct, and instinctual needs insist on satisfaction. I am clear, however, that I am not an animal chasing her prey over open prairies, or mating with a male for the sole purpose of procreation. I am a woman—a Black woman—who must separate the instinctual from the societal, the individual from the stereotype, the truth from the assumed. And I must find myself amidst these contradictions. I must be willing to ask myself the hard question: By which am I motivated—fear or love?

Will I ever be totally free of this demon? Who knows? What I do know is this: I want to be free of it enough to love whom I love, and secure enough to accept someone else's choice if they decide not to love me.

Different Ways of Saying I Love You

by Rochelle Spencer

This is embarrassing to admit, but I've never been too good at relationships. I'm the sort of person who scours through *Essence* and *Cosmo* and actually takes the quizzes. Most of my relationships have the shelf life of milk; the very few I'm in that last longer than six months always seem to end disastrously. Still, even though I'm bad with long-term relationships, for the most part, I enjoy dating. I was a late bloomer, so dating is still new and exciting for me. Consequently, I'm known as the girl who's gone out with *everybody* (including an ex-boyfriend who thought he was a space alien and a brother who thought he was God and wanted to be known only as "Divine"). Still, sometimes I feel that it might be time for me to settle down. Most of my girlfriends have had the same calm, steady boyfriends for five years or more (now that we're entering our mid-twenties, it looks like their calm, steady boyfriends will soon evolve into calm, steady husbands). Thus, my girlfriends have never known what it's like to be stood up on Valentine's Day. And they've never gone out on a blind date with their coworker's brother's best friend. And they've never limped home in five-inch heels because they were just that tired of dealing with their coworker's brother's best friend.

Usually, when I meet a new man, he'll say something like, "You're charming and attractive, how come you don't have a man?"

And I'll look at the guy like he's crazy because, hey, I want to know that too.

But, then again, maybe a part of me already knows the answer. At twenty-five, I've finally recognized that I have issues. Serious, serious issues. Often times, when I enter into a relationship, I lose part of myself, and become needy in a way that frightens me. I need continual reassurances that the man I'm with genuinely cares about me. I want cards, flowers, and constant "I love you's" whispered in my ears. Oddly, if the guy I'm with does all the things that I want him to do, then I feel myself cool towards him.

Where did these strange and conflicting feelings come from?

Because I've run out of guilt trips to place on my mother, I now fling them, rather furiously, at my father. There is a problem with this logic, however. My father—unlike good old mom—refuses to feel guilty.

If I tell my father that I feel unloved because he never verbally expresses his love for me, he reminds me that he paid for my college tuition. If I blame him for my inability to maintain stable relationships, he reminds me, again, that he paid for my college tuition, and also, that he did the best job he could. *The best job that he could.*

Who can argue with that?

This was my childhood—suburbs, Brownies, private school, ballet lessons, debutante balls, and a living room that resembled Toys 'R Us every Christmas. I was a happy kid with a supportive family, and in college, when I needed a car, I got one, even though I didn't technically know how to drive.

This was my father's childhood—inner city, bitter family feuds, and rivalries, all of his close friends and family either dead or in jail, including his lifelong best friend who was murdered while still in his early twenties. My father once described his childhood as a blur of deaths and funerals, and to this day this man—whom I admire more than anyone else in this world—has trouble expressing his emotions. Maybe somewhere in my father's childhood, he learned to bury his emotions and accept the fact that the things and people he loves most might not be there tomorrow. And maybe, somewhere in mine, I learned to value verbal, highly emotional expressions of love because it seems as though that's what I missed most from my father.

I'm always initially attracted to men who are the exact opposite of my father. My boyfriends are the artsy, Afrocentric, poetic types. You know, the kind of brother who recites a heartfelt poem at a spoken word event and afterward everyone murmurs "that was deep," because no one understood exactly what he was saying. I'm attracted to these guys because they don't seem to have as much of a problem showing emotion. But my relationships with these men never last. Either they are so emotional that every day plays out like an episode of *All My Children*, or a lot of other affection-starved women are attracted to them too—and I definitely don't want to deal with that. So then, I gravitate toward macho guys like my dad, and ultimately, I'm not happy with them either. I badger them into trying to show emotion, and then I get upset when the only emotion they show is annoyance.

So now, here is the question that I started asking myself now that I'm trying to develop serious, long-term relationships: Is my father a bad father because he doesn't communicate his emotions, thus making his two daughters vulnerable to emotionally needy relationships with men, or is he a good father who simply tries to protect his wife and children by shielding them with a façade of continual strength?

I still haven't been able to come up with a satisfactory answer.

I do not doubt—have never doubted—that my father loves me. My father has never beat me—or even spanked me. He's the man who has taught me everything from how to ride a bike to how to drive a car, and he's stayed up late many a night helping me with my homework. The problem is that I've never once heard my father say "I love you," or "I'm scared," or anything else that reveals what he's truly feeling. So, while I recognize that my father's no Cliff Huxtable, I also realize that he's no Joe Jackson. Rather, he's the strong, gruff man who reads the newspaper, mows the lawn, and doles out familiar advice.

The lack of closeness I often feel with my father is intensified by my relationship with my mother and sister. The three of us talk constantly. On Sunday afternoons, we pop popcorn and cry and laugh together over movies on Lifetime. In contrast, conversations with my father are awkward. For instance, whenever I'm away from home, my father always calls. But after we've said that first, initial hello and he asks me how my car is running, we'll sit on the phone for many long, very painful minutes with absolutely nothing to say to each other. Then, slowly, almost regretfully, my father will say, "Well, I guess you want to speak to your mother," and he'll put my mom on the phone and listen as she and I chatter away for hours.

Yet, it's more than just conversation that keeps us apart. My father is not the type to demonstrate affection: hugs and kisses are rare; punches on the arm or heavy-handed pats on the shoulder are much more frequent. When I look at my girlfriends who grew up as "daddy's girls," the girls who were the apples of their fathers' eyes, the ones who actually had the affectionate, doting dads, I feel robbed. These girls—no matter what they look like or what they accomplish later in life—have confidence that's unsurpassed. A daddy's girl is the plain or average-looking girl who arrives at the year's hottest party with the Morris Chestnut look-alike on her arm. A daddy's girl is the woman who argues vehemently with the supermarket cashier that she hasn't been given the right amount of change, despite the growing line in back of her; a daddy's girl is the woman who automatically feels at ease with herself.

It's funny how our world forgets how important a father is to girls and young women. In books and films, on billboards and in our day-to-day lives, we're haunted by images of lonely little boys searching for their fathers; our society itself has become a reminder of how much a boy needs a father to become a man. While this may be true, the media never mentions how equally important fathers are to their daughters—and they should. I remember reading a study many years ago that suggested that many girls are promiscuous because they are simply longing to be touched, in a loving way, by a male. I think, also, that along with this loving touch, many young women are longing for some sense of male approval. These young women, from popular rapper Lil' Kim to the anonymous sister on the street, need to know that they matter to someone, not for what they look like, but simply for who they are. And this is where fathers come in. If the one male figure who looks most like you in the world doesn't believe that you're the most beautiful, the most perfect creature in the entire world, then who else will? There's an entire generation of Black women with emotionally distant or physically absent fathers who feel unattractive and unloved and, thus, enter into loveless relationships.

But how do we begin forming loving relationships? How do we get past the emotional distance that separates us from each other? Maybe the first step is to acknowledge that we have different ways of communicating.

Black men are told that they need to be tough in order to survive, and it doesn't help that we still live in a world that praises men—of all races—for being cool and noncommunicative, and ridicules them for showing any sign of emotion. And yet, the more I examine my relationship with my father, the more I'm slowly recognizing that there is more than one way of communicating and more than one way of saying "I love you."

My father said a silent "I love you" to me a few weeks ago, during an evening when it was growing dark and cold outside, so cold, in fact, that my breath turned to ice the moment I stepped outside. I had my keys in my hand; I was going to get something out the trunk of my car. As I walked out onto my front porch, there was my father, in the cold, in the dark, quietly working on my car. I hadn't asked him to do anything, but he had changed my oil and washed and waxed the fading paint job on my little red Toyota until it gleamed.

I'll never be a daddy's girl, but maybe by not offering constant nurturing and by forcing me to be independent and tough, my father has made me aware that I shouldn't settle for less in life—or in a relationship—even if that means dating the occasional deity or extraterrestrial. And while I'll never have a father who is generous with his "I love you's," I'm safe in the knowledge that he did do the best job that he could, the best way that he knew how.

Las Cartas del Alma de Pedro Valentín Carol Almeraz . . .

by Taigi Smith

Imagine a country where the old have faces that tell no stories and tongues that speak no words. Imagine a place where los viejos *sit on verandas, expressionless and dazed, and watch as the world revolves around them in a way that is motionless and steady. Imagine laughter, imagine music, imagine dance, imagine poverty. Imagine a nation of Black people who have spent a lifetime in Castro's Cuba while the opportunity for freedom has come and gone. They are too old to flee, too weak to fight, and too wise to pretend as if communism has proven itself the great equalizer. Imagine a country where the elderly say nothing, and instead, watch as life and liberty dissipate before them like steam on a cold winter day. They see tourists come and go as they please, and realize that the dreams of equality Fidel Castro promised for his people have been nothing more than political propaganda, lies. Imagine a country full of brown people too afraid to demand the political freedom they deserve. Imagine a nation of citizens full of beans, rice, bread, nicotine, and rum, who have literally been starved to a point where they are physically unable to fight for that freedom. Imagine a country where children without shoes dance in the streets as old men make music that is soulful and sweet. Imagine rusty horns and guitars without strings, a place where the voice is an instrument of the hills and the countryside. Imagine a place where people's freedom has been stolen, but not their souls, and when you wake up, you'll find yourself in Cuba.*

April 12, 2001

It is a balmy afternoon in Habana Vieja, and like all days, there is music. On curbs sit old men who chain-smoke cigars, while laughing *abuelas* watch the latest episode of a Brazilian *telenovela* just a few doors away. Beside ice-cream stands sit laughing children who nickel and dime tourists like me, while the rhythms of congas, trumpets, and maracas fill the air. A boy rides past on a rickety bike wearing sneakers that are holey and black and his smile tells me that he is in love—on his handlebars sits his *novia*. I watch two men repair a '59 Caddy using rusty tools while a gang of teenagers play a mean game of stickball just a few feet away. I am on a street named Obrapia in Old Havana and at this moment, Cuba seems surreal; almost like a daydream that just goes on forever. Yet for me, Cuba is that dream. For the past year, I have been obsessed with the *Buena Vista Social Club* album and have been on a Cuban binge of sorts. I have purchased every piece of Cuban music I could get my hands on and have spent countless nights dancing passionately with myself to *cubano* rhythms, and even as I sleep, visions of crowded nightclubs and dancing men fill me. At night, I lie in my bed alone and listen as the voices of old men sing songs with names like *"Dos Gardenias Para Tí"* and *"Chan Chan,"* all the while yearning to visit the mythical place I have come to love simply for its music.

My definition of Cuba is wholly based on the music I have heard and nothing more. I do not know that most of the people in Cuba are of African descent, and I do not understand the complexities of Cuba's government. I know nothing of the country's poverty, and I do not understand why the Cubans in Miami fought so hard to liberate Elian Gonzales. Over midnight glasses of merlot, I fantasize about singers like Compay Segundo and Ibrahim Ferrer serenading me with lullabies in voices so sweet and seductive, and finally, after months of contemplation, I pick up the telephone and charge a five-hundred-dollar ticket to Cuba from a Canadian named Wlodek. Weeks later, I board a commuter flight from New York to Toronto, and eventually connect with Cubana Airlines flight 1855 to Havana. My friends Harold and Duron join me on this journey and after a year of dreaming, it is from Cuba I write.

I am standing in an open-air bar sipping mojitos and listening to the rhythms of a five-piece band—the echoes of rusty horns sing rugged and crisp. I am self-conscious because people are staring at me, the foreigner, but my fascination with the music is stronger than my fear, and before long, I am lost in a world filled with song. The singer's voice is a slow, deep wail, and as he sings, he dances. I am in Cuba. I am in Cuba. I am in Cuba. These words play themselves in my mind until I am interrupted.

"Want some action?" are the only words that the thin, dark man standing before me can eke out . . . he says "action," like *"acción,"* and he's giving me this strange, semi-rehearsed, b-boy stance. The white parts of his shirt have turned a dirty gray and I can see spaces in his mouth where teeth used to be. His voice is deep and his English is broken and heavily accented—at the moment, it all seems so strangely sexy. Yet, the proximity of this man unnerves me and I'm starting to feel nervous because I am a single woman standing alone in a Third World bar. The Havana humidity has caused my press n' curl to frizz and my tank top, emblazoned with the words "Little Black Kitty Cat," is letting all the Cubans know that I ain't from these parts. Back at home, I wouldn't have given this brotha the time of day, but I take a risk and go with the flow. I am intrigued with the possibilities that this conversation may bring and I am, quite frankly, relieved to have met someone who speaks English. When I look up from my mojito, he's looking me dead in the eyes.

Over drinks, I learn more about Pedro. In his search for Americana, Pedro calls himself Peter, but he's Afro-Cuban and Black—like the midnight sky. *Pedro Valentín Carol Almeraz.* Such a beautiful name, I say to myself, and wonder why a man with a name like Pedro Valentín would reduce himself to "Peter." Throughout my trip, I call him Pedro, but even at this moment, in 2003, I still think of him as Valentine. Pedro speaks relatively fluent English and has taught the language to generations of Havana's children, and everyone—adults, children, and *los viejos*—call him "the Teacher." Pedro, a country boy at heart, was born in Mantanzas, but grew up in Habana Vieja and has lived there for most of his forty-seven years. I learn that Pedro is a reader and an intellectual, a former soldier with a bullet hole in his leg from the years he spent fighting in Angola during the seventies.

This man is so intense, his words so calculated, his voice so deep. He touches me when he speaks, wanting to know that I understand his words, needing to know that I am listening. And I am listening to him and hanging on to his every word. I am trying to decipher his origins and mine, all the while, trying to understand where his road and mine forked, needing to know why his ancestors' journey from Africa led them to Cuba, while my ancestors' journey brought me to the United States. These are circumstances in which we had no control, but because of that forked road, he speaks Spanish and I speak English, he is poor and, I am, to Pedro, rich, and most importantly, he is imprisoned within the confines of his country and I am free to roam.

✂   ✂   ✂

Pedro spent several years in a Cuban prison for owning a pair of Levis given to him years ago by an American tourist—this was back when hanging out with Americans meant a quick ticket to jail. And yes, that was after he fought the war in Angola. He is a student of aikido, a man born on Valentine's Day, *un hombre* of few words. That afternoon, Pedro takes Harold, Duron, and me to the tiny apartment he shares with his sister, aunt, niece, great-niece, niece's boyfriend, mother, and other family members—the relatives total about nine. He lives in an apartment that is built off an alley in one of Habana Vieja's old buildings. In the alley, everyone leaves their doors open, and like most places in Havana, there are stray dogs everywhere. Laundry hangs from clotheslines and people spend warm, humid days watching *telenovelas* and looking out their windows. The apartment is old, dingy, and dark. There is no stove or running water and it is infested with roaches. The floors are concrete and other than a few plastic folding chairs and a television, the one room in Pedro's apartment is bare. There is a ladder that leads to an upstairs space where everyone sleeps and it appears that there is little room for privacy or peace.

Everything about Pedro's home makes me uncomfortable, from the roaches to the folding chairs to the shame I feel. Pedro's invitation makes me think of all the times I have denied friends entry into my home because it was "dirty," or because I simply felt my apartment was too small, and when I think about this, I feel shallow, almost as if I've forgotten the true meaning of hospitality in my quest to acquire material things. Later I learn that Pedro's invite was more the rule than the exception and that Cuban people are almost always willing to open their doors to strangers no matter how humble their abodes may be. Pedro's open door would be the first of many.

It is not long before I learn that Pedro wants nothing more than to leave Cuba. He is a man trapped in a country that does not value him and makes a mere fifteen dollars per month teaching English. He is an amazing dancer whose skin shines black even under the pressures of age and dire circumstances. He wants to know everything there is to know about America and envisions it, as so many foreigners do, as a place where there are movie stars everywhere, a country where prosperity is abundant and life is good. He asks me to tell him about Brooklyn and I start to feel shallow, again, and inadequate as I tell him about the way I live. I tell him about my travels and my apartment. I tell him about my friends and the mundane things about my life, but as I tell him these things, I realize that my world is as foreign to him as his world is to me.

I start to notice that although Pedro holds a job as a teacher, he hardly ever goes to work. Instead, Pedro, Harold, Duron, Yamila (Pedro's cousin), and I hang out day and night, wandering the streets of Havana listening to music, dancing, drinking, and discussing life. Through Pedro, I meet Cubans who have art galleries in the backs of their homes, participate in spiritual cleansing ceremonies with a *santero*, and go to a birthday party where blown-up condoms masquerade as balloons. When I ask him about money and how he makes it, he pretends not to hear me and then, eventually, tells me that to him, money is not important. I take a mental note and try to decipher the importance of these words. Back in the United States, I live in a world that revolves totally around money, but for him, in a country where most people are poor, it is life and love that matter, and not dollars and cents. Do not get me wrong, this is not the celebrated cliché of the happy poor person. Pedro certainly yearns for a different, better way of life, but he also realizes that there is more to life than working fifty hours per week and chasing dollar bills. For someone who has grown up in a capitalist society, this concept baffles me. When I'm with Pedro, I feel as though I'm really living life and appreciating things for what they really are. Then I realize that I'm on vacation, and when I go back home, money, and time clocks, and work will all become part of my reality once again. When I look at Pedro, I see a man who is angry and dejected because he lives in a society that has literally stripped him of his dignity, but somehow, I am amazed to find, his soul remains intact.

April 13, 2001

Pedro and I are lying on a beach called La Playa de Santa María drinking Cuban beer and contemplating life under the Caribbean sunshine while policeman with big guns stare us down through binoculars. The bullets are not meant for American tourists like me, but instead for Cubans, like Pedro, bold enough to risk death in the pursuit of freedom. Duron, my other travel companion, is listening to music on his MP3 player, and Harold is flirting with Yamila. In the water, when we go out to pee, Yamila tells me that months ago, Pedro fell in love with a *gringa* from España who promised to marry him. For months, Pedro corresponded with this woman by telephone, and then one day, she stopped calling, and all of Pedro's dreams for freedom went up in smoke. Back on the beach, I begin to bombard Pedro with questions, needing to understand his way of life, and most importantly, wanting to come to terms with the guilt that has started to consume me. I question him because he speaks English and can help me understand those things about Cuba I desperately need to comprehend before this trip is over. I need to understand why the White Cubans we're lodging with have a penthouse full of American accoutrements, while Pedro lives in an apartment with no water or stove. The struggle to understand the way the economic system works in Cuba nags at me. My conscience will not rest. I do not understand Castro's strange system of food rationing nor am I able to comprehend why basic necessities must be purchased on the black market. This is not the Cuba that I learned to love from the songs that blasted from my CD player back in Brooklyn. Yes, there really are old men who sing these soulful songs on the streets, back alleys, and bars of Cuba, but these old men wear holey shoes, live in ramshackle homes, and are constricted by the laws laid down by Fidel Castro.

By chance, I meet a few of these men and have the opportunity to tell them what their music means to me. I look in their eyes and tell them that they are the reasons I am in Cuba and try to make them understand that back at home, their songs have brought me happiness when things in my life were anything but happy. Their love songs gave me hope and provided respite from the constant barrage of misogynist messages that had come to define my generation's brand of music. It is the irony of Cuba that amazes me; the irony that allows the most beautiful music I've ever heard to be born in a country where Black people are not allowed on certain beaches or in tourist hotels and no matter how hard I try to understand Castro's communism, I just don't get it. I need to understand why the police are everywhere. And most of all, I want to know why Pedro looks down when he walks and why he rarely looks me in the eye when he speaks.

And so, I fire off my questions, demanding answers, hungry for information. It does not matter that we are still sitting on the beach—me in a pink bikini, Duron still lost in his MP3-driven world, Harold and Yamila frolicking in the water like new lovers. Pedro says nothing, but instead, runs white grains of sand through his fingers. In America, I tell him, most liberals consider Castro a folk hero, a great equalizer of sorts. I tell Pedro that some members of the American Left praise Fidel for his extraordinary health-care initiatives and educational system. I tell him that most Americans blame Cuba's poverty on U.S–inflicted economic sanctions. Still, Pedro is quiet and says nothing. He sings quietly to himself in Spanish. He's away somewhere in another world, and although I am sure he hears me, he does not answer. It is just as I've been told so many times before. People in this country do not denounce Fidel Castro publicly. The consequences are just too great. Finally, Pedro says something. "He wants it that way."

"Who wants it that way?" I ask.

"Fidel." And this time, he looks at me.

❄   ❄   ❄

I'm pouring Coppertone on my body, basking in the sun, and now Pedro's asking the questions. He wants to know about New York City, and I tell him what it's really like for people, Black people. I need him to understand that beneath the bright lights and glamour of New York lie racism and discrimination. I try to explain that there is more to New York than Jay-Z, Foxy Brown, Jennifer Lopez, and rap videos. I tell him about Amadou Diallo and police brutality. I tell him about the young men who have to sell crack because they can't get jobs. I tell him about welfare lines, homeless people, and I try to explain to him that, in America, the police will shoot you or beat you simply because you're Black. Pedro seems neither shocked nor amazed by my accounts of America and it's because he knows that in truth, no amount of police brutality could match what he's lived through for the past forty-seven years of his life. After a while, Pedro takes a piece of paper from my notebook and draws me a map. "This is Little Italy." Yes. "And this is Soho." Yes. "And over here is Tribeca, near Soho." Yes. "And way over here is Central Park?" Yes. "Taigi, where do you live?" I take the pen and draw a bridge that connects Manhattan to another mythic city. "I live all the way over here . . . in Brooklyn."

Two weeks later

As Harold and I near the end of our trip, it feels as if we must find a way to take our friends with us. In just a few weeks, Pedro has grown close to Harold and the two men have become kindred spirits, bound by the ties that connect Black men born into the unsavory circumstances of economic injustice. Pedro and Harold are connected not by the struggle, but by the hustle. Both men have learned to make money on the street and have found ways to survive any which way they can. Harold is loud, boisterous, and always laughing, while Pedro is quiet, sullen, and intense. The two men have become fast friends simply because opposites really do attract. Although it has only been a few weeks, I am seriously contemplating marrying Pedro so that he can have the life he so deserves, but my desire to live a "normal" life holds me back. There are moments when I feel as though I really have nothing to lose by giving him a chance at freedom, because beneath all of my material possessions, college degree, big apartment, designer wardrobe, and impressive career, I really am alone. Back in New York, I am involved in a lackluster relationship, but I know that this person is not husband or father material. There really is no *real* man waiting for me back in Brooklyn, no boyfriend contemplating marriage, no lovers, suitors, or Mr. Right signing up to marry me. Like many women I know, I go to the movies alone, eat out by myself, and often times find myself dateless for months on end. My phone is not ringing off the hook and I've certainly had my share of disappointments when it comes to relationships. Regardless of what people may think, I actually get quite lonely and would like nothing more than to have a *real* relationship, and so, this decision to marry someone, even if that union is driven by necessity, is a hard one.

In three short weeks, Pedro has started telling me that he loves me, and there are moments when I actually believe him. I believe him because I really do want someone to love me, but at the same time, I'm rejecting Pedro's love because my Mr. Right isn't supposed to be a poor man from a Third World country. Or is he? I am torn because deep down inside, I'm afraid that Pedro could be my Mr. Right and that my fear of the unknown may actually be blocking my blessing. In the back of my mind, I wonder if this relationship really could turn into something viable and the conflict that arises within me is real because deep inside, I realize that most people would dismiss my relationship with Pedro as a case of a vacation fling gone awry. But to say this would be dismissive of the fact that for a moment, I felt as if the creator had perhaps chosen me to give this man a taste of freedom—to restore within him the life he never really had. *Reality check*. No matter how attractive I may think I am and how sexy I may feel within the confines of my own home, my love story is a sad one, full of heartbreak, emotional turmoil, and drama. When I really look at my situation, I feel hopeless, as if I don't have much to lose by marrying Pedro, but at the same time, I just can't bring myself to give up on the life I want for myself. It's the life that includes a wedding, a nice house, an SUV, a few kids, a successful career, and a husband who is an intellectual and social equal. But right now, in Cuba, at age twenty-eight, this life seems out of my reach, almost as far away as Pedro's quest for freedom, and so we are both living our lives in pursuit of pipe dreams that may never become reality. We move forth with the masquerade, hoping that at the end of my trip, things will become clearer for both of us.

Beneath the cover of mojitos and jazz, we start to hatch escape plans. While we sit on the Malecon, we discuss escape. While we eat at Paladar de Julia, we discuss escape. At the Buena Vista Social Club, we discuss escape. Time is running out and Harold and I realize that when we leave, all means of communicating with Pedro and Yamila will virtually be cut off. There is talk of false identities, doctored passports, social security cards, and of course, marriage. Over drinks, Harold and I joke halfheartedly with Pedro and Yamila about marriage, but deep inside, we know that the situation is anything but funny. From my place on the curb, I watch Harold and Pedro speak in hushed whispers like brothers. I imagine that Harold is asking Pedro why he has not bought himself a place on a raft that will leave him on the shores of Key Largo, or why he has not purchased an inner tube, and sailed dangerously towards freedom. After waiting almost fifty years to gain her freedom, Pedro's mother obtained a visa to visit her long-lost sister in Spain. It has been several weeks since she's left, and instinctively, Pedro knows his mother is gone for good. I ask him when he thinks she will return, and like most questions I ask, he does not answer.

Last night, Pedro and I escaped to the Malecon to talk privately. The water on the Malecon was angry and fierce, and as we sat on the Malecon's edge, the water crashed against its crumbling concrete. Unlike days past, Pedro spares no words. He tells me things that shake my existence and pierce me in a way that is painful and real. He says that without me, he may never leave the country that traps him, and may forever be doomed to a life of food rations and poverty. He is asking me to marry him, to return for him, but instead of lying, I tell him the truth. I tell him that at home, I have a boyfriend, a life, and obligations. I promise him that Harold and I will do our best to get him out, that we will never forget him, and that with some luck, we will also return for Yamila. I tell Pedro that I cannot be held responsible for the conditions under which he was born, and I beg him, with everything I have in me, not to hate me for leaving him behind.

"You can leave, but I have to stay here," are the last words he whispers to me that night as the water crashes behind us. There is something about Pedro's honesty that makes me question myself. While he has said that he loves me, he never pretends as if this is his reason for wanting to get married. I respect the fact that he has made his intentions quite clear, but there is no way that I can imagine my love story being totally devoid of *real* love. My husband is supposed to live in the United States. My husband is supposed to have a college degree. My husband is not supposed to be forty-seven years old. And, my husband should want to marry me simply because he loves me. But I am still unclear on where I stand, no matter what words come out of my mouth. I really do want to help Pedro escape, but at what cost? Selfishly, I decide that my happiness is worth more than Pedro's freedom and I am ashamed of myself, not because I'm a bleeding-heart liberal (because I'm not), but because I do not possess the ability to be totally selfless.

On the Malecon, I remind Pedro that I hardly know him and privately think, I am not like those White women who used you and promised to marry you, but then took their planes back to Spain and left you for dead with only the clothes on your back. I try to tell Pedro that I am an American and was raised as such, and that because of this, I am just too selfish to give up my dreams of a cookie-cutter life, but he does not understand. So, I make half-assed peace with my decision to go home alone, but remain torn. There really is no peace to be found when a woman must walk away from someone who could possibly be her future. Pedro kisses me on the lips and I am reminded of everything that could be. There is a scenario that plays through my mind in which Pedro moves to New York City and becomes a famous lecturer. People come from all over the City to hear him talk about the years he spent in a Cuban prison. They want to hear what life was like back in Cuba from a real-life Afro-Cuban. He charges a thousand dollars per lecture. In this fantasy, Pedro and I team up to write a book about his life in Cuba and it becomes a *New York Times* best-seller. It is this fantasy that drives me to continue thinking about how life could be if I married Pedro. If we worked really, really hard, maybe we could create a life for ourselves as a couple. Would it really matter that he was a forty-seven-year-old man who loved me for all the wrong reasons? The other scenario that plays through my mind is more daunting and the ending, less happy. I marry Pedro and he moves to New York City but is unable to find work because he does not possess the skills needed to be a productive member of the American work force. In this scenario, my family disowns me, I become pregnant, and my friends abandon me because they feel that I've somehow fallen off the deep end. Pedro leaves me for another woman and I am left alone—again.

As we sit on the Malecon, I am moved to a moment of intense self-evaluation and reflection. I flash to my Brooklyn apartment with wall-to-wall closets full of expensive shoes, $130 jeans, leather jackets, and Louis Vuitton luggage. I flash to my Brooklyn refrigerator full of bottled waters, gourmet ice creams, and leftover food from trendy restaurants. I flash to my Brooklyn bedroom full of fresh flowers, goose-down quilts, vintage furniture, and a Kenwood sound system. I flash to my Brooklyn bathroom and see my scented candles, handmade soaps, and medicine cabinet full of aspirin, nail polish, tampons, vitamins, sixteen-dollar lipsticks, and cotton balls and realize that, in a world where people have *nothing*, I have everything. And for a moment, one very long moment, I am consumed with guilt and unsure about the person that I have become.

Earlier that evening, we dance the night away at a dark, dingy night-club called La Red. We move naturally together, dancing salsa steps until the sun comes up. We dance as if our lives depend on it, each of us realizing that the time we have together will soon be cut short. Pedro has his hand on the small of my back and as we dance, he sings words so sensuous and pure into my waiting ears. He laughs at times, telling me that I dance like an American, and so in order to help me with my salsa, he makes small *click click* sounds in my ears, instructing me to follow the sounds of his rhythm. It is amazing to be in a country where Black men love Black women more than life itself.

During this trip, I've started to believe that people love deeper in Cuba because they have few material possessions to distract them. Perhaps that's why Black men and Black women have such a hard time interacting with each other in America. The bling-bling culture that has worked to infect so many relationships amongst my American peers really has no place in a country where most people have few material possessions to begin with. The notion of having few material possessions is a foreign concept to me. Seeing people for who they are instead of what they have is something that has challenged most, if not all, members of my generation. Without the cars, money, big jobs, and fancy clothes, we are all just people. Pure and simple. I make no excuses for my own materialism, but start to realize that when it comes to my personal relationships back in New York, I may actually be more symbolic of the problem than the solution. Perhaps for the first time in my life, I'm actually looking at a man for who he is instead of who he could be or for what he does or doesn't have. Realistically, it is this materialism that prevents me from even considering Pedro's proposal of marriage. I look at him and realize that there is no place in my life for a man from a Third World country. Our economic inequality is just too much for me to handle; our language barriers and economic differences are just too great. It's all so superficial, but I just can't seem to get past the particulars. As I look at this man, who's asking me to essentially give him back the life he's really never had, I am forced to evaluate who I am as a woman and a human being. It is my personal fear of what people will say or think that prevents me from taking Pedro's request seriously. But at the same time, I am not sure that a Black American man will ever love me the way that I imagine Pedro loves me.

Without our clothes, we're all just people. Naked people. By midnight, I realize that Pedro cannot come home with me.

I have always looked down on those women who married men for reasons having more to do with immigration than with love, but, for a very short period of time, I became one of those women. When I think back to the times Pedro and I spent together over that three-week period, I smile. Salsa dancing at La Casa de la Música. Live jazz at the Buena Vista Social Club. Beers and sandwiches at La Playa de Santa María. Mojitos at hole-in-the-wall bars in Habana Vieja. Long talks on the Malecon. Animal sacrifices and birthday parties in Mantilla. What a blessing to have met a man such as he.

I think back to a day when Pedro and I were sitting on the Malecon. The wind is blowing and I am seated unsteadily on a concrete ledge. The

Caribbean is crashing against concrete below us and I am afraid because I cannot swim. For the first time, Pedro begins to tell me the story of the two horses. One horse is black and the other is white. He says that at some point, one must choose between the horses, but whatever the choice, it is destiny that will ultimately direct the path of the chosen horse. At the time, it all seemed so esoteric—almost surreal. I wasn't really listening, but instead concentrating on my balance. *Don't wanna fall off this ledge . . . can't swim . . . can't swim . . .* Now, I realize the meaning of Pedro's story.

The memories come back to me the day I check the mail and find Pedro's letter sitting in my mailbox as if it belongs there. This is one of many letters Pedro has sent since my departure from Cuba, but the very presence of this letter, with its postmark from England, makes me realize that something good had happened in this crazy, crazy, war-torn world. And so I open the letter, cautiously at first, determined to understand the feelings I am about to experience before I do. The letters from Pedro have become more passionate and more demanding, and it is still flattering to receive the notes that proclaim Pedro's undying love for me and state that there is no woman more deserving of passion, courtship, and companionship than I. I have kept the letters close to me, using them to lift my spirits when life was rocky and turbulent. But this time, something is different. I open the envelope, expecting to find a letter, but out falls a photo. Of Pedro. There he is in shorts, lying on a white lounge chair grinning a sly grin. His eyes are closed. He is wearing new white sneakers and a Walkman, lying beneath a flower bush shrouded from the sun. And then, I read his note and am amazed, because at that moment it becomes clear that something really is different in this world. His letter is written in broken English and I read it several times hoping to understand exactly what he is trying to say. He tells me he is living in London and looking for work. And then he apologizes, telling me that the decision to marry the White woman was the only way he could escape Castro's communistic regime.

A White woman? I read between the lines and realize that Pedro did what he needed to do to save his life and to rescue his soul before it died. This story begins almost mythically, in Havana, Cuba, and ends somewhere between New York and England. I stare at Pedro's picture and forgive him, albeit briefly, for doing the unspeakable—for marrying a White woman. In his note, he reminds me of the story he shared almost three years ago about the two horses. The picture and the letter tell me everything I need to know, but leave out enough details to allow my imagination to wander. I imagine Pedro in a dusty London flat, in the arms of an older White woman. I envision her with blonde hair—streaks of gray are highlighted . . . she is about forty-five and her skin is weathered from the sun. She's one of those earthy types, an old hippie, perhaps even a liberal. She wears tie-dye skirts and beaded thong sandals. She married Pedro and took him back with her to England. *This part is true.* What an exotic prize, I think. A souvenir unlike any other. God bless her, I say to myself and realize just how special this day really is. Pedro has escaped Fidel Castro's oppression. He is finally free.

Pedro's note is a bittersweet declaration of love and freedom. His words recount the story of the two horses and ask me cryptically, of course, not to chastise him for the choices he's made. He is married now, to a White woman brave enough to rescue him from the communism that crushed his spirit for many years of his life. He has married a woman brave enough to accept him for who he is, a woman unafraid to face her critics. His letter forces me to face the possibilities of my own life, once again, and to take stock of the fact that, at thirty years old, I am still unmarried—still without children. I cannot help but think about what could have been, and rely on his words for the guidance needed to direct my feelings. He knows that I am upset because he has chosen the white horse, but asks me to understand his reasons for doing so. Freedom. A part of me is angry because as a Black American woman who has seen too many "good" brothers overlook sisters for White women, I cannot help but feel like another brother, regardless of his country of origin, has bitten the dust. But, as I read his letter, and look at him, sitting so smugly on that lawn chair, I cannot help but feel a bit guilty about my mixed emotions. I hold his picture in my hand for a few minutes, and slowly see Pedro Valentín Carol Almeraz's situation exactly for what it is—a chance at freedom—a chance at life.

The Bride Price

by Corrie Claiborne

I have always been a romantic. In fact, most of my adolescence was spent under the comforter of my twin bed pouring over romance novels pilfered from my mother's bedroom. Although none of the heroines in those novels were Black, I'd always thought that I'd somehow be the star of my own romance, that a truly great love affair would be my destiny. It didn't matter that I was an average, cinnamon-brown girl from South Carolina.

All that I learned about romance came from these books that usually featured White women with long hair and ripped dresses on the covers. These women were always in the passionate embrace of their hero, invariably a pirate, a soldier in the Union Army, a duke, lord, or maybe even a prince. If the book happened to be a modern-day romance, then the hero was always a CEO, a doctor, or, somehow, just plain old rich. I had no real-life models of romance, especially not romance between Black people, to compare these images to. My parents divorced when I was eight, which at the time seemed long overdue. Their marriage had been very contentious—marked by frequent arguments about money—arguments that seemed to go on twenty years after their separation. "It's your father's turn to pay your tuition," my mother would scream. "I always take the kids on trips and buy them whatever they want," my father would reply. My father was always good for things like exotic excursions to Africa, but not so good when it came to mundane things like rent. Back and forth they would go until eventually my brother, sister, and I hated to ask for anything. The only thing that I learned from my parents was how easy it was to disappoint each other.

In the romance novels of my youth, the loving characters fought over lots of things: an unwanted arranged marriage, whether or not an innocent girl would surrender her virginity, or whether or not it was better to fight for the North or South during the Civil War. Ironically, they never fought over money. Even if the heroine was dirt poor, which was often the case, the hero wouldn't mind forking over the cash—paying for a whole new wardrobe for her after she had, for example, been hit over the head, developed a bad case of amnesia, and washed up in a river on the hero's plantation. I came to understand that love meant being taken care of financially. If I were to have a great love affair, then I would need to have a man that could afford me. Everything that my parents were, in their fights over money, was not love. Love was green.

I also know that I am not so different from many women. Other women in this modern materialistic culture often equate money with love. For example, I and several of my sisters have remarked, upon seeing a girlfriend's huge three-carat diamond engagement ring, "Oh, girl, your man sure does love you!" And, we've whispered among ourselves about the men we know who actually let their wives stay home with their kids after they've married. "You know (blank) told (blank) that he will support the family and that her only job will be being his wife." We all sigh, and wonder what God we need to make sacrifices to in order for this to be our fate. It is not that we don't want to work or that we cannot make it on our own. I have a Ph.D. and am pretty happy being a college professor. I have friends who are doctors, lawyers, engineers, and politicians, all of whom are doing quite well on their own, but are unwilling, for whatever reason, to forgo the dream of the man with means.

My girlfriends and I discuss the fact that we worked hard to get where we are and we want a man with the same ambition. "I refuse to compromise," one friend declared. "Either I get what I want or I am going to be by myself!" Unfortunately finding a man who is attractive enough and "good on paper" has proved difficult. Often, it has meant that women determined enough to hold out for a Black Prince Charming usually end up waiting in vain.

For example, I have always known the qualities of my ideal man. In my mind's eye, my Black prince is tall, handsome, college educated, emotionally mature, financially stable, and artsy. Many times, I have been close to my ideal, but I never have quite found someone who is the total package. There was the lawyer who was too short and the handsome doctor that was just too—I don't know, there was just something wrong with him. And then, there was the man who was several years younger than I who provided me with loads of good sex, but juggled several part-time jobs that he tried to string together into something that could only be loosely called a career. No matter what else might have been at fault with these men, the deal breaker was often money.

In fact, as a woman who is still single at thirty-two, I have embarrassingly few experiences to draw upon with men who couldn't or wouldn't bear the financial burden of our relationship. Given the economic disparity between Black men and women, I was sure that this could not be the case because, statistically speaking, Black women have more financial opportunity than Black men. My sister and too many of my Black women friends can tell you war stories about having to pay for everything from meals to college tuitions and child support for the men they were dating or had married. I used to joke with my sister, who is a doctor, that she should set up her own foundation for "underprivileged Black men" because she seemed to purposely look for boyfriends that needed financial support. Surely, I thought, being that my sister and I were raised in the same household, we must have some dating similarities. I must have had some experience paying for dates or helping a man out in a financial crisis that I can draw on. I must have either repressed those memories or forgotten them.

I told my sister that I was writing an essay about Black women and materialism and I wanted to know what her thoughts were about the impact of money on our romantic relationships. Since she has seen me through all the years of my dating life, I asked her to tell me how I behave with men who don't make as much money as I do or in situations in which I have to pick up the tab. My sister laughed. "You, date a man with no money? Corrie, you have *never* dated a man without money." Maybe not, I thought, but at least once I must have had the experience that so many other Black women can relate to, the type of experience that Erykah Badu talks about in her hit song "Tyrone," which is all about breaking up with a man because of his lack of cash.

During my conversation with my sister, I finally remembered the time I went out with an engineer whom I had been dating for well over a year while I was in grad school. As I recall, we were at dinner when he'd realized that he had left the house without his wallet. When the check came, he looked shyly over at me and asked if I could pay the bill. I looked back at him and smiled. Always trying to be the semblance of the independent woman, I reached for my purse without saying anything, but inside I was thinking, If he lets me pay for this, then he "better call Tyrone," because I seriously doubt that we can continue seeing each other. This thought was totally irrational, because he is one of the most generous men that I have ever known. I also knew he was going to pay me back for the inexpensive meal. He had, in the year that we had been going out, purchased plane tickets for our trips, bought me more expensive presents than I had ever bought him, and had always, and I mean always, paid for our movies, meals, concerts, and anything else we did as a couple. It shouldn't have been a big deal for me to pick up the check for him this one time, but I remember feeling hurt that he would even ask.

Before the waitress could come and take my credit card, my boyfriend stopped me so he could go outside to his car to see if his wallet was in the glove compartment. He came back in with his wallet and apologized, paid the check, and I was left still not knowing what it felt like to take any financial responsibility with men. This whole incident, which I had almost forgotten or wanted to forget, made me aware of the fact that I have some real issues surrounding money. I was, of course, too ashamed to share any of this with my sister.

In fact, this is the first time I have publicly admitted the importance I placed on money as it relates to romance. In the past, I have always scoffed at women who sleep with rappers or athletes, trying to get pregnant in the hopes of making a living through child support. I usually look at women who sidle up to any man with a Lexus and a platinum chain with a mixture of contempt and pity. I've never sung along when women would chant at the top of their lungs that there's "no romance without finance!" I thought that there were the Lil' Kims of the world and then there was me. I wasn't a gold-digger, I reasoned, because I wouldn't just attach myself to *any* man who had money. The men in my life would have to have money plus something more—be it Ivy League–educations, devotion to their mothers, or interest in their communities (for a while my sister and I refused to date any Black man who lived on the East Coast and didn't go to the Million Man March!). But what I have come to understand is that Lil' Kim and I have more in common than we could ever realize.

How ironic is it that Lil' Kim raps about everything that men can give her when it is clear by the longevity of her career that she can more than likely give those things to herself? How ridiculous is it that I would get upset about spending thirty dollars for one dinner after the same man has treated me to meals for over a year? As ironic and ridiculous as both these scenarios are, they are very real. Moreover, neither one is really about the money. When my boyfriend asked me to pay for dinner, I was subconsciously reliving in my mind all the fights my parents had when I was a child—the fights where my mother would accuse my father of shirking his financial responsibilities. I always felt in some ways that my father's abandonment of our family was my fault, and that if I was worth it, he would have paid whatever my mother asked him without arguing. I felt his love for me should have overshadowed his attachment to money. I found my value through what my father valued. In the end, it looked like he valued money. In a weird way, then, money became my enemy. It seemed that I had lost to it when I was a child, so, as an adult, I became determined to win.

Money is never *just* money. Money is energy and an amplifier. Whatever else is wrong with your life will often be magnified in the area of money. The sense of lack and the desire to know that someone else is capable of supporting you, even when you can support yourself, more often than not symbolizes a lack of self-esteem and a fear of abandonment in Black women. We, meaning women, want men to prove that they are committed to us by putting their money where their mouths are. We resent the idea of supporting men because in essence it will mean that we care more about men than they care about us. What Lil' Kim and I have in common is that we both grew up as women who knew what it meant to be abandoned and hurt by Black men. Moreover, we both manifest this hurt and abandonment through our attitude toward Black men and the materialistic way we approach our relationships.

In *Whatever Happened to Daddy's Little Girl?* by Jonetta Rose Barras (which should be, as far as I am concerned, required reading for all Black people) the reason for the formation of this unhealthy connection between love and money is made plain. Because we are a nation of women, Barras argues, who grew up without fathers, Black women often cannot recognize true love when we see it. We often think that sex is love, or that pain is love, or that a man's absence is normal, because in some ways we are subconsciously pushed to recreate our childhood existence. So for women who grew up without fathers, the urge to substitute money for love is strong.

Although people often cite money as one of the greatest reasons for divorce, I know that money is not the problem. Money is only the symptom. I have come to understand that all arguments about money are really arguments about not feeling loved. Women who grew up without fathers often feel unloved by men and are frequently troubled by money issues. We put money in the place of love and believe that "if he loved me he would buy me this car, or house, or ring . . ."

It is obvious by watching any number of commercials on television that this culture encourages the substitution of money for love, and we buy into this idea wholeheartedly. We also believe, as is witnessed by the rising tide of obesity in this country, that we can substitute food for love. The problem with substitution, however, is that it doesn't work very well. Substitutes don't necessarily take away our longing for the real thing.

In love, Black women are too afraid to go for what they want so they settle for the cheap imitation. We are running scared and we don't even realize it. So we shop compulsively, eat compulsively, and watch a lot of television in an attempt to grab happiness wherever we can find it. Ironically, Black women will only be happy when they hold out for the love they seek.

However, I don't want to give the impression that the relationship between love and money is only negative. In fact, the two have been necessarily intertwined throughout history. Marriage was first considered to be a financial arrangement. Thus, in African, Asian, and many other societies, both past and present, in order to enter into an official love relationship, the man had to be mentally, physically, as well as financially fit. If a man could not present five hundred head of cattle in certain African tribes, for example, he could not get married. The reasons for these types of tests are obvious. Simply put, it was believed that if a man had to work hard to get you, then he would work hard to keep you.

There is something smart about making sure that a man is serious in his intention to be married. The "bride price" that men were historically forced to pay ensured in some small way that the bride knew she was valuable. I think that if we still had this practice among African Americans today, a lot of the conflict over money in our relationships would cease. This is not to say that a bride price would be a cure-all and prevent women from substituting other things for love, but it would be a demonstration of commitment through money that would lessen some of Black women's insecurity. While it is easy, on the one hand, to talk about the destructive effect of materialism on relationships, the flipside of that argument is that there is something valuable in holding men financially responsible for the choices they make.

By not holding men accountable for being good providers, we are in essence (once again) selling ourselves too cheaply. I think it is important that we recognize the complexity of the money issue and recognize that Black women's desire to be taken care of is valid. I don't want to pretend, even though many women do, that in this post-feminist era, we don't need men for anything. The question becomes whether or not having a man with money will ultimately fulfill all of our needs. I know for a fact that this dilemma will not be resolved if Black people simply insist on reducing women who love men and their money to opportunistic gold-diggers, or worse, in rap music, to "trick-ass hoes."

I think it is about time we do away with the myth that Black women's desire to date and marry men with money only symbolizes, on the woman's part, laziness, antifeminism, and a lack of morals. The rhetoric goes: "Black women are too picky"; "Sisters are just too difficult"; and "Black women overlook the blue-collar brother, thereby ensuring their own loneliness." And, despite Black women's magazines telling us for years that if we date men who make less money, if we take some of the pressure off men, if we just watch our attitudes, that the relationships between men and women will be healed—our relationships are still very flawed. The reason that Black women's magazines are not helpful in this area (in addition to their anxiety-inducing reports on the shortage of good Black men, which I believe are blatantly untrue) is because they insist that Black women are simply wrong for feeling the way that they do. These magazines do not seem interested in investigating why Black women are so materialistic and attitudinal in the first place. Of course, nothing is quite as obvious as it seems.

Finally, I am not in any way suggesting that women shouldn't have their own and work. However, I am suggesting that we look at Black women's materialism through new, more compassionate eyes and to make our views of that materialism more culturally specific. How much of Black women's desire for men with money has to do with the wisdom of our African ancestors? How much are we looking to the material to prove that we are loved? How does daddy-hunger drive our choices? I just know too many high-achieving, got-it-together Black women who are singularly unhappy because of the quality of their relationships. These women have made their own money and feel okay about every other aspect of their lives, but they still want men to prove to them that they are valuable. Furthermore, these women are comfortable asking men for a seafood dinner, rent, and child support, but they do not know how to ask for the love they truly desire. In many of the songs on urban radio, I hear all these women begging for material objects at a seemingly ridiculous level. However, I understand that underneath these pleas for diamonds and Prada is the desire to know that we are worth something to Black men. Black women are trying to ask Black men to love them, but it only comes out as, "Can you pay my bills?"

I do not know what can be done to unlink love and money in our minds. I just know that whatever it is, it needs to be done soon, because Black people's relationships are in crisis. Maybe the answer lies in simply remembering the words of Deepak Chopra: "When love is replaced by an object, the result is addiction." If we are clear that we are acting like addicts and not like lovers, maybe we can be conscious enough to choose new behavior. Each time I reject a man because of his lack of funds, maybe I can admit to him and myself that I am really scared that he will leave me. Maybe, even as a child of divorce whose romantic dreams were fueled by romance novels, I can find the courage to ultimately give myself the love that I wish to receive.

Bass

by Denise Burrell-Stinson

New York is a proud city with a chest that swells high and mighty on Saturday nights as the energy of possibility fills the air. As New Yorkers, we temporarily abandon the familiarity of our Monday-to-Friday routines and reinvent ourselves as sexier, better-looking beings. With our clothes a bit tighter, our heels just a touch higher, and our makeup applied with a slightly heavier hand, we adorn ourselves in hopes of possibly meeting someone even sexier and more attractive than ourselves.

It was no different on the Saturday night my sister and I traveled almost an hour on the number 6 train from downtown Manhattan to the Bronx. We were on our way to a party being held at Olivia and Jessica's apartment and as we stood in the packed subway car, radios blasted, people sang along boisterously, and sweatsuit-wearing *papis* called out brazenly to tight-jean wearing *mamis*, all the while wanting to know "Where's the party at?"

We shook our heads and laughed, but the restlessness was still infectious. The prospect of a room full of new faces on a Saturday night was more than inviting, and I wondered how I would nurture this fertile ground of possibility. We got off the train by Yankee Stadium and walked over to the Grand Concourse, past McDonald's, Burger King, and a crowded Latino diner. We walked a couple hundred feet, crossed an eight-lane intersection, and quickly found Olivia's building. We got out of the elevator and followed the sound of throbbing bass to Olivia's apartment. That bass. The even, steady syncopation of a Saturday night party where brothers and sisters are trying to blow off a little steam.

We opened the door and dissolved quickly into a sea of color. Mochas were brushing up against caramels bumping into cinnamons who were trying to get the attention of dark chocolates. A couple of hours passed easily. We nursed plastic cups of red wine and made the proverbial rounds, ending each conversation with the required "we should get together sometime." We giggled girlishly on the fringe of a makeshift dance floor, in truth, just a small section of the living room hastily cordoned off for those unable to resist the urge (induced by that soul-stirring bass, no doubt) to tangle limbs and align hips with that person who incited a different type of bass in the pit of their guts. Some were smooth and we became voyeurs, unable to look away from private moments made public. Others were more awkward, and we tried to stifle our laughter by chuckling into our plastic cups.

And then he was there. As if he had been placed next to me like a chess piece. In an instant, the broad squareness of his chest was right in front of my face. When I saw his hand extend to shake mine, I politely offered my own in return. The gesture started a long conversation about his trip from his home in South America, his plans to travel through the U.S. and Southeast Asia, and my aspiration to become a New York writer temporarily sidelined by the seven-day-a-week, twelve-hour-a-day office job I had taken in the interim to support myself.

"In America, when you meet someone and you like them, what do you do?" he asked me.

"I guess you just tell them that you like them."

"Well, then, I like you." The crescendo of a night's worth of conversation translated into a single declarative statement.

"I would like to kiss you. Right now."

"Maybe the next time," I said. Then I told him that for now, an exchange of phone numbers was as far as this encounter was going to go. I was flattered by the attention from a broad-shouldered Brazilian, chosen from a group of women who were surely better looking than I am. Despite the attention, there was a strange prickle on the back of my neck due to a new chill in the room. No longer was I the anonymous wallflower; I had suddenly become the room's celebrity. Within moments, I had become the object of double-takes and lingering stares from a room full of Black men who had barely noticed me just moments before. I could feel the widespread interest in my conversation with the Brazilian; the conversation that made me the object of attention for talking to one of the only White men in the room. The reprimands were nonverbal, but icy nonetheless. I looked down as my brown fingers bristled his pink palms during the exchange of phone numbers on messy shreds of paper. Despite the stares, I was feeling smug and satisfied that my Saturday night possibility had yielded some opportunity.

But possibility did not come without incurring the scorn of at least two formerly inattentive brothers who, in paternal, tough-love tones, inquired as to how I could so openly betray my race. "How could you get caught up in something like that?" they asked. I wondered what they would have done if I had kissed him.

This wasn't the first time I had twisted and writhed through these mental gymnastics. Just a week before it was a cocky twenty-something who tried to impress me by sliding a full cocktail glass sloppily down the side of a bar. He reminded me of a bartender passing a drink to the town drunk in the saloon scene of an old western. On another snowy night, my friend and I were stalked by Joe, a White Londoner, dressed unseasonably in a wife-beater T-shirt—perhaps to show off the blurry "DJ music for life" tattoo emblazoned on his left shoulder. Joe was so smitten by us that my friend and I were sent running from the bar in which we'd met; our pursuer stopped only after a hard fall in the snow. Miraculously, he still summoned enough energy to yell, "Come back, my African queen!" as he lay on his back in the icy slush.

But this is how it's been for me from the moment I became old enough to attract the attention of men. In bars, at parties, in classes, in big cities and small towns, domestically and abroad, the men I attract are nearly always White. No matter where I am. With women, my relationships have the texture and variance of a United Nations meeting. My girlfriends speak different languages and have varying levels of melanin in their skin. Some have names that have more consonants than vowels and live thousands of miles away from the country of their birth. Others are the third generation to live along the same one-mile stretch of Brooklyn.

With men, however, my life is exponentially more segregated. The overwhelming majority of my platonic relationships with men, as well as my minuscule batch of romantic entanglements, do not and have not included Black men. With the exception of my uncle and one of my best male friends, the most important relationships with men I have ever had in my life, including my stepfather (my biological father is Black) involve White men.

While I'm not ashamed of this disparity, I will admit the difficulty of reconciling the lack of diversity in my intimate relationships with the manner in which I socialize in my day-to-day life. My friends celebrate Christmas and Hanukah and Ramadan and Kwanzaa. Some have MBAs and Ph.D.s, while others barely made it out of high school. I have relatives who live in suburban co-ops and condos and relatives who rent Section 8 apartments in the ghetto. I grew up in a house where Sunday morning TV featured *Meet the Press* and *Like It Is*. I believe the *New York Times,* the *Wall Street Journal,* the *New Yorker, Vogue,* and *Harper's Bazaar* are no less interesting than *Ebony, Jet, Essence,* and the *Amsterdam News*. I am also likely to pass on to my own children my mother's "must haves" for a complete home movie collection: *The Ten Commandments, Gone With the Wind,* and *Auntie Mame,* as well as *Shaft, Shaft in Africa,* the *Cleopatra Jones* series, and any movie with Rudy Ray Moore.

And I am quite comfortable in my own brown skin. I revel shamelessly in my negritude. I love to wear lip gloss that shows off the fullness of my lips. My glasses will always rest on my face a little awkwardly because of the broadness of my nose. I've stopped minding (as much as I used to) that no matter how much time I spend at the gym, my pants will always strain to cover the meaty ampleness of my thighs. And when Maya Angelou says I am the dream and the hope of the slave, I fight back the salty swell of tears.

Yet for all the bravado of my racial identity, it is a very rare occasion for me to be courted by, much less presented with an opportunity to have a meaningful relationship with, a Black man. There are, of course, the brothers who have catcalled on the street and told me that I looked better than a government check, but they don't count. If I consider exclusively the men that stir up the bass, that feeling that first tingles in my toes and works its way up to my gut and sends a surge of endorphins through the rest of my body, rendering me helpless to resist the urge to tangle limbs and align hips and join lips, then I have never made a real impression on a Black man. And I have no idea why. I was raised by Black women who at one time or another were loved by Black men. And when I talk about Black men, I often refer to them as brothers, not just as contemporary slang, but more as an acknowledgment of my kinship with and love of men, who, like me, acknowledge the blessings of and give no credence to the curses of our race.

And when I imagine the man I one day hope to marry and with whom I will raise children, I don't see him in my mind in any particular color. He might be Black, White, or some other shade in between. In my visions, I know him by the feelings of safety and security and warmth of everyday comfort and passion that I imagine we'll share for the duration of our lives.

Yet on more than a few occasions in my life, I was inclined to believe that some supernatural demon, some cartoonish apparition of myself, stood behind me and signaled my unavailability to brothers, much like looking at a picture and discovering that the person standing next to you has made antenna fingers over your head.

I would never betray the value of the beautiful moments that I have shared with White men, though not all of them have necessarily been love interests. The stepfather that raised me as his own, regardless of biology, is White. David, the only man that I have ever cried with, is White. So is the only man who has ever written me a love letter. The only man who has ever kissed me gently on my forehead and told me that I was beautiful is White. Of the very few times I have slept in a man's arms, only one of those times was with a man who was not White. The only man I know who lets me call in the middle of the night to talk when I just can't sleep is White. And on the occasional Friday night when I need to self-medicate through one of life's silly disappointments that I have suffered during the week, the man on the other side of the table sharing a cheap bottle of wine with me is Jack or Mark or Tim or one of the several men who can successfully coach me through a personal crisis. They are all White.

The relative brotherlessness of my existence has forced me to ask more questions about the powers and weaknesses of my own sexuality and why it has failed to register on the radar of men of my own race. How and why did I choose certain people in my life and why did certain people choose me? Has it all just been some unfortunate coincidence or has there been some great divide between the Black woman that I greet in the mirror each morning and the one that I have given to the world?

I have a vivid memory from when I was twelve years old. I was in a scholarship program that took children of color from public school and prepared them for New York City prep schools. It remains the only time in the history of my formal education that I was in an entire classroom of non-White faces. Most of the kids in the class were weathering the hormonal and physical chaos of early puberty and for the girls, this meant shedding their linear boyish frames for softer, more curvaceous feminine frames. The changing of our bodies was dramatic enough for one of the boys in the class to make up a chart for himself and his buddies and assign a numerical value to the sexual attractiveness of each girl. Our names were listed in a column, and each of us was judged on a scale of one to ten. The categories included "Girl You Most Want to Kiss," "Sexiest Girl," and "Girl You Most Want to Go Out on a Date With." There were two very small columns at the edge of the page for "Best Personality" and "Nicest Smile."

The list was originally supposed to be passed between the boys in secret, but the girls eventually got a hold of it. We burned with curiosity and
I remember when it was my turn to look at the document. I fingered
the pages gently because they were weathered and curled from so much
handling by so many different people. I would soon find out that none of
the boys looked at me like they looked at the other girls. While many of
my girlfriends were earning steady eights and nines across the board, I was
earning meager fours and fives in almost all categories, except the last two,
in which I was given nines and tens consistently. Though they acknowledged my bright smile and pleasant demeanor, I didn't have to
worry about being asked out or kissed by any of them.

Even in my childhood, then, I realized I had hit the blind spot of
males of my same race. I often remarked to myself how little this reception
had changed through my adult life. As a twelve-year-old, I could look at
my flat chest and curveless hips and see how I lagged behind the competition. But I thought that even though I was what was affectionately
called a "late bloomer," my own road towards womanhood would eventually help make up some of the difference.

For one brief moment in my adult life, sometime in my mid-twenties,
I thought I had finally overtaken my competitors. He was a thuggish
type, a brother's brother from the Bronx. He came complete with an
afro, big jeans, Timberlands, and sweatpants with one rolled-up leg. He
worked at the same company where my sister worked during her summer
vacations and I'd see him when I'd go to visit her. He was the stereotypical cool guy, the one who always knew when it was time to crack a
joke. His tiny work area was decorated with pictures of rappers and models and athletes cut out from magazines like the *Source* and *Sports Illustrated*.
He was about four years older than I was, but had the face of a teenager.
Soft and innocent with a big square smile. When he worked, his head
bobbed to the music in the headphones of his Walkman.

There was no single moment that I can recall when it happened. It
was just there one day. This thing between us. Like a blooming flower,
where the minute-to-minute movement is too subtle to detect, but it is
suddenly obvious when the petals have broadened to their full colorful expanse. A quick visit to see my sister became a long dinner or walk and our
conversations were so effortless and easy that I became giddy. It was as if
a year's worth of Saturday nights looking to meet someone had suddenly materialized into one person. We listened to each other. We could
hear the rhythm in each other's voice. I would start a joke story, and
he would take his cues from the intonations in my voice, knowing just the
right moment to finish with the punch line. When he would tell me a
story, he knew just the right moment to emphasize the importance of a

character or event with a touch on the arm. I could feel us gathering more momentum and when this thing between us reached its full colorful expanse, I would finally know what it was like to look over and see the person who stirred up my bass. I had never been so comfortable and easy around a man outside of my family, especially a man who was Black. Even still, our race existed mostly in the background. We chose to bond mostly through music, co-creating a soundtrack to our time together, filled with the wails and harmonies of brothers and sisters who could give breath and sound to words we were unable to say. He sent me Teena Marie, Rick James, R. Kelly, Chaka Khan, and the Isley Brothers. I answered with Minnie Ripperton, Prince, Terence Trent D'Arby, and Sade.

We played CDs and tapes together one night in my apartment, sitting silently together as my speakers filled the living room with our musical conversation. He couldn't look me in the eye most of the time, turning away but smiling when I tried to get his attention with some silly comment about how much I loved this song more than the one that played before it. When we talked on the phone again later that night, he told me how shamed he was by the effect of my fleshy, big, brown thighs—the thighs I'd purposefully exposed in a pair of old high school gym shorts.

"I was a gentleman. But I was having thoughts. Serious thoughts," he said. "A little bit longer and . . ." I imagined the scene. He might have reached for my thighs and I might have reached back and we would have known the compatibility of the rhythm in each other's bodies instead of just our voices. Another night after a concert, he took me home to my downtown apartment. It was a serious detour from the route he could have taken straight home and almost an hourlong train ride from his house. I was hoping he would finally pursue his more carnal intentions. "Can't let a girl as fine as you be out alone late at night," he said. Again, I imagined that this would be the time he would reach for me. But he never did. And never would.

The "little bit longer" never arrived and soon the momentum turned to lagging anticipation. The anticipation of consummation degenerated to stagnant, static sadness. What used to be short pauses between our dates turned into long gaps with the same organic ease with which they first began. Separation went from hours to days to weeks and, finally, months. I still come home on birthdays to find Champagne dropped off with the doorman, sometimes little notes dropped in my mailbox, or even a surprise subscription to a magazine he knows I like. But now he's my few-and-far-between special occasion. We no longer have the intimacy of being each other's routine. It wasn't a change I wanted to make. I rejected it at first, holding on tight to the hinges of the thing between us even though I had been pushed out the door. For months I would come home and listen to the tapes, but there was no song sad enough, no harmony somber enough, and no wail with enough melancholy that could contain the depth of my sadness.

Around the same time, I was at a family reunion, reminiscing with a distant relative who I had not seen since I was six years old. The only proof of our having spent any time together was a picture that someone took at a family barbecue almost twenty years earlier. She had been keeping up with my sister and me through my grandmother, a woman all too willing to offer frequent updates on our progress through fancy private schools and Ivy League universities. "Come over here," my cousin beckoned to her sister. "They're so cute, they talk just like White girls."

And then I knew why he was gone. And I seethed. Instead of sending my anger out and away, I wrapped myself in it like a blanket. Let it coat and contaminate me like a bad stench. I managed to convince myself that I had unknowingly exposed who I really was. I let him see something terrible inside of me that had become so much a part of my being that I couldn't remember it being any other way. I just knew that he had somehow seen how diluted I had become. He saw in me a woman living out an idolization of the White man who raised her; living and breathing the White idealism of her Upper East Side prep school and her Ivy League college; a woman sleeping in the arms of White men and loving them to take out her revenge on the little brown boys who wrote fours and fives next to her name. I had finally been betrayed for the betrayal of my race and I believed I should be punished, inheriting the scorn I believed he had intended for me.

This was more than a blemish on my short history of relationships, it was an open, bloody boil on my racial identity. Rejection, I thought, is distasteful, but rejection because I was not the ideal Black woman tasted like bile, bitter with acid, that when it bubbles up from your stomach makes you want to heave. Was I so turned on by the novelty of being with a Black man, that I fetishized him into my own personal minstrel? Had I shown my true colors, so to speak, which were much lighter than he was willing to put up with? Did I miss some cue or was there some Black relationship ritual that I was supposed to initiate? Or did he think that I acted as if our relationship was some exotic vacation from the White men that I really wanted to be with?

I attacked my body. I would run for forty-five minutes, twice a day, stomping out my self-imposed punishment on hard concrete every night and every morning until my knees almost buckled. Transfer the pain from one wound to another, I thought. Then I would ration myself salads and frozen yogurt (and, of course, a few extra glasses of wine at dinner), relying on the airy space of hunger in my stomach to reassure me that I was suffering adequately through my sentence.

By the end of the summer, I was fifteen pounds lighter, and as my skirts sagged from my hips, I received a steady stream of congratulations on how great I was looking lately. I absorbed the attention with a smile and a thank you and shoved the lump in my throat down into that airy space in my stomach, knowing secretly my shrinking waist was really the scarlet letter of my racial infidelity.

And then, one night, I had had enough. As I lay on the sofa with one of the tapes playing and an ice pack on my aching knee, I realized I could no longer afford to pay back a debt that I never really owed. Who loves you is no indication of the things that are wrong with you. In the eyes of people that really love you are written all the things that are right about you. Even if those eyes happen to be blue or green, they may be the only ones you have when it is time to summon the resolve to mourn and move on. The arms that may reach out to hold me may be White, but I will still run to their warmth and comfort instead of standing alone, shivering and cold. My love of one does not mean hatred of another. I may not be loved by a Black man, but I am not unlovable. I may not know the romance of a Black man, but my own brown arms will always reach up to wrap him. He does not have to be my lover to know that he is my brother.

I'll Sing You a Song From My Soul

The Love Stories

The Gift of Breath

by Amontaine Woods

I had begun to notice everything. All the little things I never noticed before. Like the autumn leaves dancing like wild women to the music of the wind. So trusting, those leaves were, not the least bit of resistance in them. As if they were assured that the wind would carry them to wherever they were supposed to be.

I had plenty of time to reflect on leaves because I had stopped going to work. The day Ronald died I didn't go back. I lived off of my savings and spent my days working on my novel, when I wasn't spying on leaves or counting the little decorative holes in my ceiling. In the late afternoons I'd step out on my balcony and wait for the light and dark to change places. I would sit and pray and wait for the answer to the riddle of his passing. Perhaps he didn't do it consciously, but he taught me not to take life for granted. We're not promised anything—not even another day. So resist nothing. Breathe it all in while there's still time.

Breath. What a miraculous thing breath is. I had thought I could finally stop holding mine because I'd found him: Mr. Right. Not only was he handsome and intelligent and generous and kind, he was a brother, to boot. I had struck pay dirt. *Hats off to me, ladies, I have found him—the most righteous brother on the planet.*

My girlfriends told me to be careful, but I didn't want to. The man rubbed my feet, ran bubble baths for me, picked me up in his silver Jaguar with tiger lilies in hand, and made me laugh with his Richard Pryor imitation.

But maybe my girlfriends had a point. Maybe he was too good to be true. Maybe Ronald was hiding something. So when I went to his apartment for the first time, I was on alert for any yellow or red flags pointing to deceit or disaster. When he opened the door into his spacious apartment, I was surprised to hear music filling the space where no one had been all day. "I leave the radio on during the day," he said. "I don't like coming home to quiet."

As he showed me around I took odd liberties, spontaneously opening drawers, closets, and cupboards, as if what he was hiding could be discovered among the cups and saucers or tucked neatly beneath the linens. I laughed when I saw the book on his nightstand—*Dating for Dummies*—and the yellow rubber ducky adorning his bathtub endeared me to him like you would not believe.

I made myself comfortable on his leather sofa as he placed a record on the turntable, then went to fix me a vodka martini. The leather, the drinks, the music, the repartee—it was all out of a nighttime soap. He was the smooth and dashing playboy setting a skillful trap for his next conquest. Only one problem: he wasn't smooth. I think he wanted to be, but the loneliness that hung in the shadows around him would be anathema to a real player.

I prided myself on recognizing the record he played. "That's Miles Davis," I said.

It was the original LP he'd had since he was a kid. I couldn't hear a scratch on it. "The first time I heard this record I was thirteen years old," he said. "I immediately ran out and bought it. My mother asked me why I kept playing that sad-ass music. But it wasn't sad to me. It was like I'd been living in a black-and-white movie, then I heard Miles blow and the world turned to color. Miles Davis made me want to live."

Hmmmm. Miles Davis made him want to live. Did I make him want to die? I have asked myself that over and over and over again, the same way he must've played that record until it made his mother want to come out of her skin. But how was I to reconcile that a mere seven weeks after we met he'd flown the coop for good?

So where did he go? That's what I wanted to know. I knew that wasn't him lying in that box at the funeral looking so hard and staid. After all, the body is just a shell, right? That's what my father told me when I was a little girl of about six years old. My father believed in reincarnation, and told me that this body was not me, that I had lived many lives before in other bodies, and would live again in different bodies still. Many times my father would come to the breakfast table radiant, and announce to all of us that he had been on one of his nightly expeditions. "Astral projection" was what he called it. He talked about a cord—long, silver, and diaphanous—that connected our bodies to our souls. When it was uncoiled from its secret place, it allowed our souls to travel to cosmic worlds while our bodies remained here in our little beds. Then when it came time for the soul to return, it would simply ride the silver cord like a slide and position itself back into the body. He said he could hear the soul's return to the body, like a key being turned in a lock. I shuddered when he stated his belief that we would be dead to this world if ever the cord should break.

Imagine that. Suddenly finding our silver cord severed, hanging limp like a bleeding tail, forever lost to our little beds. But what on earth would make the cord break, I wondered. An accident? Accidents happen all the time. Such a tenuous thing this life. One cord of flesh is cut and we are said to be born. Another of gossamer breaks and we are said to be dead. Our lives are literally held by a thread, aren't they? How daring and dangerous my father seemed to me; how colorful and strange the night worlds he visited. The telling of his escapades left me breathless but disappointed. Why was I not special enough to go on that magic carpet ride with him? When I awoke each morning my soul had been nowhere that I could tell. The key to my cosmic being had remained unturned, and I was utterly trapped in the black hole of my flesh.

So where was my Ronald now? And what was it like for him as he departed this world? Did he fly away? Maybe he went out spinning. I imagined his death to be no less spectacular than a comet catapulting across the night—a tail of glistening silver flapping behind him.

All of these ideas probably would have sounded very strange to my Ronald. He had more traditional beliefs. I remember the time he asked me to go to Sunday church services with him. I hadn't stepped foot in a church in years, and wouldn't have stepped foot again, except I wanted so to please him. As we were about to leave that morning I walked into his kitchen and found him pouring tomato juice in vodka.

"You're not planning to walk into church smelling like alcohol?" I said. "I mean, it just doesn't seem right somehow."

He looked at me as if I'd asked him to throw away some life-sustaining medicine. Then calmly and matter-of-factly he announced, "Maybe we shouldn't go."

But we did go, and he didn't dare take a single sip after I'd shot that disapproving scowl his way. We showed up cold sober and smelling of competing colognes. The church was so packed that morning that we were forced to sit in the balcony and I was unable to see much of the preacher and the choir. After awhile I tired of straining to see past heads rocking to the rousing spirituals, and fans whipping every which way. So I bowed my head and listened to the charismatic preacher warning the congregation against falling prey to the sensuality of this world, this modern-day Sodom and Gomorrah. I remember that the pretty teenage girl in the pew in front of us shot up out of her seat and danced around as if possessed, a strange and holy force sweeping her into a frenzy. I envied the dark mystery stirring within her.

At some point during the service, Ronald turned and looked at me for a long time. I watched him out of the corner of my eye. Then he gently took my hand. I looked up to find tears of joy glowing in his eyes.

So the eyes are the windows to the soul. Then what of the hands? His hands. The ones that did a million little things for me—stroked me a million times. The same hands that wrote me the first love letter I'd ever received. Those black, knobby knuckles and thick, sausage fingers that worked and worked to please, they told it all.

But at the very same time that we were becoming more deeply committed and trying our best to make things work between us, the disagreements over the drinking were escalating. At first I just assumed he was a person who liked to party. But after a few weeks in his company, I began to realize that he had a severe drinking problem. Several days after the church incident I threatened to call it quits if he didn't get some help. He promised he would stop. "Tomorrow," he said, "but let's drink tonight. Let's drink this one last time together." So out from beneath his cabinet he produced the Cabernet and two crystal wine glasses. He put on a CD of old school R&B, poured and poured until our two glasses held the last of the wine left in the world, or so it seemed. He savored that last bit slowly, stopping to make little circular motions so the dark red liquid could play against the sides of his glass. Then we watched a movie and went to bed.

I woke the next morning, immediately straddling myself across his chest. Startled and puzzled, I heard this great sloshing inside of him. His chest had become a sea shell through which I could hear the ocean. I asked him what that was.

"I haven't taken my water pill yet this morning."

"Oh, my God. And it sounds like that? That's bad, isn't it?"

"Well, yeah. People die from water in their lungs."

I rushed him out of bed to go and take his pill. Even then it didn't dawn on me that there could really be something wrong with him. After spotting a bill from a cardiologist on top of his kitchen cabinet, I continued to remain clueless. A real super-sleuth, right? Here I was searching for secrets in closets. All the while the truth was in plain view for anyone who had eyes to see.

But love is blind, as they say, and he wasn't by any means old. He was so energetic, the one I strained to keep up with. The one with the money, the car, the connections, the jokes. The one everyone relied on to make it all better. People like that didn't get sick. People like that didn't die. Maybe the rest of us had lives held by the whims of a gossamer thread, but not Ronald. Not *my* Ronald.

It was a Wednesday morning at 5 A.M. that I suddenly awoke in a panic. I sat straight up in bed—stupefied—as if smashed in the head with a frying pan. But it had just dawned on me I hadn't talked to Ronald yesterday, the first day we hadn't talked to one another since we'd met. I immediately called his apartment. No answer. He should have been home. Should have been home.

I tried calling again as soon as I reached the office. Still no answer at his house, so I left a message on his work phone. By noon he still had not returned my call. Now this was very strange. Ronald was extremely attentive and incredibly available for small talk any time of the day or night.

Worried, I left work at lunchtime and headed for his apartment. Along the way I looked for his car in the parking lots of bars he frequented. Funny. I hoped to find him merely drunk.

Men in white overalls were poised on scaffolding and carrying buckets of paint around his complex when I arrived. His silver Jag was parked in its regular spot. Even though I'd come here looking for him, I didn't really expect to find him at home in the middle of the day. *Breathe.* Yes, I remembered. He told me he sometimes came home for lunch.

I maneuvered past workmen, got on the elevator, walked down the long hallway with the plush brown carpeting sinking around my feet. I knocked. "Ronald, it's me. Ronald, open up, this isn't funny now." His neighbor squeaked open her door ever-so-slightly, peeking out with appetite wet, sensing some juicy tidbit on the horizon.

When he didn't answer I scrambled back down and found a young woman outside with a baby slung across her hip—the assistant manager of the complex. I told her I was worried. I told her she should let me into his apartment. It was against the rules, but she had her own reasons for being worried. It seemed a note had been posted for weeks asking residents to have their cars moved for the painters. She had been trying to reach him all morning, but to no avail.

I remember the manager, the baby still perched on her hip, knocking on his door. Then, finally, turning the key in his lock. As she tried to open the door, she was stopped midway by the chain. "He's in there," she said, stunned. We yelled his name. The manager began to weep. I found strength I didn't know I had, as I pushed and pushed against the door. She cried, "Yes! Yes!" On the third push the door gave way.

There he was. In his bed, the covers pulled up to his chin. The television was running. The drone of the TV was always a lullaby to him. I screamed his name and still he refused to acknowledge me. There was no blood. The blankets were barely mussed. His death had no smell, no real vulgarity. Only his face had turned hard as a diamond, and a thin dribble of white foam issued from the side of his mouth.

After the police had finished their questioning, after the manager had left to tend to her baby, after the painters had ceased working for the day and the body had been carried away, I wondered what was next. Where to go, what to do. I thought about going home, but no. The next obvious place was to my mother's, of course. She'd gotten me through a thousand little catastrophes. Her ample mommy breasts, her breath, her voice, all like smelling salts to my soul. Many times in the past she hadn't even known her baby girl was wounded and had come to bask in her healing rays. I had grown accustomed to breathing freely. And here it was suddenly again—this holding of the breath, this fear of existing without him. But this time it seemed different. I wasn't sure that even my mother could get me through this one.

The day after Ronald died, I had a dream about him. I was perched on a stoop in a New York ghetto waiting for him to arrive. He drove up in a long, pink Cadillac, got out wearing an electric-blue suit. Then all of a sudden we were together at the edge of the river, the waves lapping at our ankles. A mermaid emerged from the deep. She pounded her silver tail against the glistening water. She called to him. "It is time to go," she said. She was kind, but determined. As she beckoned to him, he grabbed my hand and softly pulled me with him. "No," I laughed. I believed he was teasing me, that we were playing a child's game of tug-of-war. But he suddenly was squeezing too hard. He was hurting me. His beautiful hands had turned menacing, life-threatening, as he seized my wrists in desperation. "No!" I shouted. "I won't go. I won't! Don't you understand how I love this life? That I will do anything to hold on to it? I will even fight you, my dear, for I love this life so."

As he saw my conviction, he slowly relinquished his grip. He turned his back on me, grasping the end of the mermaid's tail. The two of them dove deeper and deeper into the rippling water.

As I woke up, I lay in bed shaking with anger. I was mad, seething mad at him. It was bad enough he'd left, but how dare he ask me to go with him. "Coward" is what I called him. And worse. I screamed to the rooftop, "You wanted to leave, you wanted to bail out when the going got tough, fine! But don't expect me to cut my journey short! I suppose you think I'm selfish! Because I want to live! Because I want to stay and live!"

After a few minutes I got up and paced the floor, unable to still the rage welling up inside. My rage brought tears, and my tears brought the rains, again. That had been happening a lot. It was a gentle drizzle that fell at first, but quickly became a torrential downpour. I crawled back in bed and listened to the rush of pelts against my window.

I listened to the rain for what seemed like a long time when something strange and wonderful happened. I wasn't asleep, I swear. I was lying there fully awake, when suddenly I was no longer in my bed. Now I was sitting in my favorite chair in the living room. From there I looked into my bedroom where I just was, and saw it saturated in a bright white light. Then I was outside my window. I was the rain falling from the sky. I was not wet or cold in the way I experience rain when I am outside of it. I was *in it, of it*, the soul of rain. Its soul seemed no different than my own. Now, once again, I was in my bed. Glory. For one moment I saw behind the veil. I wasn't even scared. It is a wonderful thing to be without fear. I only hoped at that moment I would stop fearing forever.

In time it became clear that I had to forgive Ronald for leaving. I understood that he was tired in a way that a good night's sleep could not fix. He was afflicted with congestive heart failure, something he, for whatever reason, had decided not to tell me. One of the policemen on the death scene called me the day after to find out how I was doing. He told me that he had talked to Ronald's doctor, and the doctor confirmed that Ronald had had a serious heart condition for some time, and was in fact amazed that Ronald had lived as long as he did. A ticking clock had been stalking him like a predator. Maybe that's why he had so much gusto and energy for life—for he really understood that any moment it could be over. Maybe that's why he drank—a habit that was surely shortening his life, but at the same time keeping that dark, dank shadow at bay.

Would I have stayed with him if he had lived? Would I have tried to work it out? I don't think so. The drinking scared me. And for that, I've had to learn to forgive myself.

I'm left with a lot of questions: What is this road we are traveling, this bumpy, mysterious, and dubious road of pain and joy, laughter and tears? And why sometimes does the road suddenly become swallowed up in a tangle of vines seemingly gone amok? I don't have the answers. But regardless, it's okay. Okay that I have stayed. Okay that he has gone and begun anew in another place. Whether we know it or not, we are just like those leaves dancing on the wind. And what's more, we are being blown in the right direction. So let it be.

I am praying. It is a prayer that is a mixture of song, poetry, and scripture . . .

We are not bodies but spirits. We are not lost but found. Found in the sliver of green grass and the black soil from which it springs. In the rain and the sky from where it falls. In the lock and in the soul-filled key that turns it. In the leaf, soft and free in the wind, trusting it will be carried to where it's always wanted to be. I accept this gift given to me—the knowledge that every day is to be lived as if it is the last. The last. I am the first and the last. The alpha and the omega. The beginning and the end. I am the invisibility that dreams itself into flesh . . . the mother offering my ample breasts for a healing . . . the father traveling the cosmos on a silver cord. I am the tears of grief become the soul of the rain. I am the water of life sometimes stagnant in the lungs, sometimes rushing furiously through the seas. I am the force that cannot be comprehended except through the joys and pains of living. I am here and also there. I am everywhere. I am you and also me. I am everyone. We are love . . . We are love . . . We are love . . . We are love . . .

Baggage Claim

by Tina Fakhrid-Deen

They say that the apple doesn't fall far from the tree. As the daughter of a compulsive womanizer and a hardcore lesbian, it follows I would either turn out a pimp, a man-hating feminist, or Madonna. And at different stages of my life, I have been all of the above and then some, with the common thread being a strong distrust of men and a constant fight to reclaim my womanhood. I learned many important things from my parents, like how to hustle, survive, and end relationships faster than the underground train gets from London to Paris. I had no interest in being played, and even less tolerance for relationship bullshit. If I smelled shady dealings or had any inkling that my suitor was being untrue, I was out. I let them know, "This ain't working," and exited stage left. Most of my relationships ended with little explanation and no soap-opera, teary-eyed drama. I learned from my estranged parents that relationships were like a simple game of checkers, conquer before being conquered and maintain absolute control at all times if you want to win, or at least get out unscathed.

My parents met in Chicago through a family friend and got married shortly thereafter. My mother said that my father was charming, hard working, and smart. She was a feisty virgin, itching to get out from under her mother's strict, abusive roof. She cared for him and knew that he had genuinely fallen in love with her, so she took a chance, although this wasn't the ideal love situation for her, being that she was gay. Being in an openly gay relationship was unheard of, and so my mother married because it was the accepted thing to do and also because she truly wanted to have a child. She says my father was the best option at the time. They were young and struggling to survive on the harsh streets of Chicago's west side, home of the original pimps, gang-bangers, and hustlers who served up heavy doses of crime, drugs, and prostitution for its local constituents. My daddy was a Southern boy who worked extremely hard and knew how to make a way where there was none. A hazel-eyed pretty boy who went as far as women would allow—usually pretty far—his affinity for the opposite sex had him fascinated with the pimp game: a common and respected hustle where men used their intelligence, manipulation tactics, and business savvy to seduce women into using their bodies as commodities instead of waiting for a government check on the first and fifteenth. The trick was that all of the women's earnings went to the pimp who in turn provided a little loving, sweet talk, and basic essentials to keep his women loyal and in his possession. Although I don't think my daddy ever made anyone sell themselves, I'm sure many of his women sold their souls and self-esteem just to be in his arms—everyone except Mother. His own father was promiscuous and not really an active part of his life, so I don't think he ever had a model of manhood. I will never forget my grandmother telling me that inevitably my husband would cheat on me, but that the important part was that he continued to provide for the family. I'm sure that since my daddy was always a great provider, his mother's teachings gave him a green light to be promiscuous and still feel that he was a good man. And aside from his indiscretions, most would say that he was.

Caring less about how well he provided and fed up with my father's adulterous ways, my mother divorced him after about two years. From about age two until six, I remained with my mother with intervals living with her best friend when my mother's work situation got sketchy. We lived in the same housing project where my mother grew up. I have good memories from that time period in my life, but one bad event haunted my relationship with my mother for years. At about age five, I woke up in the middle of the night because I had a nightmare that dozens of snakes were suffocating me. I went scream-ing around the house for my mother, but she wasn't in the apartment. I went to the window to call her name in the quiet night air when the screen gave way and I tumbled three floors to the cold, hard ground. With a 50 percent chance that my leg growth would be stunted, I wore a full-leg cast for months while my mother nursed me back to health. To this day, there are various stories as to where my mother was that evening, but all I know is that she wasn't where she was supposed to be—beside me in bed. At age seven, I went to live with my paternal grandparents in Louisiana, then moved back to Bellwood, Illinois, to live with my father at age eight.

I was always the quintessential daddy's girl. As a baby, I wouldn't go to bed until he got home from work and then would fall asleep on his chest, so when I moved back in with him, it was like Candyland. He had purchased a home in the west suburbs complete with a garage and backyard. I had my own bedroom and all kinds of board games. He was my number-one buddy; he taught me how to ride a bike, took me to the drag strip where he raced, and bought my first training bra. I absolutely adored him—he seemed so smart, all-knowing. He wore the nicest clothes, always smelled good, deejayed parties, and owned several small businesses. We had the largest record collection in the whole neighborhood and he was so cool that he bought *Centipede* by Rebe Jackson so that I could play it over and over again. All of my friends thought he was "nickel-dime fine" and he had more girlfriends than New York has train routes. He even married five of them, but that never stopped him from having ladies on the side. He was always juggling at least three women at a time and introduced me to most of them like it was no big deal, like he wasn't exposing his innocent child to a life of dysfunction. He was the type of man that would make infamous pimp Magic Bishop Don Juan proud—flashy with a big car (a powder-blue '79 Ninety-Eight Regency) and plenty of women who catered to his every whim, even if he needed to smack them up once in a while to maintain it. A few times I witnessed "charming Charlie" lose his cool so that Bellwood's finest ended up filing a police report at our doorstep, a weeping and terrified woman in the background. Each time, my father made it seem like it was just a little lover's quarrel between a man and his overly emotional woman, and the cops went on their way.

Probably fearful that what goes around comes around, my father warned me to leave all boys alone, which meant no phone calls or sidewalk chats. He wouldn't even allow a member of the opposite sex to stand in front of our house and I had to be in by the time the street lights came on. He explained that only "street walkers" stayed out late and he had little tolerance for most of my female friends, accusing them of being too "fast" or "loose." The irony was that he seemed to like "fast" women and always bragged about how much they loved him. And I guess they did, because whenever he courted one, she ended up dropping everything she had to move into our house. Women gave him money, cars, and funded some of his businesses. They washed his clothes, cooked his food, catered to me, and did what he said. In my four years living with my father, I shared space with three of his women and three of their children. I was beginning to believe this lifestyle of my father's was okay, until a few of them came to me crying about how much they loved him and how horribly he treated them. Even still, they stayed until he kicked them out or got rid of them. I never got involved—as long as they treated me well, I wasn't in that mess. That was grown-folks' business.

Everything was going well until he married that last one. She was a few years beyond the legal age for marriage, shaped like a girl in a Jay-Z video, and super ignorant. Since I was born in the projects, I knew a certified hoodrat when I saw one. She was an incessant smoker with a noticeable drug habit. No more than nine years my senior, she stole my title as woman of the house. Being my mama's child, no one was going to take what was mine, so we went to war. When she copped an attitude, mine was bigger. When she asked me to go and get a pack of cigarettes from the store, I took my sweet time coming back. And when she tried to pull rank or get smart, I quipped, "You ain't my mama and I'm telling my daddy what you said!" It was like two women fighting over a man and, in essence, we were. I was fighting to remain the apple of my daddy's eye and she was fighting to be his wife. She won. On the eve of my twelfth birthday, my father kicked me out of his home forever. He said that I had gotten too grown and he was tired of me disrespecting his new wife, so off to my mother's one-bedroom apartment I went.

We were no longer in the projects, but we might as well have been because all of my suburban amenities were gone for good. Although there was less physical privacy, my mother respected my space. She spent a lot of time watching television in her room when she wasn't at work. She encouraged me to have company (which I resisted) and created a blanket border for my little area in the home. She tried to make me feel welcome, but it was hard for both of us. My mother was struggling to fulfill her dream to become a construction worker and paychecks for women in that industry were few and far between. It seemed to me like I always came second. I learned later that it was because she wanted to create a stable environment for me that she worked so hard. My mama, a victim of severe child abuse who received no love from the people around her, who battled with intimacy and control issues, didn't ask anybody for anything and struggled to grasp onto a life worth holding on to. She was a poor high-school dropout who had been on her own off and on since age fifteen. She kept to herself and had few friends. She was hardworking, but always seemed to be in financial trouble. The only thing she had was me, and she loved me fiercely, even if she didn't know how to show it. She said that she loved me often, but didn't dish out many hugs or public displays of affection. When I tried to hug her, she'd say things like, "Girl, get from under me, it's too hot for that." Although a closet crybaby, I became just as indifferent and hardened as she. We began to lock horns. It wasn't until recently we became close.

In my heart, I long accused her of not being there for me—from the time she let me fall out the window to the time she told me that she couldn't be present at my high-school graduation because she had to work (although she showed up anyway, complete with dirt and soot from her construction gig). Further complicating my feelings for my mother, during my Bellwood hiatus, my father had filled my head with stories of her alleged drug abuse and assured me that she would prefer the streets to caring for me. While I was living with him, my father hadn't allowed her to come see me unless he approved it, treating her more like an annoying crack-head aunt instead of my mother, which impacted my view of her as well. Regardless of resistance from both sides, she frequently came to pick me up from my father's on the weekends. We'd go to the zoo, eat celery and carrot slices at the beach, and discuss how fine Michael Jackson and New Edition were. When I was ten, she came out to me. It went something like this:

"You love Michael Jackson, right?"

"Yes," I said, with irritation that she would even ask such an asinine question. I didn't wear a jheri curl and red pleather jacket in ninety-degree weather for my health.

"Well, what if I told you that Michael was gay?"

"Then I'd call you a liar," I said snidely.

With even more caution she asked, "What if I told you that I was gay?"

I paused. "Then I'd say I don't care." But I did care. I cared a lot.

That was the end of that conversation. Mind you, I didn't even know what being "gay" really meant at the time, but I knew it was supposed to be bad and that only nasty people did it. I knew by the way kids spat out that word as an insult at school, making it sound like the dirtiest word in the world. I also had enough insight to know it had something to do with that fact that my mother never had a boyfriend around. It also explained why "Aunt Angie" lived with her. I found my eyes welling up with tears as I stared out of the bus window on the ride back home. At the time I found comfort in the fact that I didn't have to live with her.

But when I moved in with her I was forced to deal with the fact that she was gay because it was literally right in my face. She had those damn rainbow-colored candles flaming in her living room and pictures of scantily dressed women, including the diva of all time, Ms. Tina Turner, scattered around the house. I didn't know how to explain this to my friends so I seldom invited anyone over. My friends were already silly enough and I refused to be ridiculed even further. Playing the dozens was second nature and how could I make a good comeback with this riding over my shoulder? They already joked that she was a "dyke" just because of the combat boots, no bra, and the filthy construction helmet. All dead giveaways in her case, but I denied it emphatically. I often felt like *I* was the one in the closet because I was terrified of someone finding out that my mama really *was* a *homosexual* and, of course, there was always the underlying fear that I'd grow up to be gay too. I tired of referring to her live-in girlfriends as her roommates, of lying to my friends and family. I was embarrassed when people in the streets referred to my mother as "Mister" or "Sir" because she looked so masculine, and even more humiliated when she would laugh it off, poke out her chest and exclaim, "That's 'Miss'. I'm all woman." I didn't want her to come to parent-teacher conferences and craved to see her in a skirt and lipstick. I had a hard time accepting her for who she was and was even more ashamed to admit that fact out loud. This put a silent strain on our relationship, leading to frequent verbal attacks from me. Even with all my attitude, to her credit, she never turned her back on me, kicked me out, or tried to curtail my big mouth.

Although she didn't receive much of anything from her own mother, my mama did her best to teach me about being a good woman. At age thirteen, I knew how many holes I had "down there" because she locked me in the bathroom and made me look with a hand mirror. She always encouraged me to use my brain to critically analyze what was going on around me. I was so confident in my abilities that I wasn't afraid to be the smartest person in the class or try new things. Even though I got angry with her because I thought she was calling me a ho, my mother taught me how to put on a condom and take responsibility for my body. And most importantly, I knew how to kick someone's butt if they got in my face and disrespected me. We sparred on a regular basis and she constantly harassed me about taking up karate lessons. She was a certified butch lesbian, but not the stereotypical male-bashing type. She was very cordial to my male pals, had her own male friends (most were flaming), and was actually the first person I ran to an hour after I lost my virginity to share all of the gory details. She was cool (as mothers go) and laid-back. I didn't even have a curfew in her home. She trusted me to do what was right in my heart and I never let her down. My mother gave sound advice about relationships, but didn't necessarily live it. She told me to trust and respect my partner unless shown otherwise, always know how valuable I am, and never lose myself in a man. The result was that my esteem and warrior spirit were up there with Queen Nzinga, and my self-appointed diva status had me convinced that I was the best thing since sliced bread. Modesty was a trait that neither my mother nor father praised.

. Women came through my mother's life like a revolving door. She loved them and they loved her, but something always seemed to go wrong. I think she was scared to love too deeply, to relinquish full control. She didn't want to control the other person, but she had to be in control of her own emotions and feelings at all times. She assumed that she was right most of the time in arguments and never put up with much drama, which is necessary sometimes in order to work out the kinks. She'd rather leave the situation and be alone, always quipping, "I can do bad all by myself." Along with my father, she seemed incapable of loving with any longevity. Because her mother failed at motherhood and her father left the picture before he could get on the page, my mom had to catch on by herself. Inevitably, there was a lot that she missed as it relates to developing healthy relationships.

From observing my parents' interactions with various partners, I learned at a young age to keep men at a distance, trust none of them, be fiercely independent, and maintain control of my relationships at all times. Although my mother encouraged me to be trusting, my baggage with my father was too heavy—what I had witnessed while in his home had scarred me to the point I felt like men weren't worthy of trust. So I kept my legs and heart firmly closed until my sophomore year in college.

My excuse was that I needed to focus on my education, but the reality was I didn't know the first thing about being in a relationship, and the thought of ending up some wannabe pimp's sperm receptacle terrified me. On my campus's crudely titled "Dick List," an anonymously distributed list that provided annual updates on campus sexual activity among Black students, I was voted "padlock queen" and popped up in the "most wanted" section. What they didn't know was that I *was* having sex, but I'd only "do it" with so-called "friends" that I knew cared about me, and I would only "do it" once to maintain friendship status. Needless to say, this was a faulty arrangement based on my need for control. The campus "dicklisters" also didn't know that I was so traumatized by the act of sex and by intimacy that I had begun doing the unthinkable in the Black community: I began seeing the campus therapist. And even worse, she was a White woman. I couldn't go talk to the pastor like most Blacks because I had decided early on to shun the Black church like it shunned my mother for being gay. I began weekly therapy because I was having recurrent nightmares about my father raping and killing me. He never violated me like that in real life. However, in his attempt to keep me disinterested and frightened of boys, he repeatedly threatened I would become a prostitute if I ever kissed a boy or if one came in the house after dark. So I was sure that I was doing wrong and thought that I was no better than Charlie's girls. In my mind, I had gone from being an innocent daddy's girl to a whore. I knew that he wouldn't be proud of me—all of his warnings had been in vain. I equated being sexual with being weak, powerless, vulnerable, and out of control, the way I thought my father's women were when they lost his respect. Subconsciously, I saw intimacy as dirty and shameful. The nightmares got so bad that I would wake up sobbing, looking around for my father, praying for his forgiveness. The therapist suggested that I take a hard look at my relationships with my parents and at my perception of men. At that point, I decided to take a vow of celibacy and try to get my stuff together. It was obvious that I had a lot of healing and soul searching to do.

I began frantically writing poetry and performing as a way to release some of my internal pain. One of my best pieces was a monologue titled "Losing Virginia," about losing my virginity but reclaiming myself, that I performed for a talent show. That performance opened up a new world. Dozens of young ladies came up to me for years to come, sharing their very personal stories about losing their virginity and how difficult, emotionally and physically, it had been. I learned to celebrate and mourn my chastity without rejecting my new sexual being. I also re-evaluated the dynamics between my parents and myself and recognized that I had inherited some bad relationship habits or misinterpreted their ways. My father had unhealthy relationships due to his refusal to be faithful and my mother had short relationships because she never learned how to work through the rough spots. Neither of them was taught to love the way they do in the movies— tenderly and forever. They were both probably immobilized by the fear of being hurt due to past heartache and their own families' dysfunctional histories. I couldn't blame them for what they didn't teach me. I made the choice to fill the void on my own so that I wouldn't repeat the cycle, and stopped making excuses for having unhealthy relationships. As a grown woman, daddy and mama were no more to blame. I was accountable for the things I wanted to know.

I began to research, read about, and observe other relationships around me. I asked questions about intimacy and what it took to give and receive good loving. Through much exploration, the answers came strong and clear. It seemed as if most people's needs, regardless of their varying backgrounds, were quite similar, and that there were some basic principles to the successful navigation of relationships. Black women and men wanted unconditional love, understanding, respect, trust, support, and open communication. They wanted someone to have their backs when things got rough and to accept them for who they were.

Equipped with this guidance, I slowly entered the dating game again. There was the convict that ended up in jail for life after only six months of dating. There was the frat boy who cheated on me and broke my heart. There was the pushover who would have asked, "Can I say goodbye to my mother first?" if I told him to jump from the Sears Tower. There was the British-Pakistani that treated me like a queen, but couldn't share our relationship with his parents because I wasn't Muslim. Then there was the deejay that was a lot of fun, but who wouldn't commit. Each of these relationships, bad or good, prepared me to open my heart to meet my soul mate.

I met Jashed in 1994 while in a summer research program. He was everything I liked in a man: confident, intelligent, soft-spoken, unassuming, gentle, and single. We became fast friends and then pen pals once he went back to school in Atlanta. We discussed intriguing topics like alien life on earth, building Black-owned water and electricity companies so that we weren't SOL if White folks ever took those resources away, spiritual cleansing from a Yoruban perspective, and going to Jamaica to live in a shanty and teach the shorties math and English. He seemed to be the yin to my yang, the candle to my flame. But I didn't pull the old "let's do it once" routine this time; we remained strictly platonic for four years until we were wholly ready to be in a relationship. Both of us felt the need to mature first as individuals and come correct or not at all.

Our first year in a committed relationship was the most difficult, when my control and trust issues almost sabotaged our union and some of Jashed's manhood issues threatened to do the same. Not trusting my father had impacted each of my relationships and this one was no different. When Jashed didn't share his feelings enough and a "friend" sent him roses on his birthday a few months after we got together, I was quick to say it wasn't going to work. I thought that he didn't really know how to communicate with a real woman and worse, that he might be unfaithful. I wasn't ready or willing to tolerate either. Jashed gently reminded me that I wasn't perfect either, and that he was not my father. He taught me that I couldn't fully love him until I trusted him completely. He was secure in my being independent, but let me know that he would always be at my side. I had to unpack my daddy-baggage at the door and find the rightful owner of my distrust instead of passing it on to my man. I also couldn't control everything and quit at the first sign of troubled waters like my mother. Our relationship survived and grew. Shortly after our engagement, my foul temper flared again and I threw my ring at him. I don't even remember what we were arguing over, but I was a minute away from walking away forever. I told him that I refused to commit to bullshit. Translation: "You are not doing what I want you to do so it must be wrong because, of course, I'm always right." He forgave me *again* and taught me to work things through. Maturity taught me that I didn't always have to get my way and I had to learn to be okay with that for the sake of the relationship. This was definitely no place for my selfish streak or my amazing ability to cut men off when I realized they weren't perfect. Compromise was the key to saving this delicate union.

Jashed, also, entered with his luggage tightly packed. Like many Black men, he had spent a lifetime being challenged as a man by his family, women, and White society. He would accuse me of berating him like countless others had before. The sad part is that sometimes, I did, and my sister-girl attitude didn't help the situation. When this occurred, Jashed would get defensive and totally shut me out while I pleaded with him to communicate. We went days without speaking sometimes because he refused to be yelled at by me or say anything that he would later regret. Jashed says that I taught him to let go and speak his mind more, but I had to learn to be disciplined enough to *listen* once he did finally open up. We were both so sensitive and strong-headed that we had to constantly put ego aside and work it out without the dramatics. The acting belonged on the stage, not in our bedroom. We knew that this was the only way we would survive. We began talking more about problems before they got out of hand and we each let down our guard. Jashed vowed to never just walk out while we each were in an argument and I promised to keep my voice to a level where the neighbors couldn't hear me. (I'm loud by nature so *believe* that this was a difficult feat.)

I firmly believe that the two most important things that stopped us from walking away from the relationship when things got rough were our foundation of friendship and our commitment to fluid and respectful communication. A closed mouth doesn't get fed and a relationship with no communication doesn't either. We all have baggage, but we have to be willing to muddle through it and help each other to heal. I have been married now for almost three years to the most beautiful, honest, kind, supportive, spiritual, and self-aware man that I know. We truly have a God-sent relationship that is magical and enriching. I am learning how to be a better partner, friend, wife, and now, mother. We have a beautiful six-month-old daughter and it fills my heart with joy to know that she will learn beautiful things from her father, like how to treat a woman, not only from him telling her, but by her watching our relationship and how wonderfully he treats me.

However, it doesn't all come easy. There is a Rwandan proverb that asks, if you are building a house and a nail breaks, do you stop building or do you change the nail? Jashed and I work at our relationship daily so that we can keep building. We have a baby girl who watches our every move, so we have to make those adjustments and be sure not to place our baggage on her. I have learned to always put God at the center of all that we do and keep a positive outlook on our relationship, even when things look foggy. I always try to look for the best in my partner, even when he's acting like he ain't got no sense. I also try to support his dreams, be sexually free, compromise like crazy, keep family first, maintain my own identity, and communicate like our relationship depends on it, because it does. Quality relationships take a lot of hard work, as does anything that is worth having, and our love is definitely worth the sweat. We will try to continue to love each other fearlessly, confront our issues, and work together to make our love stand the test of time, God willing.

Pack Light

By Kimberly Virginia Hoskins

I release the judgment that I am wrong because I don't want to cook every day. I release the judgment that I can't be a good wife because I am physically challenged. I release the judgment that David is wrong for wanting a divorce. I release the judgment that because David can't or won't love me as I am, no other man will either. I accept God's judgment on these matters.

I say these words to trigger the flow of emotions that will vibrate heartlessness out of my body. Heartlessness that wants to replace the vibrant red pulsing in my chest with sludge eager to kill me sooner, rather than later. I say these words, or some variant thereof, until ignition is reached and tears rush rapids, screams erupt whirlwinds, or the deep rumble of heartbreak's moans shake me like an erupting volcano. His judgments against me must leave my body. The judgments I hold against myself must change into compassion and understanding. The red life pulsing throughout my body must stay vibrant.

See, I have always liked brown boys. There has usually been one or two in my life as boyfriend or friend; I have pledged my undying allegiance and love to them. This failed relationship, this unequally yoked union, will not succeed in tampering with my love of the brown boys of my past, or bar the brown men of my future. I will unpack these bags of pain. I will maintain clarity. It isn't them I am disappointed with. It is him. David.

At the time, I believed I was at the airport to see my mother off for her trip to Egypt. Now, I believe fate brought me to the airport so I could get a glimpse of my future. As I walked over to say hello to a former coworker, I passed within ten feet of David, quickly glanced in his direction, and took a mental, intuitive note: He is an African-centered college student, whose "I'm a hard Black man" façade grandly masked the gentle spirit living within him. *He will become a part of your life.* We never made eye contact, and I had not known then if he had even noticed me. The group boarded the plane and I went home and immediately forgot about Mr. Berry-Black, until three weeks later when they returned from their trip. I had gone to the airport in a black spandex cat suit hoping to be introduced to the young, bald, berry-black man. It didn't happen. I went away to graduate school wondering if I would ever see him again. Christmas break, I returned home, and my friend Veronica and I went to visit her friend Alma. When Alma learned of my interest in Egypt, she said I might be interested in meeting her friend David, who had gone to Egypt the previous summer. Five minutes later, the phone rang. "This is David."

"Here," she passed me the phone. "Ya'll talk." And with some awkwardness, we did. Later that day, I wondered if he was Mr. Berry-Black from the airport. My mother had told me his name was David. She had also told me that he told her he thought I was pretty.

A few days after the fateful phone call, my mother and I saw David at a Kwanzaa festival, and we were finally introduced. We confirmed that we had indeed talked to each other on the phone days before, and we exchanged telephone numbers. Nothing became of our game of phone tag, and I returned to school for the spring semester. Valentine's Day weekend, I'd come home to hear Ivan Van Sertima lecture about the African presence in the Americas before Columbus. I saw David enter the lecture hall, look around, and leave. "Mama, I'll be back," I said, and went in search of my future. I found him standing among the countless vendors and people searching for jewelry, clothing, and other wares. I touched his arm. David smiled and embraced me like he was greeting an old friend. As he let me go, I could feel a subtle hesitation as his mouth passed my cheek. He later confessed he had wanted to kiss me, but he thought better of it. Any indignation I would have displayed would've been feigned, because I felt like I knew him. I gave him my out-of-state number, and the next day, we talked on the phone for two hours. Finally, the party had started.

✁ ✁ ✁

Late-night phone calls, three-hour interstate bus rides, and poetic letters helped us forge a strong friendship. Yet while we basked in our growing love, my body was changing. When I bent my neck forward, my spine tingled. The once simple task of walking the three and one-half miles to and from campus was now becoming exhausting, and for a couple of weeks, the central vision in my left eye disappeared. I went to the doctor. David sat by my side as the doctor explained the diagnosis. "Multiple sclerosis is a progressively degenerative disease that affects the central nervous system," he began. "In essence, there is an electrical short in your body. Fatigue and muscle weakness are common. Maybe you'll have to use a wheelchair, maybe you won't. There's no way of knowing how the disease will progress in any one individual case. There is no cure, but some people spontaneously remit. Go home and live your life like normal." *Well. What do you say about that?* David and I had been dating for eight months.

When we returned to my apartment, I told him I would completely understand if he wanted to break up. "No. No," he assured me. "I love you, and I'm going to be here for you. We're going to get through this." Acquainted with people who are conversant in alternative healing, David would bring me herbs and vitamins that could help strengthen my body and encourage self-healing. While I had some belief that I could heal myself, David seemed to have definitive faith that it could be done, and that it would be done. I am sure he hoped that it would happen quickly. While I worked on my degree, and grew accustomed to my weakened legs, we continued our long-distance courtship. Where we had once walked around the small campus town, we now rode the bus and took cabs to get us to the movie theater or to a restaurant. And the days when depression threatened to pull me under, he anchored me to solid ground either by phone or in person. A year after I was diagnosed, I completed my degree and moved back home, secure in David's and my love for one another.

I hadn't been home long when David began to point out what he didn't like about me. He was mainly uncomfortable with my introversion. Often, he would have to coax me out of the house. He stated on more than one occasion, "I don't know, babe, maybe you're not the woman for me. Maybe we should just be friends." When I asked him if he truly wanted to be just friends, he insisted that he wanted to continue the relationship. Why didn't I break up with him, since I felt he didn't like my core personality? My fear of not being able to find another mate was one reason. I did not want to lose his support. But more importantly, I liked him. His personality. His way of being. I liked the fact that every time he smiled at me, my heart found its home. I wanted him in my life—indefinitely. My desire to be with him aside, I wanted David to make a choice.

One evening, while we were at one of the many resorts we frequented, we went to a restaurant overlooking Lake Michigan. While we dined on crab cakes, garlic mashed potatoes, and a vegetable medley, a man in a dark suit played soft jazz on a grand piano. After dinner, I ordered a glass of cranberry juice and then cane in hand, wobbled to the ladies' room. When I returned, a waitress brought my juice on a silver platter. A little black velvet box was by its side. Looking very pleased with himself, David took my hands in his and told me that he did not want to live his life without me. He told me that I was the woman he had prayed for, and he thanked God that we had found each other. Then he asked me to be his wife. "Are you sure?" I replied. It was a question meant to address two issues: I needed assurance that he had come to accept and could live with the fact that we were different people with different ways of being. I was often content sitting at home reading, watching TV, or visiting with friends. He liked to interact with the world up close and personal: Nightclubs, parties, festivals, and concerts were his choices of entertainment. I was laid-back and timid; he was exuberant and fearless. And we were both very stubborn. The second issue that concerned me was, of course, my health. Considering my limitations, when it came to running a household, he would have to take up the slack. When David visited me while I was away at school, if needed, he would go grocery shopping, sweep the floors, and if my sister-friend hadn't done it already, he would do the laundry. And because I was still being courted, and he wanted to impress me, he usually cooked. Because we spent so much time together and he had experienced some of the challenges of my life (energy drain, falls, and the dearth of handicapped-accessible venues), I believed that he had a good idea of what might lie ahead. After recovering from the abrupt halt of the romantic moment, he told me that he was sure he wanted to marry me. *He is willing to face up to the challenges of my life for the rest of his? I am blessed, and he is indeed my knight.* I accepted his proposal.

In the days approaching the wedding, we had conversations about our expectations for our household. I told him that I don't cook like grandma, nor do I clean like grandma. I assured him he would not live in a pig's sty. He told me that my ways wouldn't be a problem. He said he didn't mind cooking or cleaning. But the *reality* of our marriage didn't agree with him. Like many brothers who say they want a strong Black woman, David's ideal strong woman didn't disagree with anything he said or did. She did not display anger at him, and she didn't talk back. She cooked, cleaned, worked outside the home, and did it all with ebullience. And, when he came home from work, she met him at the door with smiles and sunshine. In our home, magazines and books sprinkled the coffee table. Sometimes there was food from my stove; sometimes there was food from the restaurant that delivered. I had told him that even if I were not physically challenged, I would not live my life like June Cleaver; everything would not be just so. I knew this because I had not always used a wheelchair. I knew this because I knew myself; things in my life didn't have to be just so. Six months before the wedding, he voiced no objections. Six months after we said, "I do," he told me of his discontent.

I balked at David's desire to have, what was in my mind, an idealized, and pre–women's movement wife. David thought I should've wanted to provide that kind of home because I loved him. I thought that because he loved me, he should've gotten off my back. Once he witnessed my tempestuous resistance of his attempts to make me accept his idea of wifedom, he was taken aback. When he witnessed my raw anger because I felt he had no respect for who I am and how I function in the world, his fantasy shattered. Once he allowed himself to see the soul of the iris that had once enchanted him, and that I wasn't going to let him make me into something I'm not, we worked to reach a happy medium—but to no avail. As I continued my efforts to please him, and he thanked me for doing so, I realized he still wanted to break up.

I had fried a batch of chicken wings. "Thank you for cooking for me," he said. "But it's not enough, is it?" I replied. He gently shook his head. *What am I doing wrong? What can I do to make him stay? Why doesn't he like me anymore? I release the judgment that because he is not willing to give us time to acclimate to marriage, there is something wrong with me. I release the judgment that because he won't give us a chance, he is weak. I release the judgment that I will never find a Black man to love me as I am . . .*

After three years of marriage, he told me, "This is not the situation for me." You ever feel a sledgehammer slam into your chest, breath escaping lungs like air fleeing a slashed tire? I will never forget the summer of '98 . . . It is late; we are the only ones in Ridge Park. The orange light shining down on the park bench makes me feel safe and exposed. He says he is having a hard time being married, that he needs to leave, but he doesn't know how to tell me. "You just did," I chuckle. My eyes close and I search for the Kleenex box sitting on the floor of my three-wheeled scooter. When he called and said he wanted to talk, I intuitively knew he would be saying goodbye, and I thought to bring tissues. Tears flow and I blow my nose with the scented, peach-colored paper and hang my head. He leans down off the back of the park bench and reaches for a tissue and blows his nose. I reach then he reaches again. We need to quickly wipe the tears away and still the running, so I place the box on the bench. He was my champion; I was his queen. *What is happening to my fairy tale?* The previous year had been tense as we danced an elaborate tangle around our troubled marriage. The separation intended to unfurl the cords of our connection, so we could feel what we really wanted to do, had indeed yielded his truth. I have spent a lot of time in this park with brown boys: at twelve, and fourteen, and sixteen, and twenty-one, and . . . twenty-nine. I'll never bring a man to this park again. *I release the judgment that all men bring heartbreak. I release the judgment that men leave. I release the judgment that men are emotionally weak. I release the judgment that I can't have my fairy tale.*

When I was twenty-nine, my world shifted on its axis. And that shift left me full of questions. David is the only one of the two of us who knows for sure why he wanted a divorce. I know he was impatient with the slow pace of our melding; he had difficulty adjusting to the one fact I presume exists in all relationships: He is not she, and she is not he. Occasionally we squabbled. He said up, I said down. He saw red, I saw burgundy. He liked it, I didn't. They were the kinds of squabbles I was accustomed to. They were the same squabbles that I had witnessed from my parents my entire life. I think he thought that I disagreed with him intentionally. When I disagreed with him, it was because I had a perception different than his. I thought it was normal. David, on the other hand, found it disconcerting.

Unfortunately, I had internalized David's dissatisfaction, made his issues with me about some internal flaw I had. I didn't show my love for him the way he wanted me to. I didn't like to be on the go as much as he did, and he insisted that we *didn't* have anything in common. Eventually, I came to believe there was some validity to his perceptions. I must not be a good wife. Maybe we didn't have anything in common. Maybe I really didn't love him. I began to doubt the validity of my own perceptions and feelings. At some time during our three-year courtship and subsequent marriage, because of his sense of responsibility, his intelligence, his loyalty to the "cause," and his support of me, I had deemed him a paragon of Black manhood. I would venture to say that David strove to be the poster boy for Black manhood. He wanted to make "the people" proud. I believed that if a paragon of Black manhood found me so displeasing and was so eager to discard our relationship, then I must be unworthy. During our courtship, he would call me his queen. I didn't like the terminology because, as I told him, that noun and people's perceptions of what a queen is sets up expectations I was not trying to meet. He may have stopped calling me queen, but he seemed to still be in search of perfection (say nothing of the fact that a queen has ladies-in-waiting and other servants). I was newly married, working on yet another graduate degree, and working out how to navigate my world while living with MS. I was not interested in notions of perfection.

As time progressed and David's complaints increased, I felt I was no longer awesome in his eyes. As I was losing my husband, my self-confidence shattered, and my sense of self teetered on the edge of David's approval. I had unknowingly equated being able to please him with my sense of worth, something I thought I would never do. Was I wrong for insisting that I be heard? Was I wrong for wanting him to accept how I showed my love for him, by letting his wings unfold so he could fly? Constantly, I questioned myself, and I began to feel like a failure. When David and I finally separated and divorced, I felt like a neon sign plastered to my forehead flashed: *Failure, Failure.*

When I told people David and I were divorcing, their usual response was, "Because of your health?" Wrapping my brain around the probability that the challenges my physical limitations present pushed David away is difficult, because what *I heard* him say was that we didn't have anything in common, I didn't keep house to his liking, and that in general, marriage shouldn't be as difficult as ours was. To me, the way we met, the fact that we both felt a soul-deep connection, the fact that he courted me and asked to marry me despite the MS, was the stuff of fairy tales. In my fairy tale, the couple living happily ever after endured trials that served to reinforce the seams of the delicate relationship garment.

Maybe the fabric of our garment, the fabric of our relationship, rotted before we married. Any garment made of weakened fabric will disintegrate no matter the reinforced seams. A marriage counselor I talked with said that whatever unresolved issues from the courtship go unresolved in the marriage will eventually kill the marriage. The issues we thought were resolved, in fact, were still chewing moth-holes in our union. Maybe David's discomfort with my health heightened, for him, our differences. Maybe David's discomfort with my personality masked his discomfort with my health. Every book I've read on MS points out that some people, family members included, have a difficult time reconciling their loved one's debilitating disorder with how healthy they appear. If I sit in a regular chair, no cane, no wheelchair in sight, one would be clueless as to my state of health. Except for the MS, I am a perfectly healthy chick. Maybe because I was diagnosed so early in our relationship, David felt obligated to stay in the relationship. Throughout our courtship and our marriage, I had asked him time and again how he was doing. Most of those times, he answered that he was okay. He also told me that he didn't want to talk to me about how he felt, because he didn't want to upset me.

Pondering David's reasons for leaving is tiring. Counterproductive. Asking why he left is another way of asking, What did I do wrong? His leaving wasn't about me. It was about him living with the choices he made in his life and their consequences. I don't doubt that when David asked to marry me, he wanted to live up to the challenges of my life. I believe he wanted to be able to live with our inherent differences. I believe he came to accept me. In his acceptance, he came to realize that I wasn't the woman for him. Even a paragon of Black manhood wants what he wants. David either wasn't willing or wasn't able to stay in our relationship, so he did what was best for him. And it's all good. Now, I have to do what is best for me. I have to continue to cut the vines of self-doubt fertilized, in part, by one man's opinion of me. On occasion, David and I asked ourselves: Why did we get married? It was a question uttered while we tried to iron out some problem. It was a question uttered while we marveled at how difficult communicating with someone you love could be. I imagine he may have pondered the question more seriously than I did, since he was having such a difficult time. I have no idea what his answer was. I, on the other hand, married the man I had asked God for, had written about in my journal, and before we met, I had even created a fictional character that mirrored him exactly. I married the man I loved, foibles and all. In my prayers, I didn't think to add—oh, and he must be able to accept me, as I am.

As the saying goes, when we enter into a relationship, it's for a reason, a season, or a lifetime; the trick is realizing which of these scenarios pertains to you. David and I were in a relationship for a reason. We knew this when we courted, because many of our life's lessons were triggered. David felt he was supposed to learn patience; I was learning about self-acceptance. Once we moved in together, the lessons intensified. That we no longer reside in the same space does not stop me from processing the experience and growing from it. David served as a conduit through whom God worked to show me where I needed to grow, and I dare say, I was a conduit for him. When we enter into a relationship, no matter how casual, the Divine presents us with an opportunity to learn a lesson, and maybe teach one. The people in our lives are reflections of ourselves, and often times those reflections send us running away. If we are brave enough to view the reflection head-on, and discern what is being offered, we embrace the opportunity to grow as spiritual beings.

When we attract situations that reflect a truth we need to see about ourselves, we are receiving an opportunity from the Divine to actualize our highest potential. I believe the most profound way that we attract people and situations is with our internal dialogue. When our internal dialogue is saturated with stereotypes about the "other"—all men are dogs, women always nag, women just want money, men leave, etc.—and we constantly visualize a scenario where these things actually happen, we open space for disappointment to enter our lives. When the thoughts and visualizations are accompanied by feelings of fear and disappointment of what might be, we are virtually guaranteed to have an experience that mirrors what we imagined and felt. After I was diagnosed with MS, because of the unpredictability of the disease and the energy and mobility drain inherent in its nature, I was petrified David would break up with me. He is a socially active man who likes to be accompanied by his significant other, so I feared my sedentary lifestyle would eventually become an issue for him. It was a fear that, on occasion, I was conscious of having and would quickly dismiss. However, after David proposed, the feeling was completely ignored, and I missed the opportunity to fully deal with it. Because I didn't express this fear as completely as possible, and judged it to be nonsense, I held it outside of myself, and it manifested.

Because of the reflective nature of relationships, I *suspect* David had his own fears: maybe of being protector and provider, or maybe he feared my health would worsen and he wouldn't be able to care for me. I suggest this only to point out that the issue at hand always, in some way, pertains to all parties involved. The details might differ, but the big picture is the same. Whether or not he dealt with his fear, I don't know. I squashed mine. Did all that fear floating between the two of us influence our breakup? I believe so. The heavy weight of denied fear was one of the many blankets that helped to smother our flame. At the very least, it was a space where we both had denial; therefore, we could not be completely honest to each other or ourselves about our relationship.

The belief system we hold about the world constantly redefines our world, good and bad. If we don't take the time to listen and to feel what our souls are saying, then we probably are not conscious of what is really going on in our hearts. Sometimes we do feel the sorrow, disappointment, anger, and fear, and we push them aside and tell ourselves that to feel them is weak and useless. Not only do we need to feel whatever emotions are present, we need to express them as well. Expressing emotions with healing intent, and in a safe, loving way is beneficial, because expressing them helps get the feelings out of our bodies. Moving emotions demagnetizes the judgments and clears the way to attract loving opportunities. By intending wholeness and allowing myself to feel and express my emotions, I gain clarity and am able to acknowledge and accept my responsibility for the events in my life. I have realized that neither David nor I was at fault; there is no right or wrong, just choices and lessons. Because of our choices and the lessons we had to learn, we *both* played a hand in dismantling our relationship. Releasing emotions is helping me relinquish the desire to play victim, and it is helping me to take back my power.

Living with MS has propelled me to cultivate a relationship with the loving God, and I am learning that when we judge ourselves, we are not embracing love. When we judge ourselves as weak because we want to cry when we are hurt and angry, we are not accepting ourselves. My friend Natasha, a divorced schoolteacher, loved her ex-husband. Pride and extenuating circumstances drove them to a divorce neither of them wanted. Four years after their divorce, she told me that she had raged and spewed venom, but she had never shed a tear. She had never cried, she said, because then, he would have won.

Natasha's words, "he would have won," conjure interesting images in my mind: war, combat, winner, and loser. In the mid–1980s, Pat Benatar's melancholic voice crooned across the airwaves that "love is a battlefield," and at fifteen and sixteen years old, some of us believed it. At twenty- and thirty-something, some of us still do. Sometimes battles are fought in love's midst, but love itself is nurturing and supportive, life-giving and healing; love is not a battlefield. The battlefield is formed on fear's terrain, terrain often fertilized with the events of our own pasts, our parents' pasts, or maybe our best friend's present. When we deny ourselves the expression of all our feelings, because then the "other" will win, we do ourselves a disservice. The "other" does not know what is going on in our homes, but the heart does. Emotional honesty can help keep communication open between the heart and the mind. Emotional honesty can support healthier lives. My girlfriend told me that as she allowed herself to feel and express her heartbreak and yearning that she became more energetic, that she stopped anesthetizing with honey-barbecue wings as often as she had been, and she was able to more easily manage her weight. Natasha realized that her temper and her inability to forgive helped to damage her marriage. Any emotion we have is a part of us and to deny that emotion helps create imbalance in ourselves and the world.

This is why I work to release judgments. I don't want the heavy weight of fear and resentment to overshadow my love of men or my love of life. I don't want to play defense and I don't want to play offense in a phenomenon that is neither game nor war. I am a gentle, sensitive lady, strong and sometimes flexible. I like me better this way. To say that I have been unlucky in love would diminish the lessons I've learned from one boy and two very different men. My experience with David taught me that love is soft and magical, that the support I desire in a mate can only come from God, and the acceptance I desire of a mate, I must first give myself. To say that I have been unlucky in love would be to deny three occasions God has blessed me with. The fear of heartbreak is a major reason that many of us run from the opportunity to grow and flourish under love's light. We don't believe ourselves worthy, we expect that being in love will hurt, or we believe that if the beloved leaves, love will never return.

Instead of having faith that if we have love in our hearts, it will manifest in our lives, we hold on to lost love like it is a medal of distinction, a symbol of our victimhood. Sometimes we wear our heartbreak as armor, thick as a turtle's shell, defying anyone to penetrate our soft places. Our soft places, our truths and vulnerabilities, our very souls, are what yearn to be touched. And witnessed. And cherished. But if we hide these spaces from ourselves, squelch our fears and disappointments like they are something to be ashamed of, we are not experiencing unconditional love. It is cliché, but, if we do not love ourselves, can we truly love anyone else?

Once we recognize our relationships as divine opportunities to grow and actualize our highest potential, perhaps the journey into love will be less painful. David was truly a God-send. He was one of my soul's mates. In the beginning of this essay, I said that we were unequally yoked. That is a perception conceived in disappointment and heartbreak. Sitting on this side of heartbreak, I am clearer. We were perfectly matched to do what needed to be done. We accompanied each other on one leg of the journey that is life, and we were utilized by loving light to help each other grow. I am not totally free of the disappointment, yet. However, now, I only have one carry-on and it gets lighter and lighter every day. I am clearer on what my union with David was truly about; it reflected my relationship with and my need to trust loving light. I thank Mother-Father-God for being present with me when I vibrate heartlessness to allow more love in.

And so it is and ever shall be. Ase. Selah. Amen.

Love Down Under

by Kristal Brent Zook

We met at Yallingup, a clear-blue-water haven on the Indian Ocean with pristine beaches and romantic, hidden caves. Ironically, Yallingup is an Aboriginal word meaning "place of love." I was living in Perth, the capital of Western Australia, and working as a visiting professor in cultural studies at Murdoch University. It was a gig I had hoped would give me a fresh perspective on the usual fixed boxes of "culture" and "race" in America. So far my plan seemed to be working. I, the child of an African-American mother from the South Side of Chicago and an Anglo-American father from the San Fernando Valley in Los Angeles, had searched my whole life for a better understanding of such terms. From the moment I arrived in Australia, it was as though the world had been turned upside down: Australia was forcing me to look at lifelong assumptions about "Blackness" from a new angle. Like doing a headstand in yoga, my worldview was being oxygenated, and I loved it. By October, more than half of my six-month appointment had gone by and I had yet to take a vacation. My favorite colleague invited me to join him, his wife, and their daughters at an Aboriginal surfing competition. It was a yearly event—a place for *nyungah* (the preferred term among Aborigines) from around the country to come together for surfing, barbecue, music, and a good time. So we piled into the car one Saturday morning, making our way some 150 miles south to Yallingup.

A few hours later, six or seven of us were drinking Cabernet on the porch of our rented cabin, just as the afternoon sky turned orange. A very sisterly woman named Mary made a point of referring to her handsome, well-traveled son who had just gone to the store, by the way, but would be back shortly so I could meet him. I liked her immediately.

Not long afterward, a fantasy man rounded the corner. Matthew. He was six feet two inches tall and perfectly muscular. He had long, curly hair and a tattoo on his right bicep with a pattern of ocean waves. My heart raced. So did his, apparently. Months later he was still reciting to me every detail of what I wore and said that first afternoon. We spoke briefly as the sun went down and then agreed to look for each other on the beach the next day.

I tossed and turned all night with images of Matthew. Shortly after sunrise, my friends and I descended the cliffs for the big surfing competition. Glistening and brown after surfing (like an "Aboriginal Adonis," as my friend Lisa used to say), Matthew planted himself so close to me that first morning that our arms touched. I placed an ice-cream cone in his large brown hands. Afterward we posed for sandy-faced pictures inside the caves. At the roasted-kangaroo and fish cookout, I slipped into his sweater and we sneaked off in the darkness. We camped out under a trillion stars that evening, just the two of us, beneath a single blanket. I remember being lulled to sleep by the crashing waves, amazed that I could fall into such a deep warmth so quickly.

For Matthew, I discovered, being a surfer was more important than any other aspect of his identity. More than being Australian or even nyungah, surfing was the very core of who he was. Later, from various shorelines, I would watch him in the distance, immersed in the silence and awe of the waves. He seemed to need the ocean in the same way that some people need churches. It was the place where he most felt the presence of God. Without it he was irritable and distracted. With it he was centered, all-knowing, infinitely compassionate.

Matthew came to visit me in Perth about a month after Yallingup. Before he arrived, I dreamed that he had given me a birthday card and was hurt that I had treated it too casually. Inside the card was a certificate for $429 that he had won surfing. He was turning it over to me in full. His surfing. His life. The message of the dream was clear. I was being told not to take him lightly when he arrived. He would be someone serious.

For two weeks we frolicked in the sun, riding bikes on Rottnest Island, making love, and drinking beer. I wrapped up my semester at Murdoch late one evening, with Matthew helping to fill in my students' grades as

I called them out. He slipped out early the next morning, bringing back fresh fruit, croissants, and flowers. We couldn't stop touching each other.

Australia is a continent only slightly smaller than the United States but with a population the size of New York State. Because there are so few people, even those who live in big cities have the luxury of space. Australians can walk into the ocean naked (which we did) or make love under a blazing sun (which we also did) and never see another human being for miles and miles. Not even a footprint. No matter where one lives, a deserted beach or mountaintop or forest is never far away.

With so much land available, Matthew could rent a three-story five-bedroom home overlooking the ocean for about $900 a month. He worked as an artist, painting canvases and didgeridoos when the mood struck. Sometimes he took temporary jobs with friends in construction. He traveled. By his mid-twenties, he had already lived in England, Holland, Spain, and Germany, where he alternately laid roofs and tended bar. On a whim, he would jet to Indonesia for the weekend to surf. Part of me admired him and shared his sense of adventure. Another part of me was envious: His lifestyle represented a freedom unlike any I had ever known.

About four months after we met, we spent the weekend in an island cabin near Cape du Couedic in South Australia, where we saw seals, wallabies, and koalas. We brought no clocks with us, and there were none in the cabin or car. One day we went to town and asked a waitress if they were still serving breakfast. She looked stunned. It was three-fifteen in the afternoon. "No matter how much I try to situate him in my life, to rank or place him," I wrote in my journal, "his spirit won't allow it. He simplifies me."

Matthew's ancestors were Narangga people on his maternal grandfather's side and Pitjantjara on his maternal grandmother's. His father was an immigrant fisherman of Italian and German descent, whom Matthew only came to know at age seventeen, shortly before his father's death. Although Mary, his mother, had hoped her five children would learn something of nyungah languages, Matthew never did. His older brother had returned to "the bush," the center of the country where most Aborigines reside, and endured a painful initiation ceremony involving mutilation of the penis. Knowing that a similar fate awaited him if he went North as an adult man, Matthew refused to visit his elders. His brother had been deeply traumatized by the experience. To Matthew, such rituals of traditional men were pointless and cruel.

Although immensely proud of his lineage, Matthew had been raised in the predominantly White city of Adelaide, where he was the only Aboriginal child in his classrooms. I understood what it meant for him to straddle two cultures: He had to live outside people's boxes, in a space that is both liberating and lonely. In fact, I sometimes felt more kinship with Matthew than I did with African Americans, especially those who insisted that I wasn't *really* Black because of my color or education or other such nonsense. We were, both of us, outsiders.

But I was also full of doubts about us. I once asked Matthew if he thought we were compatible. He was silent for a moment. "I don't know," he said finally, "but I think we're good for each other." Though I admired his free-spiritedness, I realized just how much I valued order: clean sheets and towels, appointment books, and newspapers. He, in contrast, was adamantly opposed to watches and careers. No amount of encouragement I could give—such as helping him sell his artwork—was going to change that. Nor did I want it to, really. I was attracted to him, after all, because of who he was.

Still, it bothered me that Matthew never saw his art as a vehicle for the future, for us. I remember when the World Council of Churches commissioned some of Matthew's paintings. They were to become part of an exhibit that would tour the world. Ultimately they would be housed with the Pope's personal collection in Rome. Though Matthew was pleased, his art remained just something he did from time to time. "We could have houses anywhere, babe," he once told me when I was in a fretting mood. But I knew that houses required paperwork and steady jobs, things that were as foreign to him as another language. Our days together were like having plenty of money but no checkbook to measure it by. We lived well and loved deeply, but never planned for the future.

I returned to California following my six-month assignment in Perth, while Matthew remained in Adelaide. Despite my doubts, we continued our long-distance love. We would take turns making the twenty-hour trip, which, given the eighteen-hour time difference between our two worlds, meant literally two days of travel. In this way we spent weeks and months together at a time, followed by weeks and months apart. Although we entertained the idea of one of us moving, it just never seemed to be the right moment. Matthew was in serious culture shock in Los Angeles, while I couldn't imagine giving up the career I had worked so long and hard to establish. Besides, it seemed at times that the ancestral forces didn't support us.

One night as we lay sleeping in Los Angeles, I was awakened by what I felt to be distinct presences in the room. There were two or three of them, hovering in the corners of the ceiling and walls. I felt that they were ancient spirits, and it seemed to me that they were furious. Matthew awoke shortly after I did. "Do you feel them?" I whispered. "Yeah," he replied, his voice sleepy and confused. I wondered if they had come because Matthew was thinking about living in America.

Until as late as 1992, the White Australian government had continued the official fiction of *terra nullius,* arguing that the British settlers who preceded them had come to "no one's land" at the time of their 1788 invasion. It was a fiction that ignored the 50,000-year history of Aboriginal people in Australia. Now Matthew was thinking about abandoning his ancestral home. It was enough to make ancient spirits angry.

After that night, the spirits often returned to my room, even when Matthew was not in America. They would sit and wait. Once I shot up, spooked, just before the phone rang. It was Matthew calling in the middle of the night to say he had sent a ticket for me to come over. Putting down the phone, I could sense that these spirits didn't much like me. Or at the very least, they didn't care for what I represented. To them, most Americans must have seemed like a blur of rushing careers. We represented the quest for profit and crushing indifference to all that they held sacred: respect for nature and a meditative reverence for stillness.

If the spirits objected to my being with their son, Mary certainly did not. She, like Matthew, was somewhat removed from traditional Aboriginal communities. A survivor of the Stolen Generation—nyungah children who were forcibly taken from their families between 1910 and 1970—she had been one of those captured and placed in state-run foster homes. The kidnapping was part of a legal policy of assimilation, which sought to "save" light-skinned Aborigines by placing them in families where they could shed their "pagan" values and eventually intermarry with Whites.

Anecdotal accounts of gun-toting men barreling into the bush are legion. Children would scatter upon hearing the trucks that came to take them away, hiding in bushes for days at a time. Some mothers covered babies' faces with coal to prevent their removal. Once taken, many children were subjected to electric-shock treatments, maggot-infested sleeping quarters, and sexual and physical assault. After several years in such orphanages, young Mary managed to escape and return home, but not before being repeatedly told that her mother "didn't want her" and "had died." What awaited her was a dysfunctional household in which she became the primary caretaker for several younger siblings. Beyond such sketchy details, Mary did not talk about her childhood, her mother, or her time in the orphanage. Matthew wondered how I had gotten his mother to open up at all.

But we had something in common, Mary and I. At age fifty, she was pursuing a university education, a rare feat in a country that claims only 8,000 Aboriginal college graduates. Fully 25 percent of all Aborigines over age fifty-five have never been to any kind of school. On my visits to Adelaide, Mary and I would often sit in her living room for hours, talking about literature and ideas. Her grades were excellent and she intended to pursue a doctorate. To me, both she and Matthew seemed to stand apart from the cultural displacement, alcoholism, domestic violence, and epidemic suicide rates that plagued their communities. About 2 percent of the population, Aborigines were 19 percent of the men and women found in prison. Life expectancy for them was eighteen years shorter than the national average, incomes were a third lower, and unemployment was up to five times higher.

The image that most troubled me was that of young Black men getting drunk on the weekends and hanging themselves—an event that was as common in rural areas in Australia as lynching had once been in the United States. I often found myself staring at Matthew as I did at Black men in America: amazed that he was alive, healthy, and free.

It has been more than five years since I last saw him. In the end, the doubts just became too much. I could no longer pretend that our love would lead to the home and family I needed to create. Tensions ran high on my last visit to Adelaide. Attending the wedding of one of Matthew's good friends led to a particularly ugly fight between us on the way home. Perhaps because weddings provide such a brilliant glimpse of emotional clarity, they demand a similar truth from those of us who are invited to bear witness. Matthew and I understood that night that neither of us was ready to make such a commitment. The realization was bitter indeed.

Even so, I like to think that we parted as friends. Being with Matthew was one of the most profound experiences of my life. We are so anxious to be "right" in America, to plan and control. Matthew had no such investments. He taught me about a certain quiet knowing at the center of things. Like the time he sat on my living-room floor for days, painting a pattern that he would eventually describe as "my heart." His genre of painting, known in Australia as Aboriginal dot art, is literally hundreds of thousands of tiny dots dabbled from the end of a brush to form a pattern, or "dreaming" story.

I remember him hunched over the burnt oranges and lime greens of the canvas, shirtless and bald—we had both cut off our hair as part of a spiritual-cleansing exercise. And I remember thinking that he seemed so naked just then. Naked in his soul. Matthew must have known, as he painted, that he had lost me. And yet he continued to make his art as a gift for me. Patiently. Quietly. With great tenderness and faith. Without a formal religion, Matthew was, quite simply, an example of spirituality in practice. He believed in accepting things as they were meant to be. He believed in kindness and free will. And above all, he believed that I should be happy, regardless of what that might mean for us. Because as long as I was happy, as he used to say, "we're laughing, babe."

And we were.

What One Dance Can Do

by Keisha-Gaye Anderson

The scent of marijuana enveloped me at the door of the club as the straight-faced bouncer nodded stiffly for me to go in. A sea of Rastafarians swayed slowly to the bass rhythms pumped out by the reggae band, while others bopped lazily by the bar with beer in hand.

It was easy to spot my friend Mira—the only blonde head in the crowd. Working in the music industry always got her—and me, by association—free tickets to one performance or another. I figured I'd check out the show and hang until my feet gave out. It's not like I had Valentine's Day plans the next day, a lack I'd come to expect over the past couple of years.

We greeted each other with the usual hugs and air-cheek kisses and I watched the band step in unison to the rhythm. On the packed dance floor, a few couples wrapped in tight embraces two-stepped with the speed of molasses as they memorized each other's contours. Some were engrossed in more explicit demonstrations that were sure to end in the bedroom.

I smiled self-righteously at my indifference. Public displays of affection like these used to send me tumbling into an abyss of self-pity about being single, dredging up painful memories of all of the failed romances that stacked themselves like steel walls, or better yet, a glacier, around my heart.

Lately I had become that glacier, letting all idealism about love flow around me. Apparently, love didn't *love* me. Just look at my track record. There were the cheaters, the liars, abusive men, insecure men, men who didn't bother to mention they were married, men who were married and didn't care, and then there were things I didn't dare recall in my waking moments.

As a college-educated, professional Black woman, I knew that I wasn't alone in these adventures. Cocktails and commiseration about men was a favorite pastime of mine and some of my closest girlfriends', and there was sort of a sick consolation in that. It was ridiculous the number of women I knew with my credentials who were painfully single and preoccupied with finding a mate. I resolved to never ever become desperate, like those who were sharing a man, or putting up with ridiculous "baby-mama drama." The media didn't help either. An article I read in *Newsweek* said, "Black women are almost five times as likely as white women to still be unmarried at 40."

Yeah, there were a few cuties at the club tonight, but most of them seemed decidedly Rastafarian, according to their dress and demeanor. Born in Jamaica and raised in New York City, I knew quite a bit about Rasta. I knew enough to know that I could never really abide by any of the conservative rules Rastafarianism often prescribed for women, and I figured most of *these* guys came with just such prescriptions, so I didn't give them a second glance. Perhaps I was generalizing and being judgmental, but at the ripe old age of twenty-seven, I'd decided that love wasn't for me anyway, so I just rocked to the music and sang along with the band. I tried not to think about the past and what went wrong and why, but here it came, invading my head space. Mira was busy talking to someone else.

I mean, I'd dated outside my race a few times, but was usually confronted with the role of exotic sex object being projected onto me, or got the feeling that I was only temporary recreation. And my obviously "African" physique usually attracted only men of color anyway. Who was I to expect romance, marriage, and children? Surely I was dressing up in White women's ideals.

No. From now on, I would put all my energy into writing, making money, and traveling the world, with a few torrid trysts sprinkled in between for fun—I did have needs.

I was already living by my new operating principle to a small extent, working as a journalist for a major TV network and writing regularly for national magazines. I had applied to graduate school for my master's in creative writing and I was in the process of buying my first co-op in an up-and-coming section of Brooklyn. But more importantly, I was doing what I loved most on a regular basis—performing my poetry.

I was still bubbly from the reception I'd gotten at the Knitting Factory right before I came to meet Mira. I performed some of my poetry to a packed house at the Lower Manhattan bar, throwing in a few of my more cynical pieces on love, "that translucent boomerang that tears through my heart—not of my reality, or am I just out of phase with the rest of humanity?" The crowd loved it. Adulation was a good substitute for intimacy, I figured.

Mira yelled over the music and interrupted my ego trip. "Come . . . I want to introduce you to someone!" Social butterfly that she was, she was always introducing me to people. I followed her to a spot near the bar while still trying to watch the fevered tempo of the percussionist on stage.

"Keisha, this is Ralph. He works with me at the label." I turned around and suddenly stood face to face with a tall, lean, ginger-brown man with a broad smile and quiet eyes. He stretched his hand out to shake mine as I climbed the steps toward the bar. I was immediately drawn to him like a bear to honey. I didn't understand it. I just knew I had to fight it.

"Would you like a drink?" he immediately offered with a welcoming wave of his hand, his head tilted to the side expectantly.

"Thanks," I replied. As I pressed through the crowd and followed him to the bar I realized I had been smiling and made a conscious effort to look cool. Soon, I was sipping on a Corona, and he, a Red Stripe.

Although I was very conscious of maintaining my nonchalant demeanor, due to my new personal rule—men aren't worth my energy!—this guy seemed interesting. "He must be taken," I thought to myself. "They all are." I glanced at his left hand to see if he wore a wedding ring, and felt somewhat relieved that he didn't, although I didn't want to admit it then. His glasses, full beard, and inquisitive eyes gave off the air of a scholar, someone well traveled, mysterious. Plus, I could tell that he'd be about an inch or two taller than me without the heels—at five foot eleven and two hundred twenty pounds, meeting a tall man was a rare delight.

I had serious hang-ups about my size that I masked fairly well by making sure I was always dressed to a tee in flowing, sexy clothes. Being tall and curvy, or what folks would call "thick," had always brought me attention that I didn't want, especially from men much shorter than myself. In their clumsy attempts at flattery, they'd often made me feel more like a carnival attraction than beautiful, like some sort of urban dominatrix. I had to be careful though. Height, this superficial characteristic, often had the amazing power of making me overlook glaring character flaws in the past.

As concertgoers pushed past me to get to the bar, they kept bumping me into Ralph and I found myself wanting to get even closer. "Sorry," I said sheepishly, smiling and holding his arm longer than necessary to catch my balance. He smiled and nodded that it was no bother at all. I wondered if he enjoyed this flirtation but I resisted the urge to contemplate it too much. Dealing with men always somehow left me shell-shocked.

As the night progressed, Ralph and I tried in vain to have a conversation over the blaring sound system, but I managed to get the important information anyway. My first impression was correct. He was college educated, Afrocentric, well traveled, Caribbean like myself, and a seemingly cool guy overall. We exchanged smiles, nods, and furtive eye contact as we waited for breaks in the music to coolly ask the next question. I stood there as long as I could talking with him about reggae music, politics, and other things, all the while, my diva leather boots squeezing my feet into throbbing masses. I enjoyed talking with Ralph, getting close enough to catch whiffs of the sweet oil in his beard and hair. I could tell he had a stellar mind, something I valued highly and rarely found in a physical package that pleased me.

My feet were about to give out, so I told Ralph I was going to head to the ladies room and then go home. He immediately offered to lead me through the crowd so I could get to the bathroom quickly without being harassed by the other men there, and then waited by the bathroom door for me so that he could walk me out. I thought that was an incredibly sweet gesture, but my knee-jerk defenses made me take it as just that, and nothing more. Before I left, I wrote myself a reminder on the back of his business card: "Can help me with poetry CD." It was only going to be about business, I told myself. I told him we should keep in touch, then ran outside and hailed a cab. I plopped down and immediately freed my feet from the oppressive leather and threw my head back on the seat, closing my eyes.

As I rode to Penn Station, I thought about how nice Ralph seemed. Budding optimism about a new man was always stifled by the cynical ghosts in my head that piped up their disapproving voices during these times. They were the emotional shrapnel embedded deeply in my mind after each romantic fallout, and their presence always sent me on an unwilling mental journey into my past. Each time I dove into myself for clarity, an explanation for what I had gone through, I came up empty and exhausted.

My experiences with men had run the gamut from good to really horrible, like most of the sistas I knew. Overall, I came to the conclusion that either men were generally not capable of seeing women, especially Black women, as intelligent, whole human beings, or that there was something inherently wrong with me. It was Zora Neale Hurston who wrote that "Black women are the mules of the world," and that observation had always stuck with me. Having traveled throughout the Caribbean, southern Africa, and South America, that metaphor came to life over and over right in front of my eyes. Black women everywhere seemed to be experiencing the same things in terms of poverty, sexual exploitation, and overall lack of freedom. It all seemed so overwhelming and futile. Where would I be lovingly cherished and adored for being me—smart, beautiful, tall, thick, and Black?

I mulled over some of the more memorable train wrecks of my personal life as the cab dipped and swerved up to 34th Street. There was the athletic Mr. Perfect who, after softening my defenses for six months with witty conversation and daily "I love you's," turned out to be engaged. When I busted him, he appealed to me, "but I love you *both* equally . . ." There was the sexy divorcé who promptly told me he wasn't gonna "work for pussy" when I suggested he pick me up for our date, since he had the car and I didn't. And, I couldn't forget the hot-shot M.B.A. who felt I should be honored that a catch like him wanted to redeem some perceived booty-call privilege after reluctantly paying for my soul-food dinner in Harlem. I gave him his $12.95 back.

These jokers I could laugh at, as well as the colorful ways in which I'd dismissed them from my life. But in the deeper recesses of my mind lay memories I didn't want to access, but which always surfaced once the door of recollection was slightly ajar. Their acridness further reinforced my new Valentine's Day mantra—You were not meant for love!

Scenes from that July night seven years prior flooded my mind. Realizing I had been drugged . . . hallucinating in a dingy Brooklyn apartment at 4 A.M. . . . pleading humorously to be taken home so as not to anger the naked bull of a man charging toward me . . . my spaghetti arms drawing my pants on crookedly as I staggered across the room . . . he, pulling my pants back down, agitated, calling me a "college girl" with contempt . . . muscular, tattooed arms restraining me as he forced himself where I didn't invite him . . . floating out of my body when his weight and liquor-laden breath became too oppressive . . . covering the bruises on my neck the next day with foundation . . . telling my girlfriend the date went "okay."

The irrationality of that incident stirred up my most raw emotions, validated all that I thought was wrong with me, and the only response I could manage was numbness. The slim pickings of potential partners and my own poor choices filled me with a feeling of hopelessness. It wasn't like I had some history of abuse to explain my bad judgment when it came to men. Mine was a sterling example of an intact Black family, my parents having been married thirty years, a rarity these days. People had always told me I was beautiful and intelligent, yet I somehow felt isolated and out of place with men. I'd gotten an array of responses when just being myself, from being accused of "sounding White," to mocking my more scholarly interests. My need to be warmed by what I thought was love always left me scorched.

What I didn't realize is that, up to that point, I'd only been timidly dabbling with caricatures of love. All that I thought I understood about love changed when I started letting Ralph seep into my life, like mist overflowing a river with thirsty banks.

"Happy Valentine's Day!" a deep, raspy voice cheerfully greeted me through the phone early the next day.

"Who is this?" I asked sharply. And what the hell was he so happy about this day anyway? I thought to myself. Work was a zoo and I hadn't gotten sufficient sleep the night before. I think all that ganja in the club had given me a contact high.

"It's Ralph. We met last night at the show—"

"Oh yeah, the record label guy." I paused and looked at my computer. "Didn't you *just* e-mail me too?" I said. I pulled up his similarly cheerful e-mail, laden with smiley faces, which had arrived at my job before I did. I didn't let on but I was impressed by his writing skills. I could actually see the way his mind worked—the perfect balance between logic and imagination, maturity and playfulness—and I liked it. Yet I remained irritable, torn between secret excitement over him calling and blatant suspicion about his motives. It was just like a man to come along and test you when you'd made a decision to swear them off. I had a feeling he was not interested in frivolity. But I had no intention of wavering from my new way of living. It took many hurts to bring me to the stance I'd taken and I wasn't going to be moved, only to be disappointed again.

He chuckled at my rude retort. "So we work in the same neighborhood. We should definitely get together or have—"

"So what exactly *do* you do again?" I interrupted, half listening, half watching CNN on the TV in my cubicle. He proceeded to explain his job in much more detail than I'd hoped for. Then, he came back to the point of getting together.

My bad attitude didn't faze him. He was still as cheerful as ever. I tried again to dissuade him. "I don't know when I'm free. I have a writing class tomorrow, drinks with some friends on Friday, a book reading I really want to go to. I dunno . . . maybe next week, the week after that?"

"That's cool," he said, lingering silently on the phone for a few seconds more. "Yeah . . . so . . . let me know."

"Okay . . . *Byeeee*," I said in an exaggerated tone. I decided I wasn't going to call him.

Ralph called persistently every day before our date the following week. My reactions to him gradually shifted from annoyance to intrigue as we had lengthy conversations on topics such as Black history, literature, and politics. I viewed the exchanges as a healthy intellectual exercise. I was brutally candid when expressing my views about women's issues, including the sexual freedoms a liberated woman should be able to enjoy without the stigma generated by patriarchy. I thought for sure this would scare him off. My interest in him escalated when I realized that he not only shared this and many of my other viewpoints, but he was attracted to my honesty and free spirit. It's a side of myself I really hadn't shown men before for fear of being misunderstood or judged harshly. Now I sort of wanted to scare Ralph off with the real me, especially since I had a hunch that he was eight or nine years older than me, but it did nothing but reel him in.

When we finally met for dinner I studied the hard lines of his face, a long African mask cradled by a wiry ebony beard; soft sleepy brown eyes; full, cocoa-colored lips. I couldn't deny my attraction. I started to tell him something about a literary device in one of the short stories I was working on. He had picked up his fork to eat but put it down to listen to what I had to say. When I was finished, he proceeded to eat. He's actually listening to me, I thought to myself. Could this be something viable?

We communicated quite well. The attraction was certainly there physically, intellectually. I felt like I was about to overload on anticipation. But soon, the cynical voices began to bubble up in my head again. *There must be something wrong . . . too good to be true*. I ignored them.

"So, do you have a girlfriend?" I asked, focusing on my plate.

Of course he does, stupid . . . when are you gonna learn? Those nagging voices tested me.

"Well . . ." He paused. I slowly impaled a piece of broccoli on the edge of my plate, bracing myself for disappointment. "I've been seeing someone for a while but it's on the outs."

I thought that was acceptable. Aren't most people usually seeing "someone," one way or another? I know I had my own little midnight-rendezvous lover on standby. The voices quieted.

"You know, when I take my little girl ice skating—" he continued. Upon hearing those words, my heart sank. I knew all too well about baby-mama drama and I wanted *no* part of it—no jealous ex, no bratty children, no losing sleep wondering if your man is still screwing the ex—none of that. I was above that. I deserved better than that. I needed to be the first and the last and that was all there was to it.

Ha! Told you so. I knew he was too good to be true! my inner critic jeered.

"When you take *who*?" I asked him, knowing the whole time what he would say.

"My little girl. She's ten. She loves ice skating. You should come with us one day. Think you would like that?"

"Oh . . . Um, no I don't think so. I don't want to disrupt your time together," I said, visibly disappointed. I'd decided to take this for what it was, a nice date with a nice, intelligent guy but with no real future in sight. I definitely was not going to complicate things with sex either, although I would have loved to bend over and kiss his perfectly carved lips. But I bristled at the thought of coming second in someone's life when I so often felt "second" in my relationships, even when there was no child involved. My fragile ego couldn't stand it. I wanted desperately to be somebody's one-and-only, all-important darling after the horrendous experiences I'd been through with liars, cheaters, and worse, a rapist. And although I had no basis for my feeling, I suspected the child—especially a little girl—would be an obstacle to the fulfillment of my need to feel valued. I remember how attached I was to my father. I had to let Ralph go, and fast. I should have known better than to waste time dating anyway.

"You wanna go dancing?" he asked eagerly, noticing a change in my mood. I loved dancing. I figured, why not. I'll go and have a good time.

When we were inside the club down by Union Square, slow '80s reggae vibrated the walls and Beres Hammond's silky voice penetrated every corner of the room. I was still having a good time, enjoying Ralph's company. We started to dance and he decisively drew me close to him. I liked his directness. I felt butterflies tickle my stomach as I nestled comfortably in his arms. I could feel the base of his heartbeat—among other things—against my body. Our sweat-covered cheeks remained fastened as Beres crooned the chorus, "I'd like to tell you a story about / what one dance can do . . ." I already knew what this dance did to me. Our lips found each other simultaneously and didn't part for the rest of the night. It's like he quenched a thirst I never knew I had.

I couldn't just walk away from such a safe, sensual, enlivening feeling, all rolled into one. What was I getting myself into this time? I remembered the couples dancing closely in the club the night we met. We had certainly memorized each other's curves by the end of the night.

From that point on, the relationship blossomed at breakneck speed. If we weren't having lunch together, we were meeting after work to go home together, talking endlessly about art, writing, current affairs, culture . . . I spent many nights lying in his arms, drinking in the perfume of his breath, falling asleep to the beating of his heart as his wiry beard tickled my forehead. I was terrified yet invigorated by the comfort of being loved for who I was, physically, spiritually, and intellectually, and being able to drop the mask of indifference. I didn't wear it well, especially when I was feeling lonely. Not only did I stop feeling lonely while I was with Ralph, I rediscovered my beautiful qualities in my solitude because he shined a spotlight on a side of myself I kept tightly under wraps. His honesty, compassion, humor, optimism, and sensitivity freed me to be myself, to be vulnerable without fear of being used and abused. I couldn't explain why. I just knew I was loved and I couldn't walk away from it.

My little cynical ghosts of relationships past were still taunting me, though, causing me to display some resistance to deeper intimacy, due to the existence of the child, among other things. I'll admit, it was a lot to deal with all at once. Ralph *was* older—by fourteen years. He had a pre-teen on his hands. I was just about to move out of mommy's basement, trying to figure out where to take my career next, and here I was embarking on a real "relationship," which might lead to my becoming a step-mother? Hadn't I made a vow to myself to put my all into my professional and educational pursuits? Wouldn't this derail me? Cause unnecessary stress? It was all a poor excuse to mask my fear of getting my heart broken. Ralph worked double-time to allay my fears, and assured me he would keep his promise never to hurt me.

One night, about a month or two into our relationship as I tried to pack neatly for a business trip in the middle of my messy room, Ralph reclined on my bed to keep me company. As usual, he was reading some dense book about politics. He put the book down, looked over at me, and said, "I think I love you." I stopped and looked at him with that Black girl face that basically says, "brotha . . . *puhleeze!*" The last one who convinced me I was his "soul mate" dropped me like a hot potato when I refused to keep sleeping with him. Apparently, he didn't see his new live-in girlfriend as an obstacle. But Ralph went on to articulate that he thought he'd found the person he wanted to be with for the long haul, a.k.a, marriage! I immediately became uncomfortable, hopeful, suspicious, elated, and angry all at the same time, and my defensive wall shot up.

"That's nice, but . . . what am I supposed to do with that information? I mean, are you really sure? Or are you just saying that because you think it's what I want to hear? Because you want to keep me for sex? Because if you are, it's kind of insulting. Maybe we shouldn't have slept together so soon. Are you sure? Love?" *He's just playing with your head,* my internal bitter twin whispered. But he insisted he was being sincere. My skeptical questions continued in rapid succession. I couldn't control it. I didn't want to be made a fool of yet again just because my need to be loved was so great as to make me believe anything he said. If he told me he was an alien, was I going to believe that too?

I employed avoidance as my coping mechanism. "That's nice. I appreciate the thought," I said, "but why don't we just live in the now, have fun? Tomorrow is not promised. Right?" He smiled, held my face in his huge hands and kissed me, brushing my frizzy, untamed hair back. I don't think I was fooling anyone but myself.

Not shortly after I began to accept without fear that I was fully head-over-heels in love, other aspects of my life began to fall completely apart. The co-op board denied me the apartment I'd been sacrificing for so long to buy, and all the nonrefundable bank and lawyer fees put me about two thousand dollars in the hole. None of the graduate programs I'd applied to accepted me. The shaky economy was making my job security shaky as well and I wasn't sure if I would be kept on at the network. I got nothing but rejection letters from publishers and poetry contests where I'd submitted my manuscript. All my well-laid plans that would substitute for this thing called love began to disintegrate and I had no idea where I should be heading and what to do next. Never before had so many things gone wrong simultaneously in my life.

In the face of such disappointment, I was usually content to nurse my wounds alone or vent to a few choice girlfriends, but the day I got the call saying I was denied the co-op, it was the last straw. After unsuccessfully holding back the tears at work, I went straight to Ralph's office, stood in his doorway, and cried even harder.

With swollen red eyes and wild hand gestures, I paced back and forth and told him what had happened in one wheezing, run-on sentence, punctuated by sniffs and the type of hyperventilating I did in my childhood when I knew I was in for a spanking.

"After six months of going through *all* this work to find that place and going through the process and looking at it over and over and giving them all the documents they wanted and going to the interview those bastards have the nerve to deny me based on what? I don't know! I am a young professional and I would be a good tenant and I have good credit and now I'm almost thirty and I'm *still* living in my mother's basement and by the time I move out I'm just going to have to move back in and take care of them because they will be old and I'll never have a life of my own or a house or kids and it's too much pressure with all the bills and how am I ever gonna make money being a writer anyway and this is all such *bullshit!*"

Ralph listened quietly. Walked over and hugged me. I shook violently as I cried. It wasn't just about the co-op. It was about the whole identity I was trying to build for myself that now was toppling before my eyes, never to materialize the way I wanted. I wasn't steel after all. Inside, I was as soft as clay and my delicate inside was beginning to rest outward in front of Ralph. I was embarrassed. I felt trapped by my gender, my race, my family obligations, my lack of money, my high level of sensitivity that made it impossible to stop the tears that were now running down my face. I felt like a failure.

"You should fight those bastards!" he said as he walked back and sat behind his desk. I finally relaxed enough to sit down. He wasn't bored or annoyed at my display. "Why don't you write an article for one of those magazines you write for? This seems like discrimination to me. Don't worry and don't give up. You'll be back on your feet soon. But don't let them get away with this."

Ralph supported me in this trying time and in the months that followed, and never took advantage of my depressed state. He attended all of my poetry readings. I talked and cried and talked and cried and he always listened patiently. He was optimistic and held my writing and overall intelligence in high esteem. I had no time to sink into my familiar depression while my inner ghosts taunted me about how stupid I was; Ralph pumped me up with loads of optimism whenever I ran low, he being a person who naturally looked on the bright side of things. And, he wasn't afraid at all to point out when I was wrong and offer me constructive criticism. I admired that too, someone who would stand up to me.

In the weeks that followed, I gradually got back on my feet and started looking for a place again, as well as a new job. For the first time, I was able to express a vulnerability that freed me to be myself without fear. Ralph's compassion and honesty showed me there was no danger in being me. This was love and it was brand new to me. I liked it.

As for his little girl? I never did go ice skating with him and his daughter, but I did meet her after about four months. Despite the usual awkwardness of first meetings, I felt optimistic about forming a relationship with his child, mostly because it was evident in speaking with her that Ralph had explained how special I was in his life. "He talks about you *all* the time," she said once.

I felt honored that he loved me enough to introduce me to his daughter, his mother, and eventually, his whole family. He has never once made me feel "second" as I feared would be the case when dating a man with a child. In a way, looking at her was like looking into a mirror. Here was a tall, intelligent, beautiful young girl on the cusp of self-awareness, a time when young Black girls learn to hate themselves as prevailing Western beauty aesthetics permeate so many spheres of their daily lives. I became excited at the prospect of helping her steer clear of some of the pitfalls of low self-esteem that made me regard myself as so much less than I actually was.

There were times when she expressed discomfort with having to share her dad—she is an adolescent after all—but these bumps were never enough to scare me away from what was developing into a beautiful relationship with Ralph. Love was the fuel that kept me sailing into uncharted waters. First, learning to release my fear and open up. Now, forming a relationship with his child. After two years, I don't regret either of those things. And I am prepared for challenges that may come.

It's true you don't choose love—love chooses you. But as long as you are brave enough to become the truest expression of yourself, you'll always be ready for it when it comes.

For Better or Worse

African-American Marriages
Under the Microscope

Me and My Marine:
Holding Fast in Love and Faith

by Shrona Foreman Sheppard

Standing beneath a rented archway adorned with silk flowers and garlands, I inhale deeply as I turn to face the 250 people gathered for the day. I have just exchanged vows with my lover and best friend. We stand together, waiting for our brother-in-law Eddie to begin singing Leon Patillo's popular wedding tune, "Security." I had initial reservations about including the song in our wedding program because I had not yet heard it. But I relented when my wedding coordinator—Eddie's wife and my future sister-in-law—convinced me of the beauty in the melody. I scan the crowd of family and friends and see my mother weeping—her face a blend of pride and sorrow. Eddie's voice—rich and smooth—seems to fill the room with exquisite velvet. Yet, it is the tune's sentiment that I will not soon forget: "When a man has found a wife, he has found good thing for his life. And a woman will agree, companionship has made her feel so complete."

I am experiencing an onslaught of emotions: a joyful anticipation at the start of something new and a wistful melancholy for the only life I had known. My husband Hector takes my hand and helps me from the dais to the unity candle we are to light together. I am thinking how beautiful and perfect Eddie's tenor is when the full force of the song's chorus hits me: "With you and me and the Lord up above, we have security." His voice growing stronger, Eddie continues, "What God has joined together let no man put asunder. Nothing can separate you from me. I worship and adore you, put no one else before you. This is my vow to you my love through all Eternity." It has been ten years, but the emotions I felt on my wedding day are still palpable and the memories remain vivid in my mind's eye. The songwriter speaks of a security that can abide only in the faithful. I understood even then that the security I enjoy in my relationship with Hector is guaranteed only if the two of us can share a mutual faith in our spiritual union.

I am trembling as Hector and I walk away from the unity candle. Once we are standing again under the archway, I turn to my bridegroom and he sees the tears beginning to slip from my eyes. He whispers, "Don't cry, baby." But, it is too late. We are holding hands now, but Hector slips his from mine and wipes away my tears. There is a collective sigh from the audience and, later, several people remark that it is this moment that will be forever etched in their memory of our special day. Furthermore, I have come to view my husband's spontaneous gesture as a metaphor for the care and concern he has demonstrated throughout our marriage. Every day since has not been as beautiful, nor every sentiment as heartwarming, but the good days have far outnumbered the bad. I am blessed to have made it through the dark hours to the sunshine and now I am able to appreciate the moments of despair because I know now that it is through these periods of struggle that my husband and I have been able to forge an intimacy far greater than anything we could have known the day we wed.

In the rose-colored heyday of early romance, newlyweds are often unable to see their partners as persons who will—at some point—visit hurt or disappointment upon them. Throughout our six-year courtship, Hector's love and dedication were so true and perfect that I could not imagine a day when our love would be anything short of wonderful. I had been seduced by his sincere affection, and, in many respects, I remain so enthralled. Yet, I no longer view our love with the same Pollyanna optimism or youthful naiveté that I did in those incunabular days. While there was no clear line of demarcation as we transitioned from bride and groom to wife and husband, I noted the unmistakable shift, at once subtle and swift. Our transformation came in the form of compromises and sacrifices that we were willing to make as we merged our disparate lives. It came in the acceptance and tolerance of both the unique gifts and the peculiar personality traits that we each bring to this relationship. The shift from autonomy to connection also manifested in the considerable flexibility with which we tailored our individual aspirations to a new, coupled reality. It is the unconditional love and acceptance we share that make the compromises and sacrifices that much easier to bear.

The first major compromise in our union came just weeks before our wedding when Hector was offered an engineering internship in our hometown of Augusta, Georgia. This opportunity came on the cusp of our decision to make Pensacola, Florida, our post-nuptial home. I had lived and worked in the Panhandle city for three years—enjoying my first job as a cub reporter for the local newspaper. Having spent great distances apart during our courtship, Hector and I promised to never voluntarily spend any significant time apart once we were wed. However, we decided that this opportunity to gain valuable work experience would be worth a short separation. Opting to endure our first three months of marriage geographically separated has since been reduced to a cakewalk along our lives' journey. The real challenges lay ahead—the first of which came several months later when Hector became a commissioned officer in the United States Marine Corps. I understood Hector's decision to become an active-duty Marine as this option had always been on the table; but he agreed to exercise it only if he was unable to secure another viable job opportunity.

Still, the decision had immediate consequences and required us to accept a lifestyle far different from anything we had envisioned heretofore. First, there was the potential for danger in the event of military conflict—an especially difficult issue for me because Hector and I were only recently engaged when his reserve unit was called to serve in the 1991 Gulf War. I had terrible memories of the all-consuming fear that gripped me throughout Operation Desert Storm when I spent countless hours watching the Cable News Network for any word on units in or near the port of Al Jubail, Saudi Arabia. Of course, I was no less fearful now that Hector was embarking upon a career in the Corps. Secondly, I was chagrined that Hector's career path would have a decided impact on my career aspirations, as it would force me to adapt my career goals and prepare for the frequent relocations. Often, I would second-guess our decision and wonder if I would ever secure my dream reporting job at a large, metropolitan daily. Finally, I loathed the protracted family separations necessitated by military life, fearing that I would have to go it alone in the event that Hector and I had children. This was not something I wanted for my future children or me. Still, I faced this disquieting prospect with some ambivalence. On some level I welcomed the excitement of global travel since, as Hector pointed out, we could live in any of the U.S.-operated bases in Asia, Africa, and Europe—if only for a short time. Ultimately, Hector enjoyed my full support, as I shared his desire to secure financial stability for the two of us. I am pleased that, for the most part, the experience has had a positive impact on our life together.

In fact, our family has been fortunate that throughout Hector's time in service the separations have been short and infrequent. Furthermore, aside from the recent Operation Iraqi Freedom, most of Hector's deployments have been relatively stress-free. Nevertheless, our children—Shamaal, seven, and Tirzah, five—probably suffer the most during extended deployments. Shamaal lost a coach for his Bad-News-Bears basketball team when his father's squadron was sent to Kuwait just prior to the end of the season and Tirzah performed her first dance recital without her Daddy's proud face amid the audience. The worst moments come when my daughter wakes at night with tears streaming down her face. "Mommy, I'm missing Daddy too much." Or, when I must address the anxiety in my son's face because he wants an answer to a rather tough question: "Will Daddy die in the Gulf?" I am honest with my children and I tell them that I don't know when Daddy will be home and that I don't know if he will perish in a faraway land. I tell them that the most we can do now is pray for the courage and safety of the men and women who have been called to arms, and I find myself reminding them of all the good times they have shared with their Daddy and of the hopes and dreams the two of us share for them. My heart is filled with joy when I see in my son the same tender compassion that made me fall in love with his Dad. It leaps again when I see that my daughter has been blessed with her Daddy's cheekbones. Often, I remind my children how lucky they are to have a Daddy who is attentive and engaged whether he is near or far. I even share with them the anguish I know Hector feels when he has to spend time away from them. He says it pains him that he can neither delight in their amusing conversations nor enjoy their race to greet him each day.

Shamaal and Tirzah have certainly brought immeasurable joy and happiness to our lives and have added a new dimension to our concept of family and responsibility. Yet, I do not think that either Hector or I fully appreciated the demands—physical, emotional, and financial—that children would place on us. I was surprised most by the sheer constancy of their needs and the staggering burden they can place upon a young couple. In our case, we worked hard to achieve an equitable balance. My primary roles include planning and preparing our meals, while Hector's primary tasks include cleaning and vacuuming the house. Meanwhile, we often share the other duties and responsibilities. I cherish my husband's role in our home. One of my most endearing memories of our early days as new parents is of Hector waking to retrieve the babies for their nighttime feedings. I nursed both of our children and, for all practical purposes, there was no real role for Hector during feedings. I recall that several of our friends teased us—arguing that there was absolutely no reason for both parents to endure sleepless nights when the mother is nursing. I understand that our routine may not work for everyone and, in fact, I had several nursing mothers tell me that they would prefer their husbands get a full night's sleep as he was the only one working outside the home. But Hector's stock soared with me because I found his actions especially considerate. Today, Hector maintains that assisting in the late-night feedings allowed him to feel important in the babies' lives. "You were nursing and, obviously, I couldn't do that, but I wanted to share in the bonding," he said.

Nevertheless, the most difficult times in our marriage occurred in the months immediately following the birth of our second child. I had spent just five months with our newborn before I accepted a full-time job as an education reporter at the *Washington Times*. Having only recently purchased our first home, it was becoming decidedly tougher to juggle family finances. So, I agreed to return to work in an effort to provide some relief to the situation, ambitiously hoping to also eliminate some of our debt. But, after several months, this proved not to be the case as our daycare expenses rivaled my new salary. In reality, my return to the workforce resulted in little more than a major disruption to our family routine. I would spend nearly three hours each day—assuming all the planets were aligned—commuting between our home and the paper's Washington office. The stress became overwhelming and when I was accepted into the graduate program at Georgetown University I jumped at the opportunity to attend school full-time.

I had completed my first year of studies in the Communication, Culture and Technology program when I was confronted with this notion that for some White Americans my Black husband and the love and support he demonstrates for his family is an apparent anomaly. The incident occurred shortly after my husband joined me at a school-sponsored social. Later, one of my classmates, an affable White guy who worked for a Washington, D.C., law firm, said he was surprised that my husband was Black. Puzzled, I asked, "Why is that?"

He said, "I guess it's just the way you talk about him." Becoming somewhat flustered, he added quickly, "Don't get me wrong, he sounded like a great guy and a tremendous support system. It's just that I assumed he was European. Maybe, it's because you lived abroad for a time."

I considered his comment and was able to recall only one occasion when this man could have heard me speak of my husband. The conversation came after several classmates remarked how impressed they were that I was able to manage my studies while raising two toddlers. I responded that I had a lot of support from home and explained how my husband and I tag-teamed duties. I told how I cared for the children during the day and he cared for them at night when I had class. Meanwhile, Hector attended only weekend classes in his graduate program. In addition, the kids were also enrolled part-time in a home daycare program. It was I who described my husband as a personal cheerleader, of sorts—a great source of support and encouragement. So, I thought, a White European? I had never lived in Europe. I had lived in Japan and this information was public knowledge in our program as it had been included in the introductory biography I posted to the program's website. Still, my classmate did not assume that I was married to a Japanese man. It was at this realization that my classmate's comment disturbed and saddened me the most because the man I described—caring, loving, and supportive—is not the Black man with which White America is familiar. Yet, it is the only one I know intimately.

The feature I most appreciate of my marriage is the strength of my husband. I do not have to be the Strong Black Woman—carrying her man and her children on her back. I can be vulnerable and needy and express my weaknesses in the full softness of my femininity. I have seen the SBW up close and personal and I have seen how she masks her pains and disappointments with superwoman heroism. I have seen the Strong Black Woman—as mother, aunt, and friend—reduced to anger and bitterness as she seeks comfort in drugs, drink, and, in some cases, the arms of another. Society can have its SBW for the annals of history. I will honor her and attest to her fortitude in the preservation of the race, but I cannot make her my reality for I have seen the SBW buckle under the weight of her own strength. I have seen how society will harness her strength to do battle with her helpmate, and I want no part in this legacy.

On several occasions I have addressed the SBW concept with many of my married friends—some of who candidly acknowledge their own fall into the SBW trap.

"I have the same hyper-self-sufficiency that my mother had," says Andrea, a working mother with two small children. "As Black women, we are simply accustomed to being nurturers and caretakers. It is how we protect our men."

While Andrea seeks to remove the burdensome SBW cloak, another friend gladly assumes the armor, arguing that without it her marriage would have failed: "The wife is chiefly responsible in the instrumentation of the marriage. She is the drums, and for us, as Black people, without the drums there is no music," she says. "I had to assume the lead, otherwise we would not have made it twelve years."

In the weeks preceding our wedding, Hector and I attended a series of premarital counseling sessions. During one session, the minister asked us to describe our role models for marriage and apply these ideals to our expectations for each other. I had some difficulty identifying a single someone as my ideal husband. Instead, I offered a composite of the kind of husband I desired based on the marriages and relationships of the people closest to me. I longed for the ultra-masculinity of my uncle Anthony and the macho bravado with which he cares for my aunt Joan—his bride of thirty-five years. I sought the humor and tolerance of my uncle Herman, who married my aunt Lynne a quarter century ago. I also coveted the quiet confidence exuded by my stepfather Donnie in the thirteen years he shared with my mother, Juanita. Certainly, I craved the intense passion of the shorter-lived love affairs of countless other relatives and friends. While each of these relationships experienced its own unique challenges, in many respects they still serve as beautiful and remarkable instances of successful Black love. I am pleased that my husband and I now count among them. I marvel that after a lifetime together, my aunts and uncles can still enjoy decades-old jokes. In their laughter, there are forgotten memories of past hurts and battles that no longer matter. It is their spirit of ebullient camaraderie that I hope to share with my husband until we are old and gray. Once, when we were living in Japan, Hector and I found ourselves entertaining some American musicians booked for a gig at a plush Japanese resort. One of the band members joked that he could see Hector and me together at ages ninety-five and ninety-seven. "You'll be together until Hector falls down the steps and cracks his hip and you have to put him in a home," he said, only half-joking, adding, "Somehow you just know couples that will be together forever, and you guys are one of them."

I smile at this memory and I pray that we will forever have the *je ne sais quoi* that this California drummer noted. So, some may ask: What are the secrets to marital success? I posed a similar question to students in the interpersonal communications class I teach at the local community college. The question was posed as part of a lecture on romantic love and relationships. I asked my students to consider why some marriages endure the test of time. They offered a variety of reasons, including love, money, fear of loneliness, and sex; certainly there are as many reasons as there are marriages. However, I suggested to my students that there is a common thread that connects all enduring marriages, be they good or bad: They feature partners committed to making it work. Commitment is not represented by the piece of paper known as a marriage license. It is, instead, the active decision to stay together even after the butterflies in the stomach have subsided. These people are willing to stay the course despite their troubles and a lucky few manage to sustain the passion that heated their embrace when love was new.

It takes effort, but it is possible to sustain the spark of young love if partners remember to treat each other as they did when they dated—with kindness and consideration. I still see in Hector the charmingly sweet young man who escorted me to my senior prom sixteen years ago, and he still makes me feel like the girl with the sparkling eyes and sexy hips that he spotted across the school cafeteria. Our marriage and the life we share together are everything I ever wanted and more. I am thrilled and blessed to have a husband who supports and encourages me. No matter the circumstances, I know he is in my corner and that he has my back.

I am especially fortunate to be in this place because it was just three years ago that my husband and I weathered the first real storm of our marital life together. Indeed, it was a particularly chaotic time in our lives as we had both returned to school. I was working part-time at a digital production studio and Hector, of course, was pulling twenty-four-hour duty in his role as a Marine. Meanwhile, we were juggling home responsibilities as well as rearing our two children. Then, in the midst of our well-orchestrated bedlam, my husband began a disturbing conversation that brought my world crashing down. It was just the two of us driving from our Virginia home into Washington, D.C., where we were conducting rehearsals for a play I produced as part of my graduate studies. It was my second trip into the city that day and I was drained. But, the hours in this day grew longer still as Hector proceeded to reveal that he had been unfaithful. I was stunned to hear that the love of my life, my best friend, had betrayed me.

Hector began his revelation with some innocuous discussion about whether I could forgive him if he did something really stupid. I, in turn, offered a playful challenge before the words I never thought I would hear began to spill from his lips. In an instant, the air escaped from my chest and my heart began to beat rapidly. I could not stop the tears that stung my eyes. I began to sob as my husband pleaded with me to stop crying, because there is more. Now, the words crept ever so slowly from Hector's mouth and I was trying desperately to concentrate while the ache that began in my stomach moved up to choke in my throat. Hector told me that just two weeks after a sexual encounter with a woman at his office, he began to suspect that he had contracted a sexually transmitted disease. A test in his doctor's office confirmed that he had chlamydia. I was, in a word, devastated. I screamed out and sobbed louder then because, for sure, a bomb had exploded in my chest. I recoiled away from Hector in the driver's seat, and gripped the passenger-side door. Even this seemed too close to him and his sordid tale.

My husband tried desperately to calm me saying that this news is not the end of the world. I am incensed because for me that's exactly what it feels like. I had always counted myself among the lucky when friends or relatives faced similar news. Of course, I would offer them words of comfort while feeling just a bit superior that nothing of that nature had ever happened to me. I remember that one of my dearest high school friends faced a similar predicament when her boyfriend paid her a surprise visit to announce that he may have exposed her to herpes. My girlfriend was distraught and went immediately to see her doctor. After being immobilized with fear and dread, my friend was able to rejoice when medical tests revealed that she did not have the virus. While I had great sympathy for my friend, I secretly felt that she was among those liberated women who took the whole idea of sexual freedom just a bit too far. Hence, I found her negative test result both a stroke of pure luck and a wake-up call that begged for her attention. Now, facing my own perilous situation, I could hardly take up the same sanctimonious posture. Instead, I shouted at my husband, telling him what he must already know, that he risked my health for some cheap thrill with a girl at the office. I retrieved my cell phone from my purse and dialed my doctor's office, but the receptionist had difficulty understanding me through my sobs. Once I managed to secure an appointment for the following day, I told Hector he would need to join me. I began to wipe my tears as we were approaching the rehearsal site and I was forced to put a lid on my heated anger. Our practice was intense as I was experiencing—in real-time—the kind of hurt and disappointment that the student actors must bring to stage in the play, which had been so aptly titled *Living History: Virtual Narratives of a Georgia Family*. The play features a series of vignettes based on the real-life experiences of my mother and her sisters.

Later, that same night—after the children have been put to bed—I am able to unleash the pain that I bottled during the rehearsal. It is an extremely unpleasant ordeal as I confront my husband about his actions and challenge his commitment to me. I ask all the important questions: Who, When, Where, Why, and How? I wish I could say that Hector answered my concerns effectively. The sheer inadequacy of his responses troubled me then and puzzles me now. It took several weeks of intense discussions like these before I realized that Hector's responses could never remedy my disquiet because there is no good reason to violate the sanctity of one's marriage—not when a partner is giving the same 100 percent that has been extended. Until that night, I never knew I could cry so many tears. I remember that at one point I was on our living room couch crying into a pillow and my husband was on his knees crying and hugging me and telling me that he loved me more than life itself and that he could not imagine life without me at his side. I am consumed with rage because I am recalling a similar posture when he asked my hand in marriage. There were no tears then—although it was a watershed event of another sort—a very rainy night in Georgia at the Augusta Riverwalk. I didn't want to see his pain as it could never rival my own, and I certainly didn't want to offer comfort or even acknowledge his search for forgiveness—not at the moment I was feeling such vitriol toward him. So, I pushed him away and buried myself again into my pillows.

I would become increasingly disheartened as the details of Hector's infidelity were laid out. My husband told me that he and a female colleague had sex in *our* car after taking a dinner break together. Because the break was taken as Hector was preparing for overnight field exercises, he didn't have to face me until nearly twenty-four hours later. He described an initial flirtation and attraction with the woman who had revealed to him that she and another colleague often referred to him as "Cutie" when he was not within earshot. Hector said he invited the woman to grab dinner from a nearby McDonald's before the training was slated to begin. He said they talked about work, the woman's upcoming wedding, and our kids. I probably knew before I asked that this woman was White. It was part hunch and part educated guess, since there were few Black women in his company. I still don't know why but my upper lip curled and my husband must have felt my disgust.

"What differences does her color make?" he asked. Too incensed, I just shook my head screaming, "A White woman!" over and over again. Finally, Hector asks if I was more upset that the other woman was White than I was of the actual infidelity. This is, of course, not the case at all. I would be equally upset if the other woman was Black. I suppose I simply found his actions so hypocritical as Hector has himself commented how startling it is to find so many Black officers married to White and Asian women. If this situation made him uncomfortable, why then did he find himself in the arms of a White woman? In the months that followed my husband's startling announcement, I questioned every aspect of our relationship. I questioned the wisdom of our long-distance courtship and I began to recall the well-intentioned admonitions from friends and family. There is one aunt, known for her acerbic tongue, who challenged my sanity when Hector and I became engaged while I was still attending Howard University in Washington and Hector was in Atlanta at Georgia Tech. She said, "My darling niecey, I know that you are in love, but don't be no fool. A man is going to be a man all day long." When I replied that I trusted Hector completely, she laughed uproariously. "That's so sweet, it's almost quaint." Now, the idea that I may have been played left a very bitter taste in my mouth, particularly as I recalled conversations with friends who marveled at Hector's and my decision to maintain a long-distance relationship—an effort fraught with temptation since college campuses are little more than hotbeds of post-adolescent lust. I considered for the first time that perhaps our "monogamy" had, in fact, been one-sided as this is the insidious nature of betrayal; it legitimately calls into question every aspect of one's relationship. I repeatedly challenged my husband's versions of the facts as they related to his infidelities. Through the tears and recriminations, I began to pray and seek guidance from the Lord. It was at this point that I began to make a few baby steps toward true forgiveness.

Our road to recovery was rough and, at times, uncertain. But there is one day in particular that I will never forget. I was home alone working on a paper when my thoughts turned to Hector's deceit. It had been just a few weeks since my husband's revelation and I was still simmering with some unsettling emotions when the phone rang. It was my mother. We began to talk about a variety of things when she brought up the subject of infidelity. I had interviewed her just a few months earlier for the play and we had discussed her first husband, George, a notorious philanderer. Our conversation was on her mind and she said, "You know, George and I could have made it, but I was stubborn. Of course, I was and I still am. I'm a Taurus. The problem was I decided early that there were certain things I would not tolerate. So, I left and I started over, but I should have done things differently. We don't need to keep starting over. Whatever happens, y'all try to work it out. Stay there and work together to stay together." The conversation ended almost as quickly as it began. My mother's words—surprising in their timeliness—proved infinitely more valuable when she died just six months later at the age of forty-six. When we hung up, I stared at the phone for several moments and wondered how it was that my mother knew what I had never spoken. Today, I simply appreciate the wisdom that she shared. I have come to understand that all relationships are tested, but the good ones can survive—so long as the partners remain committed. I decided then that I could not allow anything to destroy what I share with my husband. I could not imagine this connection and tenderness with anyone else. The man I married is funny and ambitious, sexy and confident—an interested and engaging lover, a concerned and loving father. I could not in good conscience walk away from our life together. There are problems in a marriage because there are people in it. Each of us—in our humanity—brings a boatload of issues into our relationships. There is childhood baggage, the burdens of previous romantic relationships, and the odd coupling of interesting idiosyncrasies that become maddening differences as time progresses.

Throughout our ordeal, I surprised myself when I didn't turn to my mother, my best friend, or even my pastor. Outside of my physician—who not only treated me for the STD but encouraged Hector and me to work through the rough patch—I never spoke of the incident with anyone. Instead, I turned to my husband and challenged him to share the cause and effects of his actions as he saw them. I was comforted by his contrition and more than that I felt secure in his reaffirmation of our vows. He is committed to the life we share together and is willing to work hard to sustain it. This hard work includes an ingredient critical to any successful relationship: communication.

Today, there are no off-limit subjects with my husband. We talk—ad nauseam—about everything. If I need to seek clarity on a matter relating to his infidelity, I talk to him. He may not always be comfortable with my questions, but he is willing to indulge my inquiries and dissect both his actions and my feelings in order to put the matter to rest. I think it is important that partners expose their vulnerabilities to one another. It is only under such circumstances that couples can enjoy a deeper, richer intimacy. I know others who have taken a very different approach to a spouse's transgressions. I have a very close friend who acknowledges that she was unfaithful just three years into her marriage. Her husband became aware of the affair and discussed the matter only once with his wife—to secure her promise that the relationship had ended. My friend credits her husband's forgiveness with saving her marriage. "I have to give it to him. He has never thrown it in my face—not once," she said. "He has truly been able to forgive and forget. He simply never brought it up again."

Forgiving and forgetting is no easy task and is, in fact, a very high calling. The grace I have extended to my husband has been its own reward as I am now rid of the bitter rancor that threatened to steal the joy out of the life we share. There were many times when I questioned whether Hector's careless and irresponsible actions even deserved forgiveness. I know now that the pain and hurt of betrayal can cause a deep wound in the spirit of a relationship, but it does not have to cause an irreparable chasm. For me, the path toward forgiveness began with prayer, unceasing prayer—an undertaking that has led to a bedtime ritual of devotion that I now share with my husband. Each night we clasp hands with fingers interlocking and pray aloud. Our supplications allow us to share communion and fellowship with God while articulating the petitions of our heart to one another. I learn so much about my husband, his hopes and dreams for himself and our family just by listening to his prayers. We added another element to this ritual after watching Rob Reiner's film *The Story of Us*. The film's main characters—a troubled suburban couple played by Michelle Pfeiffer and Bruce Willis—routinely shared their highs and lows for the day, verbalizing the day's best and worst aspects. I was pleasantly surprised when my husband asked to incorporate a similar feature into our nighttime prayer routine. It is quite interesting to me that after ten years of marriage I can still learn anew of the things that make my husband happiest and the things that disappoint and aggravate him. The routine has become a vital aspect of our life together because it has established a continuing dialogue about our inspirations and disillusionments as we navigate this thing called life.

I look forward to the conversations that arise as a result of our inquiries. These discussions allow us to share our successes and failures and articulate our hearts' desires. There are days when we point the finger at each other and detail petty annoyances and offenses committed against each other.

Me: "My low point was having to come home to a dirty kitchen when you were home all day."

Him: "My low point was when you snapped at me when I forgot to take the trash out."

It is puzzling to me that so many of us—single and married—expect the person we love to intuitively know how we feel about something. There are so many dimensions to *you* that the minute someone starts making assumptions about your feelings, values, and motivations, they lock you into a box; no one can ever really know all there is to know about another human being because we grow and change and our values shift.

Once, when we were dating, I asked Hector what he liked best about me. He said that I made him feel important, that his opinion mattered. "You ask me my opinion about everything from world affairs to gender politics. You make me feel like everything I think matters to you." I want to preserve this quality in our relationship and our bedtime ritual allows us to do that. While it may seem odd to some, I trust my husband more now that he has been unfaithful. I believe he is more aware of the hazards of so-called harmless flirtations. A few years ago, one of our friend's apologized profusely after his wife called our home quizzing my relationship with her husband. She had found my name and number among her husband's belongings and though she had been introduced to Hector and me at a military function, she was unaware of my nickname, which was written on the paper. Later, our friend confided to my husband that he had once betrayed his wife's trust, and now she was especially sensitive to anything remotely suggestive of infidelity. He told my husband, "I don't even flirt anymore, because I know where it can lead." My husband has since learned his own very painful lesson. I hope that he disappointed himself far more than he disappointed me and that there will be no repeat of his transgression. He tells me now, "I love you so much that I never want to hurt you like that again. I cannot bear the thought of living my life without you." He calls the incident the biggest mistake of his life.

I turn my thoughts now to the recent twenty-fifth wedding anniversary of our new friends, the Mozons, a prominent couple who live near our home in Jacksonville, North Carolina. The pair was feted at a beautiful affair attended by family and friends who testified to their enduring bond of love and friendship. It was heartwarming to hear their sweet tale of burgeoning romance amid just a handful of other Black students at Wake Forest University during the 1970s. I smiled broadly as the Mozons were serenaded by another couple singing my beloved wedding tune, "Security." I grabbed my husband's hand: "They're playing our song." I had forgotten that the song's last verse holds the hope and promise of lovers the world over: "Now, at last, I understand our love was made in Heaven before the world began. And as we dream as lovers do, I pray that all we hope for will come true."

Yes, love can be as beautiful as the picture I have painted here, but the image can be swiftly and not-so-gently transmogrified by the realities of life. The union Hector and I share, which began with such grace and beauty, endures and is now our greatest reward. My husband has stood at my side through some of life's most difficult moments: the deaths of my mother, grandfather, and godmother. He has seen me through many crises with strength and fortitude. He holds me tightly in the night when the death of my mother strikes anew and the ache of loneliness seems too much to bear. He has both silenced my sobs and cried along with me. I am fortunate to have him in these moments of despair and disappointment. When my heartache has been at his own hands, I never allowed my disillusionment to pull me away from him and our life together. I have chosen to stay the course and the journey has been made less arduous through faith and prayer.

I have discovered that the beauty and promise of our wedding day can be realized only if we are willing to do the hard work to make love last and our love is hard-won. Marriages that endure are those where partners can share faith and commitment in their union. Faith has certainly allowed my husband and me to successfully navigate the storms that have come our way because sharing and abiding in the peace and comfort of something greater than us have been critical as it challenges us to love more, to give more, and to share more so that we may be rewarded with love, laughter, and joy in abundance. I am, simply, grateful that there is still a leap in my chest when I see my man at the end of the day and fall into his embrace—safe and warm. It is, indeed, a blessing should he remain part of my life forever.

Don't Judge a Brother By His Cover

by Thembisa S. Mshaka

Single sisters amaze me sometimes. They talk endlessly about how badly they want a relationship (read: husband), but once a brother comes into the picture, he's immediately eliminated based on what he doesn't have. He doesn't have the right background, the right job, the right education, the right family. That's just the beginning; he doesn't have the right house, car, or bank account either. And just like that, he's not even dating material, never mind husband material.

These same sisters are often the ones in awe of my marriage, asking me how I did it or complimenting me on what a great husband I have. In these moments, two things happen: I send up a silent prayer for the blessing of my husband. And, I laugh to myself at the irony of relationships. Because if they had known him when I met him, they would not have given him the time of day.

Anthony Morris, or "Tmor" as he was called on the streets of San Francisco's Fillmore district, was a ruggedly handsome, fiercely intelligent young man. He was nineteen when we met, working as a production assistant at KRON-TV Channel 4. He was a gifted writer of poetry and a brilliant emcee as half of a rap duo called Elements of Change. That's what

I knew when we exchanged numbers. Here's what I found out later: He lived in Oakland with a woman who had taken him in after his own mother, a twenty-four-year-old heroin addict, kicked him out once he accused her of stealing drugs from his room. He had sold drugs since he was twelve. He stopped selling because he had started using, from powder and mushrooms to Ecstasy and crack cocaine. He never worked a regular job. He was in school at San Francisco State, but was uninspired. What he really wanted was a record deal to launch the production company he had started. My college girlfriends thought I was crazy for associating with him. (I won't even go into what my parents thought when they heard about him.) My girls called him "that dusty rapper." He might have owned three, maybe four pairs of pants, tops. Aside from his box of lyrics, Tmor could carry everything he owned in a duffel bag. He drove an old white Scirocco that sounded like a diesel eighteen-wheeler; it was his address until Chris Metcalfe, the aforementioned woman and a producer at KRON, gave him a place to live, on the condition that he work around the house as a handyman.

Tmor called shortly after I gave him my number. I wanted him to be a panelist at an event I was holding at school about Black men and hip-hop. He wanted to have me over and cook me dinner. Hearing my mother's voice in the background say, "You don't know him from a hole in the ground!" I counter-offered with an evening of Stanley Turrentine's jazz at Kimball's East. Since jazz was much of what he sampled for his music and he'd never heard it live, he accepted. We clicked instantly. From that evening on, I called him Tone.

Our friendship continued for years, evolving gradually from us being "potnas" to me working as his group's publicist, then manager. I saw so much more than his past in him. I was totally excited by all the possibilities his life held. Our conversations were rich and wide-ranging. Tmor taught me more than I ever thought any man could about life, the streets, reading people, music, politics, the system, the importance of family, and above all, loyalty. He was a perfect gentleman as my friend, and even gave me advice on the tired men I was involved with. (I found out later that he had an ulterior motive for becoming my relationship counselor—getting those cats out of the picture.)

Eventually, our friendship became amorous. I remember when I first let it show: He kissed his then-girlfriend in front of me; I was furious and let him know it. His cards hit the table when his rhyming partner said, "If you want to get with her, she can't be our manager." I was promptly fired and reinstated as "his girl."

Our courtship was now in full swing. He supported me after graduating from college and before getting my first official job as a music trade magazine editor. I had his back through a near-fatal car crash and the ensuing lawsuit, his custody battle for his troubled teenage cousin, and his return to undergraduate study. Before I knew it, we had co-founded a successful music marketing company, and had been living together for three years. I had dropped many a hint about wanting an engagement ring. I was ready to take our bond to the level every woman who has invested years into a relationship longs for: the marital one. I tried not to press too hard though, because money was tight and Tone was no pushover. He had already told me that the ring I picked out when we window-shopped months ago was out of his price range, and a long shot at best. (Subtlety was not his strong suit.)

One day, he picked me up from my Saturday morning workout. My birthday was three days away and I just knew a proposal would be my present (we live-in girlfriends get so smug!). Well, I got an argument instead. He asked me what I wanted to do for my birthday. I played it cool and said, "Something low-key, like a nice dinner out, that's all." He went into a tirade about how we couldn't afford it, and I'd have to wait until some money came in for an extravagant dinner. I was livid. *Wait?* For *my* birthday dinner? He knew that Sagittarian women celebrate their arrival to the world in grand style, even if it has to be done on a budget. In my head I was saying, *This cheapskate betta recognize!* But to him I exhaled and said, "Why can't I have a nice dinner out?" I braced myself for a verbal slugfest as he pulled up in front of our house.

He replied, "Because I spent every last dime I have on this, baby." He extended a small, black velvet box. My face was cracked and on the ground. My growing indignation and boiling fury were transformed to tears, completely neutralized by his curveball. I would not be denied my revenge for this stunt, however, ladies. I had to go there. "After what you just pulled, you'll have to get up out this car and take a knee, brotha." He obliged, opening the passenger door for me before kneeling on the sidewalk in front of me, without ever letting go of my hand. He opened the tiny box, revealing the ring I wanted to my total surprise (and relief). With that he said, "I want to spend the rest of my life with you, T. Will you be my wife?" Of course, I said yes. We took our vows on April 13, 1997.

He has never ceased to amaze me from that day forward. The next year, I got my dream job in advertising at Sony Music and my husband made the ultimate sacrifice. He left San Francisco, his home of twenty-six years, and relocated to New York with me. The relocation was tough on Tone; school was unaffordable as an out-of-state resident, and work was scarce. With steady income still eluding him, he was determined to reduce our monthly expenses. In the face of being unemployed, Tone masterminded the purchase of our home, a three-family building in Brooklyn. After nearly two years of jobs that never worked out, he went to real estate school and joined one of New York's top firms. He's one of the hottest new agents in his office. All that work he put in on the streets and in the music business is finally paying off big. He continued his education beyond real estate school. He completed the Landmark Curriculum for Living in less than six months. He is a great cook and a loving father.

We've been fed all the statistics about how unavailable brothers are, all the hype that so many of our men are already married, gay, in jail, or dead. We've also bought hook, line, and sinker the notion that our men are triflin', irresponsible dogs who only think of themselves, and with their head in their pants instead of with the one above the neck. But I submit that these challenges to finding a committed relationship pale in comparison to a sister's judgments and expectations of the men that *are* still here, right under their noses. Now don't get me wrong, I made my list of qualities I want in a man. I am all for knowing what you want in a mate and not settling just for the sake of being with someone. But sisters have to look at the man for the man himself. After all, the list is supposed to focus on his qualities, not his acquisitions. My list included that "the One" be respectful of his mother, degreed, Muslim, self-sufficient, and well traveled. At the time we met, Tone was none of the above. What kept me from passing him over? Other characteristics, like his creativity, sense of humor, resilience, and keen intellect. I was willing to start there and nurture a friendship to see what else might develop. I had spent entirely too much time on men who fit the profile but were neither ready nor healthy for me. Tone did not bum-rush me for the panties. He treated me with respect. I had nothing to lose by putting in some quality time with him. And when I think back to what inside of him called out to me, it was the manhood that could not be squelched by misfortune or mistreatment. He wasn't stopped by the step-correct-or-git-ta-steppin' defenses I had up; he was bold about getting past them, and that posed a welcome challenge. I was also drawn to how fiercely, how completely he loved the things that he made himself vulnerable enough to love: music, lyrics. His boys from the set. His mom, who he loved so much, he let her go. Chris, "Metcalfe" as he called her, as if to safeguard the space in his heart he kept for her. I stepped out on pure faith that he would carve out another space for me. Because for as long as I can remember, I've wanted to fall in love with and marry a true friend. There was no denying it. Tone had been that and more, lack of material assets notwithstanding.

My single sista, it's time to get real, time to look deeper. It is vitally important that women not confuse settling for compromising as we seek to find the man of our dreams. He may not have a degree, but still makes five figures driving the city bus. He may be a child of divorce who is committed to having family relationships that work. He may not be outfitted like a model or drive a car, but he does own his apartment. He may have a son or daughter from a past relationship, but be willing to be a father to that child. But if what you see on the outside keeps you from giving the man the opportunity to put his best foot forward, you'll never know.

The brothers that have the "complete package" with all the bells and whistles are usually already attached. That's how so many of us end up in dead-end affairs with emotionally and maritally unavailable men, with all kinds of clocks ticking all the while. Biological. Socioeconomic. Psychological. There ain't enough independent-woman rhetoric or designer accessories in the world to stop 'em either. It was the presence of the wife that aided him in the acquisition of the aforementioned bells and whistles! Two of my favorite examples are Juanita Jordan (wife of Michael) and Pauletta Washington (wife of Denzel). In the marriages I've seen, the secure men don't need or want their women to lose themselves for the sake of the relationship. They want to support, and yes—be supported. Quiet as all the ass-shakin' videos keep it, those games get tired. Faceless sex gets boring. Brothers are longing to share in building something totally new with you. But sista-girl, you've got to get out of your own way.

If we want relationships that last, we have to be open to a great man coming to share and enrich our lives, however different he may be from our fantasies. Leave Prince Charming in the fairy tales and let your man be a human being. And yes, this means that we must acknowledge that we ourselves are not pure, flawless ladies-in-waiting unencumbered by shortcomings. In fact, it will be his understanding and acceptance of you in your least flattering moments (like without your weave or during your C-section delivery) that makes all the difference. Take it from me. I may be a nationally known music executive and hip-hop culture expert, a strong sista who has it all—successfully balancing career and family. But my husband is right beside me all the time, helping me maintain that balance. If I had let his "dusty rapper" cover fool me, only God knows where I'd be. Though we are blessed to have one another, I'm the one who really lucked out.

Co-Parenting:
Stay-at-Home Dads and Other Family Constructs

by Misumbo Byrd

I always wanted to be a single mother. In spite of the obvious hardships, I yearned to replicate the extreme closeness that my mother and I shared. Today, I have a son who is fifteen months old; I am married and engaged in a co-parenting relationship with his father. The difference between raising a child together or alone and co-parenting is simple. As a co-parent, my partner does all the things that neither our fathers nor grandfathers did. He knows that being a man requires emotional and physical availability and he also knows that being a male parent is about more than changing diapers and "helping out." As a co-parent, my husband is more than a father by virtue of his sperm, his presence in our household, or the fact that he is married to his son's mother. My husband's willingness to step outside of traditional gender roles and responsibilities, and my willingness to allow him to, while I do the same, are what make us partners in caring for and raising our child.

For the past twelve months my husband has been our son's primary caretaker, an opportunity that most men miss or would not take. While this is not a prerequisite for co-parenting or a definitive indicator that the roles and responsibilities of parenting a child are being shared, it is one of the ways that my husband manifests our commitment to raising our child together. As a stay-at-home father who also works part-time from home, my husband wakes up with our son, feeds him breakfast, and plays with him until his morning nap. He bathes our son, cares for his eczema-prone skin, and comforts him when he misses his mother and only wants to nurse in my arms. On a typical day they will play secret games that my husband makes up for hours. These games give our son confidence, build his physical strength and mobility, and help him communicate through motion and sound. The first person my son ever kissed was his father, and the first step he ever took was at his father's encouragement. His laugh grew out of the silly games that they've played and when I look at our son, spend time with him, and watch him interact with others, I know that in addition to the very joyful spirit that he was born with, spending his days with his father, an easy and cheerful person, has helped to shape his personality into one that I am proud of. Yet, I always planned to be a single mother. It was what I knew and how I expected things to be.

My mother had me when she was twenty and raised me alone with the help of her birth family. She met my father at a party when she was nineteen, shortly after ending an affair with an older man she'd moved in with the day she graduated from high school. Outspoken, nonconventional, and definitely strong-willed, my mother was one of two people in her upper-middle-class peer group to have children out of wedlock. When I ask her how they met, my mother tells me that she met my father at a party. She describes him as short, almost elfin, wearing pink satin pants and carrying a staff. Oh, how he danced, he was a great dancer, she says. According to my mother, they did not marry because they didn't want to become legal partners while Nixon was president. But childhood friends of my mother have told me that there is no way she intended to stay with my father. "She wanted a baby, not your father" they say, and "no one ever expected them to stay together." Years later I chose to begin a relationship with the man who would father my children based on the fact that he is intelligent, has a kind face, comes from a strong family, and is obviously good with children. I chose him because I wanted a partner, and he told me that he wanted one too. I saw him taking care of his family and community in ways that none of the men in my immediate family have. I chose him with the intent to build a family, to stay together.

The majority of my childhood friends were raised by their mothers while their fathers were rarely in contact, if at all. At the time, this didn't seem odd to me, and I never consciously considered that parenting could or should be done any other way. None of my friends cried about their father's absence or even talked about it and neither did I. Contrary to the media image of the struggling single Black mother who constantly dogs or pines for the absentee deadbeat dad, my mother treated my father's absence as a non-issue. She never filed for child support and she never complained about his absence or the fact that he in no way contributed to my day-to-day upbringing. During my childhood I can only remember one occasion when she mentioned my father as a potential partner in my upbringing: It was in a moment when she was very angry with me and she grabbed my shoulders and shook me, screaming, "You're going to live with your father!" Because I had little to no contact with my father and as far as I knew, neither did she, I took this as an irrational threat. After that incident my mother never mentioned my father again, except for the rare and awkward times that he would call. I sometimes wondered where my father was and why he couldn't be with me.

In my pre-teen years, I fantasized that he was the musician Prince. Prince fit the physical description my mother had given: small, odd, and talented. Although I knew my father wasn't Prince, I didn't have enough of a relationship with him to know who he was so I created an image of him to replace the void. Making him a rock star also gave me a fantasy explanation for his absence; after all, Prince was on tour.

The decision to co-parent was hard for me. I had no healthy non-single parenting models and I didn't think that it was wise or desirable to bind myself to a man. I was afraid to give up my freedom by making the commitment to raise children with someone. I also feared being disappointed by my mate and hurt or abandoned if things didn't work out between us. For a long time I felt that I'd rather not risk failing at a relationship or being rejected and left behind. I had low expectations of men as parents and didn't expect them to make a commitment. I maintained the "I can do this myself, who needs a man?" attitude about parenting as a way to unconsciously protect myself from the risks associated with building a family with someone.

Then I met my husband and this slowly began to change. My husband's loyalty to his birth family, loving nature, and commitment to building a strong family—in short, his values—greatly influenced my transition from wanting and expecting to raise a child alone to my willingness to co-parent. Had I not met my husband or someone like him, I may not have been willing to face the very scary vulnerability that comes with forming a family, and I would have manifested my early goal of parenting alone.

My initial fear of partnering with someone to raise a child, and my lack of clarity about how to sustain a lasting, healthy relationship was influenced by, if not a result of, the ways in which my immediate and ancestral family has been wounded by history. In addition to my mother's choices, I link slavery—the systematic, long-term destruction of African families in America and throughout the African Diaspora—to my initial desire to be a single mother by acknowledging the ways in which four hundred years of terror and the inability to define our own destiny has shaped African-American people's expectations of family, co-parenting, gender roles, and romantic partnership. What slavery taught Africans in America was to expect *not* to stay together. Black love was not (and still isn't) respected or affirmed by the dominant culture. This is made evident by the fact that five generations of African men and women were put together to breed children and consistently separated from their families without regard for the emotional or genetic bonds that bound them. African women and men were tortured and terrorized into expecting *not* to raise their children as a couple or family because they could be sold and separated at any time. The institution of slavery taught Africans that their children did not belong to them, that their mates could not commit to them, and that the creation of a lasting family structure was a goal that often required the risk of one's life or some other extraordinary act of courage. As the great-great granddaughter of an enslaved woman, I know that this legacy affects me and the other members of my family.

Like so many Black women, the dysfunctional intimate relationships in my immediate family and the history of my people made me leery of trying my hand at marriage and co-parenting. The only reference for marriage and childrearing was my grandparents' relationship, which had ended in shambles, devastating my grandmother and some, if not all, of their children. My grandfather and grandmother married in 1948. My grandmother came from a prominent family in the Midwest and my grandfather from a working-class and sometimes poor family in the South. Years after their divorce, in an upscale restaurant in the Bay Area, my grandfather would tell me that he married my grandmother not because he loved her, but because he thought she was going to be an heiress. Hearing this broke my heart, shattering my intimate relationship with my grandfather and distancing me further from the notion of partnering and building a family with someone. I began to fear that along with the threat of abandonment and abuse, disingenuous intentions could color a man's desire to make a lifelong commitment to me.

In a previous conversation, my grandfather shared that by age ten, he had decided as a poor, dark-skinned Black boy growing up in the South, he had to make friends based on status, not emotion. The class and color constructs he inherited from his ancestors shaped his inability to be intimate and authentic in his relationships, including the one with his wife. Eventually at the height of his career and earning capacity, my grandfather left my grandmother. My mother tells me that he simply did not come home one day, leaving Armani suits and all the trappings of wealth and family in their Manhattan apartment.

So why co-parent when the road is so much less traveled? Why partner when intimacy is so easily destroyed? The benefits of raising a child with a loving, participating partner are numerous, from the easy disposition that my son has, to the calm and confidence that I feel as a parent as a result of my husband's support. The fact that I can be away from our son and know that he's okay because he's with his father and, most importantly, the fact that I have a partner who really contributes 50 to 60 percent of the labor of running our household and raising our child, make the risks and work of co-parenting worthwhile. My husband takes an active role in the childrearing process that shapes our son's values, beliefs, likes, and dislikes. And with the support of his consistent, non-macho contribution to the care of our son, I am able to have a social life, pursue my career goals, continue to spend time alone, and do a host of other things that many other mothers, single and married, simply don't have the time or support to do. Still, while I consider my circumstances lucky, my relationship has its own unique challenges. Ironically, the absence of rigid gender roles, which helps to facilitate co-parenting, is also the source of most of our difficulties.

Before I knew what it would feel like to be a mother who worked outside the home fulltime, I watched my husband's passionate metamorphosis into Mr. Mom with romanticism and a new respect. Then as the months passed and I struggled to work, nurse, be close to my son, and watch him grow without missing the priceless milestones that so many working parents never experience, my initial response to how we would balance the responsibilities of parenting turned sour. My jealousy that he got to spend the days with our son while I had to leave him to earn a living caused my stomach to ache. Our lifestyle and the financial options for upward mobility, which I always expected us to have, became stagnant as we shifted into a predominantly one-income family. This situation hadn't occurred to me when I agreed to be the only parent that had a stable income, and my awakening to this fact was no less than rude. While I had been confident that my husband would be a hands-on parent, I had not planned to be working outside of the home while he took care of our son. To some degree this happened by default. We were both freelancing when I got pregnant, the news of which inspired me to find work that paid regularly and had benefits, and him to commit himself more to being viably self-employed. By the time the baby came, his business had waned and my bi-weekly paycheck had become addictive and imperative. When my maternity leave ran out it boiled down to a simple equation; I have a good-paying job, you don't. Thus, the beginning of the most challenging aspect of gender role reversal and co-parenting that I could ever have imagined.

Having a great co-parent does not make partnering and raising a child together problem-free. In addition to the role reversal and financial issues that we face, I also struggle with what it means to have a fully participating father in my son's life, particularly since I am from a single-parent home and I know how powerful it is too make your own decisions without having to consult another person. Like my mother did, I sometimes want to have the freedom to follow my heart's desire without consulting my partner or worrying about how it will affect him. As someone who grew up in a single-parent home, I was prepared to be the alpha parent. As a co-parent, the position of alpha parent is ever shifting to meet the child's, the family's, and *then* the individual's needs. Knowing that you will not always be number one, or the most trusted parent, or the most sought out can be emotionally taxing. Knowing that your child's need for you is mitigated by your co-parent's presence and availability can be disheartening in a society where fathers are undervalued and women ascribe so much of their worth and power to the roles they play in their family, particularly as mother.

For many women, the place where we have the most influence is in our relationships with our children. For African women in America, this has been and continues to be mitigated by racism and slavery. This is true for Black men too, who often have the most influence, and some would argue power, in their relationships with their wives or women. These dynamics result in family structures where men and women often exist in polar roles: typically mother as domineering parent and father as emotionally and/or physically absent parent. The struggle to redefine these roles and create a family structure where neither of us dominates, both of us are present, and both of us share the responsibilities of breadwinning, child care, and household management is complex. Unfortunately the ominous presence of racism makes this task more difficult and sometimes our most righteous and affectionate attempts to share power in our relationships don't work.

Co-parenting and a commitment to the process of developing a lasting team challenges my husband and me to define our role as parents, earners, and lovers in a way that goes beyond swapping traditional male and female responsibilities and rises above the legacies of slavery and racism. While I am proud of some of the ways that we share the responsibility of caring for our son, I am profoundly aware that we are still struggling to move beyond a basic role reversal where we continue to exist at opposite ends of the gender-role spectrum.

To make this co-parenting team work, my husband and I must dissect the ways that we've been polarized by race, gender, and family history in order to create a third option. At best, this task is difficult. At worst, it is enough to destroy a family. My husband and I struggle to communicate about the hardships associated with this process without totally alienating one another. These conversations often spark heated disagreements that are tempting to avoid, but if we, as partners, are unable to acknowledge our differences and unmet needs then how can we honor and resolve them? As an African-American woman, I long for the day when *my* children will come first. The scars of slavery and abandonment remind me of the ways in which my daughters, sons, and even myself have come last. And sometimes every inch that I give my husband feels like a mile, no matter how much I see his good works reflected in our son.

While I admit that operating outside of traditional American gender and parenting roles seems and feels less secure than maintaining the same old painful paradigms, my experiences as a co-parent are teaching me something different. As painful and threatening as it is to my self-concept to allow my partner to occupy the role of primary parent, so too is it helping me to define myself outside of my response to racism, patriarchy, and my birth family. My choices to co-parent and to make a life commitment to developing a relationship with my partner are ones that I still question. Sometimes I long for the freedom that my mother had while raising me, as she didn't have to deal with another adult's input or commentary. And then there are times when I resent the complexity of my relationship and fantasize about how different things would be if my husband was traditionally macho in his parenting style, heading off to work each day expecting me to make no financial contribution to our household. But I know that mothers in either of those situations are just like me in their hunger for something more. I also know that I would not choose to parent my son any other way. I depend on my husband's participation and partnership (a very scary thing for a Black woman to admit) and I adore the love that shapes our family unit. As my husband and I dig deeper into ourselves and our histories in an effort to parent and partner better, my hope is that we will transcend gender-role constructs and reversals and find a way to live a life that honors our mutual desire to be with our children in a meaningful way. And though I do not advocate marriage as the solution to the hardships of parenting or life, I do feel it is my responsibility to share the ways in which partnership and co-parenting are improving my life and helping me to create a sustainable family one challenge at a time.

Notes on My First Year of Marriage

by Leah P. Hollis

October 2000

I was glad I at least kept my hair together during my cynical period. My usual stylist conditioned it the evening before. I even had a semi-regular gym routine sprinkled into my schedule with the occasional stints of eating well, yet not too healthy. I was trying to return to my collegiate-training shape. After almost five years, I was so annoyed with inconsistent love in my life. This annoyance led me to investigate adoption and artificial insemination. Why should I be denied motherhood if men in my life could not get the commitment thing right? I wanted motherhood and I was annoyed that fatherhood was on the other side of the coin. With my mother's undying encouragement, I had made most of my dreams come true over the course of about eight years. I had already moved to two major cities, held high-level jobs, and earned a doctorate on fellowship in three years flat. And yes, I'd even purchased my first house. I didn't have the obvious sexual and sensual connection a woman and man seek from each other, and my mother had in a way become the man in my life by guiding, supporting, loving, and caring for me. She even fixed the occasional mistake. Although she was a state away, my mother was still my caretaker. I was cynical because I could not reconcile the irony. My little beige mommy, at just five foot two, who was one of six kids and the youngest daughter of a steel worker, could take better care of me than any man since my father's death.

In the previous year, I was attacked in my own home. A boyfriend who once professed his love for me and promised marriage went berserk one day when I caught him in a lie. He claimed he earned a fellowship to a doctoral program, perhaps to compete with me, but when I exposed his lie, he tried to dominate me sexually. In seconds, he sprang on me, holding me down on the couch, threatening to kill me. He growled, pinning my shoulders down, forcing his weight on me. Those few seconds felt like minutes, but moments after that, I managed to get from beneath him and dial 9-1-1. Soon after the attack, he was escorted from my home by the police. The legal wrangling that followed this incident included him pleading that I return my heart to him, as if he ever owned it. Then he pleaded that I return what precious little junk he had left in my home. He left books, software, a computer, and a few papers that included letters from an estranged wife and two little ones he did not acknowledge. Through the following mess of restraining orders, court preparation, and a final court date, my mother strongly but sadly stood by me and watched the world attempt to roll over her eldest child, her only daughter. My bloodied and broken nails from the struggle with the ex-boyfriend healed and grew back. However, my heart was buried all the more deeply in my soul, under yet another layer of scar tissue. And now, here I was, over a year later, and the last thing on my mind was L-O-V-E from a man. I had decided to start fixing parts of my first house. I figured some small renovations might overhaul my attitude as well. I had booked a contractor to install a pedestal sink. In my mind, this could happen with little fanfare while I hung out in the other room watching movies. I felt cheated that I had all the trappings of a wonderful life—a house, a car, a good job—but I had no one to share it with. I had an empty heart, an empty house, and a wonderful mother.

January 13, 2001

On that bright Saturday winter morning, I did not put on makeup. I wore my eyeglasses and some ol' T-shirt, but was mildly excited to get a new somethin' somethin' in the house. Maybe the scheduled bathroom facelift would brighten my spirits. The night before, I was shopping for supplies to re-do my bathroom—new faucet, new tiles, some grout. I had no idea this expedition was a precursor of things to come. Syed, my contractor, arrived that morning. His energy was electric. No pun intended. He was not drop-dead gorgeous, but his energy was familiar. He was crafty, creative, strawberry sweet, yet strong and calm. I had felt him before, yet fear or bad timing had taken such a man away from me years earlier.

I tried not to hover in Syed's space. I didn't want to reveal my yearning for a man's love. Instead I tried to conjure up what else this contractor could do. Maybe Syed could fix something in the kitchen, change the garbage disposal, or maybe he could even rewire the entire house. I had imagined how he could build me a whole new home with his own hands. My mind wandered to the care he would take in each corner, with each pipe, and every brick and beam. But before I could think of a way to get more time from him, things literally came crashing down all around me. No, seriously. While backing his car out of the driveway onto the street to run to the store for more grout, his partner backed into my driver's side door with their contractor's van. Flecks of glass crashed all around, dented my car door, and then panicked me—the driver. Within seconds, Syed came out into the street at the sound of the crash. He was even, solved the problem, managed the crisis, and swept the glass back onto the driveway. Then, he went back to work, wrestling with those fifty-year-old pipes, despite the fact that the damage to my car now outweighed the cost of my small bathroom renovation.

Once I returned from the store with the extra grout, I tried not to hover over him, witnessing the transformation of my bathroom and of my heart. I tried not to loom around as I struggled to get a peak of him, his energy, his space, trying to peep him from another room. At the end of the day, we all had to drive forty minutes back to Newark to put my car in the shop. I got to ride with Syed in the van, while his partner drove my car because the window was busted out and it was January.

Those forty minutes sang like some lullaby. First, we discussed each other's jobs, and then out of nowhere, this rusty dusty brotha comes forth with some poetry off the top of his head. I am shocked! I don't remember what he said, though it was something about love. He was charming with speckles of tile chips clinging to his long lashes; his bright smile was the gateway to his heart. After we took my car to the body shop for repair, we swung by his shop. He held his hand out for me, assisted me over icy puddles, and gave me a tour of another job he was working. It was cold in this unheated building, but it was summer in my heart. I was so pleased to be there with him.

This story sounds so silly—it sounds like the most ridiculous, sophomoric, soap-opera, dime store–novel trash that you could pick up. This is what I think when I tell this story, but it happened to me: a divorced, workaholic, cynical lady, who did not know how to leave school. I was ready to give up on men who just did not commit—men who wouldn't commit themselves to a career or to me. Though my house had a woman's touch, with floral arrangements, wallpaper trim, and oriental rugs, it lacked the strong guidance of a man. For so long, I had been the man and the woman of the house by paying bills, cleaning gutters, baking cakes, and raking leaves, and now I was tired of the dual role. For a moment, I enjoyed the male presence in the house that Saturday—even if he was only a contractor for service.

There is more to this story; they had to come back the next day to continue. Syed had shaved his beard to frame his jaw line, brought pears and kiwis, and got back to work. It did not feel like workmen were in the house, but more like a familiar soul who had walked in to care for a broken place in my home. Although they did their work, there was more talk and friendly chatter. There were no sterile comments about timelines, money due, and bathroom material. As they closed down for the day, I was pleased with the craftsmanship. My bathroom looked wonderful. I was happy with the colors and the work they had done. As he packed his tools, Syed gave me his number and I realize in retrospect that he did the shy boy thing, saying, "Well, you can call me if you want to write poetry." I could bide my time though, as the plumbing was troublesome, and they had to come back to fix my sink three days later. We all agreed to meet at my house at 7:00 P.M. later that week.

Their last trip to the house was to replace a plumbing fixture. Afterward, we ate some fried chicken and mixed vegetables. I was embarrassed as I had spilled the salt into the veggies and tried to pass it off as the Green Giant's mistake—*not*—it didn't work. But my banana pudding was a hit. It should have been as I put my foot in that one, slaving two hours over my mother's homemade recipe. We three wound down the evening and said our goodbye as friends. Then Syed paused, commenting on the Langston Hughes on my table. I remember looking at him, trying not to stay so riveted to the gleam in his eyes. I found myself having to try not to reach for his curly hair. I was so sorry my time was up, that bathroom was complete; it was time for them to leave. In an uncustomary move, I reached out and kissed him goodbye as if I had known him for years, startling even myself. But the poetry vibe was still on, and my chance to talk with him without his contracting partner would soon come. Syed and I had agreed to get together over the next couple of weeks.

Unlike other people, Syed followed through. He came over one Saturday evening about 8:00 P.M. and chattered about a new project. That night, one of his children called; I could hear the voice saying, "I love you, too, Daddy." The snow was starting to fall, but we had a pen, a pad, and some Pat Metheny going. Doesn't it sound like the typical set up for some bumpin' and grindin'? His soul was cool and he commented early, "I can't have *relationships* with women; they always want to have sex with me." Well, I could see why. He was six foot one with hazelnut-brown eyes. Muscular. Funny. Brother had thick curly hair. Outwardly, what was not to like? His remark set the tone and he stayed on his side of the table. I was relieved; the pressure was off. This idea of male company without sex, or the eventual attempt at it, was a nice thing for me to consider.

With the smooth tunes of synthetic guitars and long looping notes falling inside, big billowing snowflakes fell outside to the tune of some five inches that evening. And we talked and wrote and wrote and laughed, neither trying to lay a finger on the other, the meeting of minds on a wintry eve. A feeling so deep, we even agreed to write a book together, which is still in the works. Over twenty poems leapt from our hearts that evening:

> *Tell me*
> *I know I have not lost my mind sublimely primed for this not so*
> *chance meeting*
>
> *To my wonderful*
> *I am so thankful for*
> *Romeo Romeo*
> *let down your hair*
> *teach me tonight*
> *it will be all right*
> *as we skip through the ribbon in the sky*
> *love means never having to say*
> *justify my love as I tell it to my heart. You are the sunshine of my*
> *life, but there's no sunshine when he's gone*
> *but don't you worry about a thing . . .*
>
> *The cacophony of sound abound, drown out anxiety except the*
> *stretch in my spirit, stretching for a glimpse, a gaze that holds me*
> *shyly mesmerized*
> *in my dreams you pervade my hopes invade my every and all any time*

When the sun rose, so did he from my couch to shovel out my drive. All he took was some tea and asked me for a quick shuttle-ride home so he could work that day. The snowpocked streets on the way back to his home in Newark were dazzling on the white, crisp sunny morn. And I recall asking, "So how many children do you have?" He answered, "Six."

Six. Let that echo in my head for a minute . . . *Six kids.*

We both joke about that now. We joke that I did not even flinch, and perhaps I was nuts, starstruck, and spellbound. Perhaps it is amazing that I did not leap from the moving car the moment I learned the extent of his flock. He spoke respectfully of his two failed marriages, but who am I to throw stones? My glass house had a divorce built into it as well.

I could spin on and tell of another eight months of poetry, which melded into real-life issues, childcare concerns, moving, religion, job changes, etcetera, which then culminated in our marriage, as understated as it was in Harlem, due to swirling chaos in the aftermath of the attack on the World Trade Center. Also, we still had to weather the continuous attacks on our relationship from the histories we both brought to the game. Three of his children moved in with us. With these children, I inherited the monumental separation anxiety they had in regard to their own biological mother. I was totally unprepared for this chaos. I could not fathom the disrespect they heaped on me because I was not their mom, because I received some of their father's love. Totally unprepared for this hurt, I was stunned to realize that my love for their father, Syed, would not soothe their own scars of divorce. I found that damn cliché, love conquers all, a farce in this case. In some ways, my love made it worse as the kids and even their father could not understand how I could love them so much and act accordingly, while their own mother barely picked up the phone. My love was a handicap of sorts as the more I gave it, the weaker and angrier these kids felt toward me.

From the outside looking in, anyone would gasp at the three divorces between us, and his six kids—three of whom were pawns in a turf war between him and his second ex-wife. I heard several folks say to me, "You're a better person than I." My mother, of course, wanted a logical reason for my decision to enter into a marriage such as this. My response? Logic had very little to do with it. I felt love in my soul, felt it in every fiber. Previously, I doubted that I could be that excited about a man after a series of sucker punches to my heart. With Syed I felt love. He had given me a chance to fill my life with marriage, family, joy, and those values that resonate so strongly in my being. I was ready to fight tooth and nail through my history and his to realize my dream. To me, this deep love was worth all those struggles to come.

My hope is that our dark days of early marriage, with those billows of smoke, asbestos, and human remains from Lower Manhattan will fade to light and reveal the love we know. In many ways, I find that I struggle to find that love we had in that first month. There is the stress of the weak economy, his three children that live with us, and the expense of the new home we bought. Factor in that our marriage comes across as an instant romance to our two families. With all these challenges, it is easy for a vibrant love to wash away into a faded watercolor. Money problems can take the stars out of anyone's eyes, and the stress of being a stepmother cannot be underestimated in the slightest.

The love I have for this man is one I am so eager to share with his three children that live with us. And that is a dangerous, dangerous place to be—to love a child whose heart is in another state, pining for a mother who, to be kind—is absent. It could make a novice crazy, unaware of the pockmarked little hearts beating in the souls of little children waiting, waiting, waiting with questions that are seldom even answered in adulthood about love, marriage, divorce, and disappointment. I grew up with a mother who lovingly prepared our breakfasts and worked two jobs for volleyball camp and saxophone lessons, while my father took care of necessities like the light, mortgage, water, and doctor's bills. My mother was not some soccer mom rolling my brother and me around in her late model Volvo, but she was the one who walked both ways uphill in the snow (and *yes* it was both ways uphill) to school, to make sure my permission slip was in on time to be in band. She was the one who raced to school to make sure my brother had a special sandwich she prepared (he was so picky). I knew as a child that we were my mother's all, her everything, and that as a product of marriage, we were loved, loved, loved. Though my mother is occasionally cantankerous, independent, and fussy, my brother and I both adore her and all her foibles. To sum it up, even on my last birthday of thirty-four, she sent me a card that read, "I loved you from the moment I saw you . . . Your face stole my heart in that first moment." Think it's some squishy love mess? Well, that is my mother's love. Therefore, my desire to give and receive love, coupled with the fact that I loved my husband, almost ensured that if I loved his children, they would love me back. I was truly misguided.

I bought clothes, dried tears, and at times defended them even as their little hearts misunderstood their own father. My heart broke when the then twelve-year-old cried, "Where is my mother?" and spent close to an hour on my phone calling across New Jersey and other states desperate to find her mommy. I listened to her make call after call. "Have you seen my mother?" I was so taken with this little spirit, and she soon was curled up on my bed at night when we heard creaks in the house. I started sharing my love of better shoes with her and started her off with her own pair of Kenneth Coles. I traded my house for a bigger one for his kids, read the Qu'ran, counseled, provided health insurance, and checked homework. I was trying so hard to be to them what my mother was to me. But I soon realized, I could not erase the hurt they had endured during their father's last divorce, and I certainly would not be loved like the woman his daughter was seeking on the other end of the phone on that horrid summer day. As they plotted their escape to their biological mom, I was reminded that despite my love, they called me by my first name, and not by some other maternal term of endearment.

July 2002

A very close friend of mine told me, before I married, about the pitfalls of being a stepmom. As he was in his early sixties, he cautioned me from his own life experience. "You will never be as good to them as the lesser biological no-good parent that they love all the more. This is the ultimate thankless job." In my blinded love, I heard the cautions. But the wake-up call for me in this unraveling epic is the runaway incident. In their desperation to be with their own mother and away from their father, the grand disciplinarian, which I deem him respectfully, my two stepdaughters had packed up their golf balls and stuffed animals in the most hideous, pink old-school luggage and run away. They thought they were going to Port Authority. They thought they would make it to their mother, who did not even know they were coming. And for seven hours, my husband and I sweated it out, calling police, talking to detectives, disseminating pictures, descriptions, and social security numbers. And we waited. A call from their girlfriend tipped us off, and after a debriefing with the police, the children were returned to us. During those seven hours, I realized, the books I had purchased for them just the night before would not make them stay. The counseling, the care, the love I thought I was giving them, the love I had learned to give from my own mother, would not make them stay. In fact, I soon learned they resented my proficiency. While I was taking off work to register them in school and run them to the doctor's office, the eldest commented, "Why are you doing this instead of my father? We appreciate it, but this is his job, not yours." I could not win. And while that was one of the most difficult days of my life, the runaway day, it made me come face to face with the fact that I was fighting on a futile love field—waging a battle I could not win. I wanted to have their hearts as my mother had mine, but I had to come to grips with the fact that their hearts were somewhere else. They were always waiting for their mother to come over the horizon, to save them from what has been their most stable environment in years, the one their father and I have created.

My love for Syed is a love that will mow me under if I am not careful. I do not regret my choices, but I feel blessed the Creator loves me enough to unfurl these scales from my eyes and show me truth before my heart is damaged by this fantasy. On occasion my husband says, "Those are your daughters," and while I used to smile, I now realize that his saying it does not make it so. They are my daughters because I love them, because they are an extension of their father. But I am not *mama, madre, mommy, mother, mom*—I am only the caretaker who comes with Dad and I must reserve my strength to pace myself through until their graduation if I expect to not drive myself crazy with the anticipation I have built in my head about giving and receiving motherly love. I have to take my cape off. I am not superwoman, leaping into broken homes and solving divorce's disappointment in a single bound. Love is my kryptonite and as a stepparent, I must keep my love-filled weakness in perspective. Instead, I struggle to make this love my strength and to persevere through what even my husband does not recognize as a somewhat thankless job . . . the job of stepmother.

And this brings me to another pitfall: It is the pitfall of being totally engulfed in a man. There really is no subtle way to describe what happened to me. I struggle to be clear about what I need. I am struggling to keep my identity, fighting to remain clear about who I am. In the state of having my nose wide open, I quickly forgot to take a stand for myself. I was so eager to give just about anything to get the love I craved. I found myself wrapping my life around his world. I would sit at a job site and watch my fine man plaster a wall in fifty-degree weather. I would shuttle him around, lend him money, and bail him out of situations, even when he did not ask for my help. I found that I was anticipating what would make him and his children happy, much like my mother did and still does for me. Yet while my mother comments on the great reward she saw in such sacrifice, I was reaping no such rewards in my constant effort to help him.

I fought my constant inclination to bring my new family little things like extra socks, designer underwear, or that unexpected pair of slacks. And when I did bring those things, I was disappointed when my gifts did not yield the love and kindness that I had expected. I baked new entrees, painted rooms, installed light fixtures, and blew my savings to take his kids shopping. I kept throwing more and more of me out there, and watched more and more of me slip away into simple acknowledgments like "gee thanks." I was forced to reevaluate how to love myself in the face of not getting the love I needed from this family. I started to take shopping trips with friends or by myself if needed even if he was still plastering walls on the weekends and into the wee hours of the night. I had to really stop feeling guilty for the trip to my cousin's house to watch my favorite professional football team. I had to embrace the occasional jaunt to the city. I had to very quickly get back to loving me before loving him swallowed me whole. His rebuttal was, "Well, you just get up and do your own thing." But I had to or else I wouldn't have my own thing left to get up.

Before I became totally engulfed in loving this man, I went to movies, shopping, and on road trips by myself. My eight-year marital hiatus had taught me to like me—to really like me. Who cared about the extra

twenty pounds? I got pedicures once in a while. I planted my favorite flowers, embraced purple, and even got an occasional makeover. I had become
a nice person and was determined to do my best. I struggled to learn
more about me every day. But now, all those lessons seemed to fly out the
window, down the drain of that pedestal sink he installed. My most difficult task was to stay that course and to not waver even under his pressure. Even now, with some waning reluctance, I take the trip to mother's
home alone, see a movie alone, even have an occasional dinner alone, so
I can hear myself consider and reconsider my place in the world. I have
stopped hesitating to plan events with friends and waiting to see when he
will be home from work before I schedule myself away from the house. I
just go about being me, with the reminder, *Yes, be me.* While we all seek
the love of our lives, we all need to remember that in our generosity,
we need to remain at the top of that list, so we can love those who love us.
At first, I thought that placing myself first was selfish. Now, it's just
straight self-preservation.

There are several other aspects of this love and marriage thing I
could share; perhaps it could spin out into a book or become the poem
that started this entire journey in the first place. But I choose to say this.
I am glad I could know love when he came to me this time and that my
love could see me standing before him. But this relationship is work.
We are so very different in many ways. We were raised differently, educated differently, and even love differently. I think this society is an in-
stamatic, zero-to-sixty-in-3.5-seconds type of world that places unrealistic
expectations on what this whole relationship thing is about. I have just figured out how to reconnect with my girlfriends for an early dinner. There
is no grandiose moral to this story, no final words to the wise, but instead,
this is just one woman's struggle with love and relationships. Simply
put, these are my notes, though abbreviated, on my first year of marriage.

Talking Back

Black Men Speak

Love Letters

by Kevin Powell

Saturday, December 28, 1996, 4:56 P.M.

Miss Nina:

So no one has ever given you a bath? Hmmm. And you melt when a man goes downtown, but you're kinda-sorta-but-not-really into reciprocating. Hah! Do I detect a selfish lover? Or a Leo who hasn't been with the right lover yet? At least you say you get as turned off as I do by the two-position-only people. I mean, damn, why did God give us joints if not to bend the damn things?

You admit that you are slightly repressed. Wassup with that, Nina? How can a woman who tells me her man "has to have penis for days" be repressed? What gives, woman? Or are you only very open with certain people, as you insist, like me?

It took me a long time to be able to discuss sex above a whisper. Most of us are taught from day one—unless we have very hip and open-minded parents—that sex is filthy and should be avoided at all costs. Maybe our parents saw the AIDS epidemic coming, huh? No matter, I cannot get with individuals who become jittery merely deliberating about the topic. That includes a lot of us Generation X-ers. I mean, where do we think we came from if our mommas and our daddies didn't get butt-naked and throw down, maybe on a bed, maybe on the kitchen table, or maybe even (gasp!) in a public place?

Later for all the herbs in the world who think it is downright immoral to talk about sex. Just as I love to discuss international relations or the latest computer technology or pro basketball, I have theories and opinions about lovemaking, and I want to hear what other folks have to say as well, know what I'm sayin'?

Peacelove&progress,
   Kpowell

Sunday, December 29, 1996
10:23 A.M.

Nina:
Note to me: I have been toying with the subject of sex but have left some things out about myself. The plan: Tell the truth no matter what.

The truth, Nina, is that I have been one miserable manchild for the past two years and I have been intolerably lonely. I can't tell you the number of times I've fallen asleep to Al Green's "Tired of Being Alone." As a result, I have slept with a few women. As I've told you, I regret some of those encounters. Nonetheless, some were real cool and, in fact, I've had some of the best sex of my life during this period. What can I say? I am a sucker for dancers (which a couple of them were), or for any woman who's in great physical shape.

In spite of being very honest with these women, except, regrettably, Amber, I still felt like I'd done something wrong by having sex with any of them.

"Why?" my friend Lorna asks me again and again. "Everyone needs a f— buddy." *Everyone?* Well, maybe. But at what cost to yourself and the person you are f—? Or is that person f— you? Or are the two of you f— each other? And what, pray tell, does "f— mean anyway, in light of the fact that we use the term so loosely in this society?

Don't get me wrong, Nina, because I thoroughly enjoy the finer details of sexual intercourse. I enjoy the velvety texture of a woman's body, the high sensitivity of her ear and neck, the delicacy of her lips, the resiliency of her butt, the wetness of her vagina. Yeah, I enjoy it immensely! But, you know what, Nina? I never went back to any of those women after one encounter, except maybe once. There was always an emptiness there, a distance between them and me and each of those women, as if we were complete strangers, our naked bodies thrown atop a bed for an hour or two or more of raw, semicensored pleasure (it is the era of AIDS after all) until our lustful bodily energy had been zapped.

The funny thing is, I usually never came during any of those sessions. In fact, if I wanted to feel *something,* I would later have to jerk myself off just to get my share of the satisfaction I assume each of those women was getting. But who knows if any of them liked it either. I could never open up, never allow myself to be *that* free. At least not to the point where I would allow an orgasm to sweep me up and take me to that place where I had journeyed before—love, or some form of it. Maybe I'm the one who's repressed, huh?

My last relationship, as I told you in one of our discussions, left me feeling miserable and absolutely convinced that love and our generation did not go together. Like the Dallas Cowboys and good public behavior. Or Michael Jordan and two bad games in a row. It was the summer of 1992—Cindy had recently graduated from college and I had just appeared on the very first season of MTV's *The Real World,* and we were both vulnerable, afraid, hungry for intimate connection. Cindy was living with this man, and I was falling hard for a woman name Toni.

Actually, "falling hard" doesn't even adequately describe how I felt about Toni. I truly adored Toni, and I felt that I was falling in love with her. Hell, *I know* I was falling in love with her. She was intellectually stimulating, and it did not hurt that she was also quite gorgeous. (People like to lie and say "looks" don't matter; that's a bunch of bull—"looks" do matter!) Toni and I never had sex, at least not during that period, and we barely ever saw each other, although Toni also lived in Brooklyn. But the things Toni and I discussed, as you and I do, on the telephone and in the letters we exchanged, had me hooked on her. We talked about everything: politics, community activism, business, racism, and sexism—Toni was and is a staunch feminist—which took up a great deal of our time. Toni was the first woman with whom I'd ever discussed, in earnest, the male-female thing and women's issues, like abortion, motherhood, rape, and incest. Although I was attempting to be as tolerant as humanly possible, there were many times that I could not take some of the things she was saying. But I listened anyway, and often I'd call Toni later and tell her that she'd made me look at women's issues in ways I'd never done before. Toni was that brilliant. The feelings I developed for Toni ran deep inside me and I wanted her bad, Nina. I wanted to be her lover, her partner, her whatever, very, very bad. But because Toni had only lately ended a relationship with a man who'd cheated on her, she could not open up, nor did she believe, as she would say to me at times, that I was completely serious. But I was. I knew my feelings for Toni were real because even after I started dating Cindy, it was Toni that I secretly yearned for.

But because I was vulnerable and needy and there were no solid in-dications I would be with Toni, I settled for Cindy. We hung out, kicked it on the telephone, and bonded. As Cindy's relationship soured and my would-be relationship hung in limbo, Cindy and I held hands, kissed, and eventually began having sex. A month after Cindy had moved out of her boyfriend's place, she moved in with me. To say the least, the rela-tionship was rocky from the very beginning.

Cindy was naïve about the harshness of New York City, especially on us artistic types, and I, well, let's just say I'd been around the block a few times, and I knew how to hustle to survive. So I found myself not only showing Cindy the ropes (like a big brother), but giving her money all the time and paying all the bills (like a father), while she pursued her singing career.

The truth is, I needed Cindy as much as she needed me. Hey, what can I say? I was mad lonely before she and I united. She was my emotional rock, you know? Or I thought she was at the time. Cindy was there when I needed her—as I was dealing with the MTV stuff, then my new gig at *Vibe* magazine and all its accompanying pressures. I was also adjusting to the mid-twenties stage of my manhood (for real) and its many com-plexities. The problem was that the kind of man I was attempting to be, until Cindy, had nothing to do with taking care of a woman. Prior to that relationship I said often and loudly that I wanted a woman who was my equal on as many levels as possible, not someone who was submissive or who relied on me to carry my weight and hers, too. That is one of the reasons why I continually thought of Toni. She was an independent woman, and I admired her greatly for that. While, again, I confess that I desperately needed Cindy's emotional and physical presence in my life, providing an adult with room and board and emotional and financial and artistic support nearly drove me to a mental institution. But I did it any-way, because somewhere in my psyche it made me feel good, Nina. That may sound strange to you, but you have to understand that, as a child, I felt so very physically and emotionally neglected by both my father and my mother. As I told you, they were never married, and that was the first insult. Not seeing my father after I was eight years old was the second. And the third, and perhaps the most devastating, was the lack of an out-ward showing of love from my mother. I remember watching family tel-evision shows and being envious of the way those television parents, no matter how rich or poor they were, showered their children with af-fection—kisses, uplifting words, hugs. I wanted that so badly, Nina. So, so bad, man. What I got instead were a lot of tongue-lashings and beat-ings whenever I was bad, and little or no praise when I was good.

Don't get me wrong, though. I know now that my mother loved

me and, in her own way, was proud of me whenever, for example, I brought home good grades from school. But hers was a distant love, out there where little children—like me—cannot possibly see that love can be, and is, a parent providing food, shelter, and life guidelines, even as their own lives and their own love lives hang precariously out the window.

How could I have possibly known back then that my mother felt as much pain, if not more than what I feel, Nina? How could I have known that the one man she loved had hurt her heart so bad that she resolved, ever so systemically, to shut down completely and not allow another male to get that close again—except for me. And she only let me in because I was her son and had come from her womb.

Because of the limitations of my mother's life—her conservative, southern upbringing, her repressed emotions, her fear of life beyond whatever she needed to survive—she could not give me what I needed and wanted. And because I didn't understand my mother's behavior, Nina, I hated her. Oh man, I hated the hell out of my mother. I don't know when it began, but it must've been sometime at the beginning of my teenage years, when I was becoming too big to be beaten, that I truly began to hate her for treating me so cruelly. So I rebelled against her. Anything my mother told me to do, I did the opposite. I wanted to punish her for punishing me. I wanted my mother to feel as unloved by me as I felt by her. And in the middle of some of our more heated arguments I would scream at my mother, loud enough for the nosy neighbors to hear, "I hate your guts, Ma!!!"

As I write this now it feels very awkward revealing all of this to you. But I have to, Nina. How could I possible accept the kind of love a woman like you might give me if I have not fully reconciled my feelings, both pro and con, for my mother? Wouldn't you, like my last girlfriend, and my girlfriend before that, and the one before that one, simply become the victim of whatever pent-up mother hostilities I've stored away in that cobwebbed corner of my mind, waiting to pounce upon the first reminder of my mom and her ways?

And you best believe my mother runs through me like a river. When I was eighteen and at college, and away from home for the first time in my life, I decided, consciously mind you, to do to women what I felt my mother had done to me. I am not saying this because I am proud of it. But it was the mindset I had throughout college and for quite a few years afterward, even when I claimed it was gone.

So: I had sex with as many women as I possibly could. Considering I was a real rookie throughout college, I'm sure many of those women would say they didn't have sex with me at all. And I used women habitually: for money, for material items, for anything I could get them to do for me, at their expense, of course. I watched the athletes, the fraternity brothers, and the student leaders very closely and took meticulous notes on the ways to mack a woman.

Those notes meshed with the notes I had taken as a boy and a teenager while combing the streets of Jersey City. The notes were basically the same: Women were men's playmates and caretakers, and only coincidentally anything else. I cursed women, belittled and laughed at women, threw things at women, and a few years after college, I pushed a girlfriend into a bathroom door. What I realize now, Nina, is that all the anger, frustration, even hatred I had felt all along for my mother had been expanded to include practically every woman I came into contact with.

This included Cindy. As a result, and I am really ashamed to admit this, Nina, I began to resent her. The communication between us was very bad because, as far as I was concerned, she wasn't on my level. She hadn't had the life experiences I'd had, and there was not much we could talk about outside the rather frivolous world of entertainment. Cindy regarded me as bossy and condescending, which, I am sure, I was. I see now that I was attempting to shape her into the kind of woman I really wanted: someone who was cosmopolitan, who read books, who had an eclectic taste in music (not just Janet Jackson or the latest greatest rap hit), and who viewed herself as an artist, not merely an entertainer. But Cindy was who she was, and I was who I was. It would have been obvious to anyone else from the very beginning that we were not compatible.

Nevertheless, Cindy and I stayed together for two years because we both were too afraid to tell each other that the relationship sucked, that we would have been better off as friends. We were both too afraid to say that we were scared to death of this crazy world we were living in and that was why we were clinging to each other. I came to love Cindy and I believe that she loved me as well. But I feel we loved each other the way a brother and a sister love each other, not as lovers do. We looked out for each other. We went to parties together. We acted our favorite television characters together. Told each other stories about our childhoods. We talked about our fathers a lot, since we both felt so abandoned by those men, and we comforted each other around that void, that blank space in our lives.

We were best friends, pals, buddies, but, according to some of my friends, after the relationship was over, Cindy and I never looked like a loving couple nor a couple in love. How could we? I felt that that space we shared, and the things we said (like "I love you," without completely understanding what those words meant), obscured the fact that Cindy and I had fallen into some very predictable gender roles. I was the breadwinning "husband" and she was the "housewife." I couldn't believe it, but it was the truth. I went to work every day, paid the bills, made sure both of us were fed. Cindy, who was often between gigs or working on her demo tape, stayed at home, did most of the cooking (which wasn't much, since we usually ate out), cleaned up the house from time to time, and, much to my chagrin, watched talk shows on a daily basis, especially Ricki Lake. Any inkling I had had of not being the "typical" man went right out the window.

I'm telling you this, Nina, because I feel it's important for you to know where I'm coming from. I am not, by any stretch of the imagination, some godsend for you. I'm far from the perfect man. And I'm not the perfect gentleman, because I'm still trying to figure out manhood and love and sex and relationships and the way my past shaped me. I care about you, Nina, unequivocally. And I want to know you and I want you to know me—the vital parts of me. Yeah, there is so much more you need to hear.

Peacelove&progress,
    Kevin

Big Time

by Victor LaValle

I made it self-destruct. My body. I destroyed it. It takes work to get as fat as I was. Not a fat child, I had to start pushing the limits in my teenage years. I'm five feet ten inches and, at my most ambitious, I weighed nearly four hundred pounds. I filled out most in my shoulders, my back. I was massive; sometimes I went sideways through a door if it was slightly narrow. I liked it. It was a presence, my girth, that split crowds even from fifteen feet away. I could be benign and friendly without getting walked on like most quiet people. The only drawback was with women. Luckily, I'm Black. And because I am, being fat wasn't the death of my sexual life. I was not quite middle class, but the pool of women I floated in as a teenager were working women: not nurses, but their assistants, secretarial trainees, cosmetologists, and foodservers at the concession stands of Yankee Stadium. In the U.S., if you're really heavy you're probably not well off. Cheap, unimaginably unhealthy food is plentiful from Jamaica, Queens to the hills of West Virginia. In this setting even two hundred fifty pounds wasn't beyond the realm of attraction. At two hundred seventy-five, I was with a single mother who was considerate, kind, and funny. These women didn't find me gorgeous, but in their lives other characteristics far overshadowed my fifty-inch waist. Loyalty, consideration, a job. I coasted on their woeful expectations for as long as I could, a chunky knight in shining stretch pants.

But then came college. Five hours upstate, I discovered another continent, one that found my fat distasteful, even offensive. And it was Black women as much as any others who rejected me. I was in the middle class, the women were self-sufficient, thus the size of my ass was as important as my personality. More. Though I made friends, socialized, I often found myself marching spitefully through a dining hall, my tray loaded with donuts and imitation Philly cheesesteaks, as if I could hide from the collective grimaces and smirks in my rising pile of candied treats. You think I'm nasty, well, watch this. That was my battle cry. The more my friends went to play basketball or jog or shotput, the more bags of Doritos, jars of peanut butter, and three-liter Pepsis I consumed. It was self-destruction, just not as sexy as cocaine or alcohol. With liquor you become loose and loquacious, but no one has ever turned charming after downing a whole bucket of extra-crispy fried chicken. It was a tantrum, but I enjoyed it. I like eating. When I'd swallowed half a log of raw cookie dough and my temples hurt, my stomach felt distended, near bursting, I would peel off the rest of the wrapper and force myself to eat the remains in front of a mirror in my dorm room. I was watching myself, chastising myself, saying, "Okay, if you're going to die like this, let's die."

The summer before my senior year of college I was three hundred and fifty. I couldn't get a date, but I couldn't be quite sure how unattractive I'd become. I was still friendly, I made jokes and, in my mind, if I saw a woman smiling at me as she laughed I still had a chance. I did not. This became clear finally when one young woman and I spent many days together in the summer of 1994. She was slight and moved easily, always, as though she'd never had to give her body a thought. At the end of the summer she told my friend that I was "her perfect man, but he's big enough to be two perfect men."

It was an alarm bell, but I ignored it. I decided that all women were bitches and I returned to my dimly lit cave with a bag of Slim Jims and a forty-ounce container of Cool Whip.

My room did have a phone. A copy of the *Village Voice* sat on my bed. I flipped through the back pages, looking at the naked girls posed in the phone sex ads (there hadn't yet been the boom in "bodywork" ads). Beside these I found another number, half a page high. The ad read: Meet real live women in your area who are horny and dying to meet you. It worked. I met some. They were not prostitutes.

The women on the line lived in the Bronx or Brooklyn. Not all the women who ever called, but all the women I ever met. The first time, I took a Shortline bus down to Manhattan from Ithaca, then a train back up to the South Bronx. I weaved through a cracked lobby door, then climbed to the second floor to meet a woman in her thirties who, based on two phone conversations, had assured me that if I wanted, she'd have my baby. I was up for the offer. Not the result of procreation, but the act that can result in it. At her door I was aware of that eye that every man gets used to, the eye of a woman's appraisal. In this case, the once-over was done quickly and expertly, like a jeweler's, though willing to accept a great many more flaws.

She wasn't pretty, but she looked better than me. We sat on her couch in the living room of her two-room apartment. We talked, but she sat far back, like an interviewer. Which she was. I lost my charm in front of her and she decided against a night of passion. She stood, went to her bedroom, unlocked the door, and let out her son. He was about six and happy to play card games with his mother and me. Eventually I cobbled together enough indignation to leave.

"I'm going," I said. She was on the phone. The next time I came down to New York City, I made sure to ask first, "Are we going to fuck?" The woman said, "If you eat my pussy first." I went to her apartment, also in the Bronx. She called herself Big Time. She was a grandmother and she was thirty-nine. Big Time met me in front of her building wearing tight pants for the same reason I did: there was no such thing as baggy for men and women like us. She was pleasant. She was business-like. I came into the apartment, she took me to the bedroom, pulled off her clothes, lay on the mattress, opened her legs and then parted the lips of her vagina.

Meanwhile, I stood there so dressed I hadn't even untied my shoelaces. She chided me. She got up to offer me a beer, but I don't drink beer so she gave me Courvoisier. We got loose. I turned off the light and ate her pussy. Then I ate her ass. Later she jerked me off. I left without sleeping over. It was like that every weekend I could put such an event together. It became expensive: calling to meet more women at fifty-five cents a minute, the cost of bus tickets. But the payoff was pretty good. I very rarely had intercourse, but handjobs and blowjobs, they work. And I enjoyed going down on the women. They weren't looking at me when I did that. Their eyes were closed. Pretty soon I was eating more pussy than a four-year lesbian. What I found most surprising was that the women weren't as ashamed as I was. They never wanted to turn off the lights. If I brought up the idea they were flummoxed, as if I'd suggested moving to another neighborhood; the possibility didn't occur to them. In our couplings, I was the demure one.

I suppose this might be seen as liberating. I was with women for whom the conventions of beauty did not apply. Isn't that the grand free space so many of us wish for? We could be blissful in our size, together. Except that they did, in fact, find me unappealing, and told me so. They let me know that they didn't usually like their men so "thick," that most often they liked burly, muscled figures. I apologized a lot. But in my mind I ridiculed them. I thought they were too stupid to know they appeared wretched and tired, that they gave off the stale odor of perspiration and nacho chips. I thought of them as animals and of myself as less than an animal, because I was beholden to them, forced to endure their mind-numbingly loud conversation the way they endured my bloated, sagging body just to bust their nut. And every woman wanted me out before dawn. There seemed to be a general agreement amongst them that I would never be allowed to spend the night. There was great shame in being rushed to collect one's clothes, ushered to the door, unceremoniously led out. I often felt they wanted me gone before their neighbors came out to see me lumber awkwardly down the hall. It was a dull, distant humiliation, but on the train back to my mother's house or the next day on the bus up to Ithaca, I assured myself that it had been a good time.

At school I discovered a great love for books. In my last year I did a lot of catching up. I don't make claims that I charted vast new intellectual territory, but I found myself very happy when I was reading, so I kept reading. Then I began to write. I came back to New York to go to graduate school, but I didn't call that number. I was living at home with my family so I didn't want the phone bill coming in screaming "Fuck Line!" when my mother opened it. More than that, I stopped wanting to go out. I didn't have energy to go bump uglies with anyone. Like a distance runner's coach, my mind was propelling me forward (go meet another one! another one!), but my body had given out. I grew fatigued at the sight of the green-line trains that ran service up to the Bronx.

Instead I went to class. I went to work. I wrote.

I wrote a book.

After some disappointments we sold it. My agent nonchalantly reminded me there would be an author photo. She was only telling me so I'd reserve the time on my calendar, but I took it differently. There would be a photo of me. I went on a diet. I am a creature of petty vanity, why lie? Living as an obtrusive, ungainly mess was one thing, but having it photographed, preserved, was another. I was pragmatic. I was a businessman. My publishing house would send me out to meet more people if they believed people would want to meet me. It was a calculation. It was also an excuse. I wanted to lose the weight. When I stopped reveling in my self-loathing long enough to contemplate my situation, I had to acknowledge that it was very hard to find clothes; I had a hard time finding seats to fit me; I was out of breath when I even thought about climbing a flight of stairs. I didn't like it anymore that people moved away from me before I'd ever met them. I was exhausted from being so large. I lost more than one hundred and fifty pounds. A wonderful photographer took my picture. I looked good. The first time I saw it I cringed, but when I held my chest and stomach in mock humiliation there was less of me to clutch and that was nice. I thought, who better than me to try being handsome? Why not me?

At a writer's retreat in drab, dear Provincetown, Massachusetts, I met a woman. This was before the book came out, while I was editing it. She wrote fiction too. We became friends, then spent a few weeks flirting, going through town window shopping, trying not to spend our stipends too quickly. It was a milquetoast paradise. Get up and write or read. Go for a jog. Go for a walk together. Come home to read. Talk with the other painters and writers. Talk with Portuguese fishermen and the aging transsexuals living on the beach. Go home to write. Then drink hooch. Wake up in the middle of the night to write down a line or idea, then while still up pour some Knob Creek in a small glass and read a bit more. Do this for seven months and be content. I was more surprised than joyous when she wanted to kiss me. It happened late one evening when I stormed out of a bar as a joke and she followed. Her face was on my chest and my first reaction was to curl up so she couldn't feel my doughy folds, but many of them were gone. Not all, but plenty. She squeezed me like there would be nothing else she would ever want to do with my body, and I was very surprised.

While it's impossible to hide the learned movements of heavier years— hiding behind towels after showering, wearing a big coat even on warm days, not wearing short-sleeved shirts, no shorts, not even sandals—I consciously tried to stop those actions, to hide them away. I thought that if I acted like a slimmer person I would eventually believe I'd become one. It worked to a degree, but like those anorexic girls in teen after-school specials, what I see in the mirror is still that weary, wider guy. My face seems puffy unless I catch it at a quick glance, before I have time to remember how it looked for so long. My body, even as my waist size plummets toward normal, never seems any more svelte. I have to touch myself with my eyes closed to feel how my stomach is flatter, how it sucks in when I lie on my back, though before it bubbled up, bubbled over. I touch my ass and it's like I'm copping a feel of someone else's. It's tight as a snare drum.

I thought for years that I simply couldn't get a date with a woman, that I had to resort to hurried, tussled fucking with someone who didn't care to know my name. But I chose that. I wanted to be treated like I felt.

And they wanted to treat someone that way. That feeling has gone for me. Or at least now when it surfaces I quickly set down to write some vile little story and get it out that way.

Only occasionally do I fantasize this plan: to run and diet and sculpt some very nice shape for myself, taking three more years to do it, until my body is perfect as it's going to be, then swallow a grenade and send the whole damn thing to hell. Very often my girlfriend, the author from Provincetown, tells me she finds me handsome. She loves me so I imagine she can't say anything else. I take her words as kindness. But I don't want to act as though I have only one face and it's a mopey one. I have many. One day I feel like I've actually put on weight, like I'm six hundred pounds and this new life is the last choked dream of my heart being crushed. But then the next day I go out and am sure there isn't a motherfucker on two feet who's sexier. On the good days I pose for my girl like I'm Steve Reeves from the old Hercules movies. And on the really good days I mean it.

Wilderness 101

by Richard Imhotep Symister

On our paths to finding our divine mates, we Black men sometimes get lost along the way. We do not always have the proper role models or the right guides in place and enter relationships unprepared, uninformed, and ill-equipped to complete our journey towards love. The quest to create and maintain a healthy, intimate relationship becomes a lot like being lost in the woods. We're not sure what to do or where to go, so we become like lost hikers, wasting time and wandering aimlessly.

My father died when I was very young and I had few, if any, Black male role models during my adolescent years. I learned all I *thought* I needed to know about life and love from my friends and television. Unfortunately, my friends knew as little as I did and Heathcliff Huxtable from the *Cosby Show,* who made it all look so easy, was a fictional character. So by age twenty-one, I was pumped full of energy, hormones, and warped, preconceived notions of what a relationship should be. I set my sights on new territory to explore, venturing out into the wilderness alone. And I got lost easily.

I traveled nomadically from one short-lived relationship to another, truly believing I knew what I was doing, that I could go it alone and could get back on the right trail. Little did I know that during this journey, I would be faced with routine bouts of confusion, fear, and even panic, as I decided whether to seek shelter or continue on my tortuous trek. Ivy was too unstable to take care of my emotional needs. Sabrina wasn't "Black enough" to push me further into my Afrikan consciousness. Daphne was *too* affectionate. Denise wasn't affectionate enough. In retrospect, I see I set each woman up to fail, thinking they could fulfill all my needs, heal my wounds, fill in the hole. When they did not live up to these unattainable expectations, I'd either exhaust or sabotage the relationships, seeking another surrogate to take over where the other left off. The wandering continued.

Through Spirit's blessing and much work, I met my divine mate and was married August 24, 2002. As happy as I am, I still look back at all the pitfalls, sand traps, and poison ivy patches I could have avoided if only I had had the proper guidance.

I have a friend from Colorado. He's a true outdoorsman who spends his days off snowshoeing, mountain biking, backpacking, and climbing the state's tallest peaks. In 2001, he climbed Mount Rainier, a 14,410–foot, snow-covered volcano in Washington State. The more I listen to his exploits, the more I understand how and why he is able to choose his trail, mountain, or slope and complete his trip safely and successfully. His secret lies in the fact that he is always prepared and willing to ask for help from others more experienced than he. "I was not skilled enough to climb Mount Rainier with friends," he said, "so I chose a guide service that led me up the mountain. They marked the route with fluorescent orange tape on bamboo sticks stuck in the snow." From him I learned that there exists an array of wilderness resources including survival guidebooks, manuals, crash courses, and websites. This got me thinking.

The answers to achieving a successful Black relationship are not clear-cut. During the course of my marital journey, I've learned certain principles that I consider essential for mutual ascension, compatibility and survival. I have compiled these lessons in a crash course entitled "Wilderness 101: The Path to Finding and Keeping Divine Love." For anyone interested in signing up, registration begins now.

Essential Gear
Wilderness survival is difficult, if not impossible,
without proper equipment.
Am I mentally ready? Brothers, stop, step back, and ask yourselves this question before venturing out into the wilderness. Humpin' and bumpin' are the easy parts. But just because your hormones say you're ready does not mean you're mentally prepared for what's out there.

While experts say that the brain is the largest sex organ, our brain serves so many other functions as well, including builder, educator, hunter, protector, and navigator. To work at peak capacity, however, the mind must be healthy and strong.

We all have issues, junk, and cobwebs in our attics that need cleaning out, but what brings us closer to clarity and understanding is how we deal with these issues. Do we bottle them up? Talk about them? Or deny that they even exist? Mental ascension, the ability to shift from lower "chakras" of emotions and sexuality to higher centers of communication, creativity, intuition, and clairvoyance is endless, yet fulfilling work. As we achieve higher levels of knowledge, maturity, and consciousness, we possess a better understanding of *why* we are seeking our divine mate, what we expect and need from this future union, and what it will take to create and maintain harmony. You do not need to make a pilgrimage to Mecca or scale the highest mountain before beginning your path toward your mate, but if you are not clear about what you want and you travel without direction and purpose, you will continue to wander aimlessly, exhausted and confused by your efforts.

If you want someone without a past, marry a robot. Otherwise, acknowledge, just as *you* have your own issues, so will your mate. The mentality that tells us we need to steer clear or abandon a relationship because of all of her "baggage" or "bullshit" is often just a cop-out for not being strong or patient enough to cradle our sisters when they need cradling. We all need cradling sometimes. Don't believe so? Then you might be forgetting where you spent the most secure nine months of your life. We all go back to the womb to some extent, seeking that maternal (and paternal) coddling, cradling, and comfort. Dr. Samuel Jones, a relationship counselor in New York, explained to me that it is not love that a child requires to thrive, but security. There is still a little boy left in each us, even if it is just through memories that crave a tender embrace or soothing words to assure us that we are safe, protected, and that everything is going to be all right.

"You cannot have a healthy relationship with me if you don't already have one with your mother." My mate said this to me when we first started dating, realizing I had some deep-rooted issues concerning my mom. I didn't listen.

You see, my family moved my older sister and me to a predominantly White community when we were very young. I did my best to fit in at school, trying to act like other White students, dress like them, talk like them. I believed, in some distorted way, I wanted to be like them—White. But I was never truly accepted, often teased or ostracized because of my skin. I suffered many years of shame, self-hatred, and racial disorientation. It wasn't until my grad-school years that I began to socialize within conscious, Black circles and attend Black lectures, readings, and events. Slowly, I started to rediscover my culture and identify with my Kemetic lineage. I put the blame on my parents for moving us to a White neighborhood, for my pain and confusion as a child. When my father died, the brunt of my blame fell upon my mother. I carried this blame into my adult years and, eventually, into my divine union. As the years passed, I gradually withdrew from my mother, but also began creating exaggerated flaws in my mate, flaws that ironically mimicked those I saw in my mother. Three years into our union, the bitterness I held for my mother went from cumbersome to carcinogenic, eating away at me while also destroying my relationship with my mate. Subconsciously, I would not and could not release my blame until my mother somehow made up for my childhood or at least acknowledged her role in my pain.

"You cannot have a healthy relationship with me if you don't already have one with your mother." I finally heard her. I did some soul searching, opening up scars from my childhood that were as painful as the original wounds. Eventually, I discovered that I had made my mom into a scapegoat for my choices, or more specifically, the consequences of my choices: confusion, seclusion, and poor self-esteem. She did not make me try to talk like my White peers, dress like them, and want to *be* them. Granted, I wished I had had a stronger Black consciousness foundation as a child, but there came a point where I needed to take responsibility for my own decisions and actions.

When I finally "released" my mother from this blame, I found it much easier to carry on a healthy, trusting relationship with my mate, my mother, and especially, myself.

Finding Shelter
Finding proper shelter is an underrated and often overlooked part of wilderness survival. Most people cannot survive unprotected from harsh weather for more than a few hours.

The sayings "you complete me" or "my other half" lead us to believe that without our wives, girlfriends, lovers, or mates, we are no longer whole. What does this say about who we were prior to our relationships or after a separation? Do we wander around as depleted, incomplete souls? We are separate entities, before, during, and after a relationship, regardless of how close we become to our mates. We enter into a union with distinct and individualized personalities, idiosyncrasies, moods, wants, and identities. Our individuality (and our connection with Spirit) is what makes us special—divine. You and your mate will not always see eye-to-eye or be on the same page. It is natural for a storm cloud to appear now and then. Don't feel guilty for wanting to seek shelter, away from your mate, particularly if some unknown tension exists between the two of you.

When we first started dating, my wife would repeatedly ask, "What's the matter?" or "Did I do something wrong?" She's come to learn that sometimes a grumpy bear (who is also a Gemini) just needs to be left alone in his cave for a while. I respect *her* moods, too. I'm not the only one who gets grumpy.

It is not a selfish act to enjoy a mini-vacation, meditation, prayer, a hike, journaling, golfing, shooting hoops, visiting Mama's house, or the four F's (friends, football, and fattening food) without your mate. In fact, it is a selfless act because you are making attempts at preserving your union by taking time out to vacillate, ponder, rethink, cry, yell, rationalize, re-energize, and revitalize. Go where you want to be, and more importantly, where you *need* to be. (Oh, and by the way, a second lover's house is not considered refuge. It's considered breaking one of the most sacred laws of your union.)

Now please recognize the difference between walking and running away from a situation. When you walk, you do so in a slow, calm pace. You understand the reasons for seeking temporary refuge: to think, to heal, center yourself, and then return to the original problem which has now become much more manageable. When you run (and I've seen some of you brothers lace up your cleats and leave a blazing trail like Carl Lewis) you do so with haste, heart beating, mind in complete disarray. You are fleeing the scene scared. You find yourself unable or unwilling to deal with the immediate problem. Before you hit the ground running, ask yourself two simple questions: One, is my relationship worth salvaging and two, is it salvageable? If you answered yes to both questions, then take a deep breath and slip into a nice pair of walking shoes.

Signaling for Help
Proper signaling can mean the difference between being rescued and being left for dead in the wilderness.
Any problem that can have a detrimental effect on your union is a problem worth addressing. Sweeping relationship issues under the rug will only create an unsightly heap that grows bigger with time. Learn to confront the issue, continue to work towards an answer and, if need be, confide in someone who can help you reach resolution.

We are a proud group, aren't we, brothers? Some would even say belligerent, especially when it comes to asking for relationship advice. God forbid we candidly discuss our sensitive or emotional issues. We don't want anyone to think we're "punking out" or "crying like a bitch," do we?

I used to think that expressing my feelings made me look soft, stupid, and less of a man. So I just stopped. Huge mistake. The pile under the rug grew to mountainous proportions.

Being sensitive in no way emasculates you. In fact, allowing ourselves to become at ease with our emotional self-expression and sensitivity frees us up and opens our minds to new venues of communication. Signaling for help is not a sign of weakness, but intelligence.

Before stepping outside your relationship for help, consider expressing your concerns with your partner (the word *"partner"* being the key word: two people working towards a common goal). Communication is the primary tool we brothers need to practice and perfect to the best of our abilities. Most elders agree that their ability to both talk and listen to their mates is what kept their marriages strong. If we can't communicate, we can't share, and if we can't share, why be in a relationship?

My wife and I have been together for almost five years now, long enough to know our limitations. Although we are spiritually connected, my wife and I understand that we cannot always handle every relationship problem on our own and at times need outside help.

When signaling for help, remember the "she did this" or "she's the one with the problem" attitude will only bog down your progress toward a solution. I am notorious for missing the whole point of a problem and, at times, waste energy finger-pointing. I've found it much more constructive to step away from a potentially volatile situation and focus less on who's wrong and instead, more on how we can work to make things right. It is not until I consciously become a sort of neutral, outside observer that I can see the situation for what it really is and respond with greater calm and rationale.

The best advice I find comes from the more "seasoned" couples—couples who have been together for some years and demonstrate that their union is strong through work, communication, and much Mir (the Kemetic name for love). I confide in my friend Lloyd. He and his wife have been together over five years. He constantly keeps me in check, reminding me that the problems my wife and I encounter in our union "ain't nothin' new" and that all couples go through them.

I learned not to depend on those brothers who always seem to be single or bouncing in and out of relationships for guidance. The only advice they can usually give is bad advice.

Instead, my aunt was there for me to sort of fill in the gap between my mother and me, acting as both sounding board and advisor. She still is a very important part of my life and knows me well enough to tell it like it is without worrying about hurting my feelings. I don't need anyone who will "yes" me to death or always take my side. I need honesty. I need wisdom.

I need someone with enough experience in a solid, healthy relationship to guide me toward the light. Older relatives often possess untapped wells of knowledge at your disposal. This familiarity of family can often work in your favor since he or she already knows a bit about your personality and character.

Every community has a place of worship. We have a church, a temple, a mosque, and two shrines within one mile of our home. I benefit greatly from sitting with a Kemetic elder guide who leads me through meditation, relaxation, and allows me to express my feelings freely and without judgment. Each counseling session brings me to a deeper understanding of who I am and the value of my sacred union.

Who do you talk to? Find someone you can trust, who you feel comfortable with, and who can offer sound, practical advice you can take back into your relationship.

Last but definitely not least, one cannot forget the creator most high. To whatever name you ascribe—God, Spirit, Ntr, Buddha, or Allah— you must acknowledge that you are part of creator and creator is a part of you. With this in mind, it is clear to see why the creator knows you best and is always present and ready for a dialogue with you. I feel closest to Spirit when I can separate myself from the rest of the world and focus on the rhythm and depth of my breathing. Whether you're attending church, meditating, taking a walk, or sitting by a lake, find a source of spirituality that works best for you. Spirituality plays an important role in our union. Our spirituality reminds us of our common goals: to do Spirit's work and support each other in this work. It also brings us back to center when chaos infiltrates our space.

Your mate's spirituality will not only reveal her ethical fiber but also your moral compatibility with one another, which can be just as important as deciding how to raise your children, where to buy a home, or financial planning. For a moment, let's bypass the initial lust and falling-in-love stages. Your mate's ethics and values will not fade, grow love handles, go bald, wrinkle, or get saggy. They will only deepen, representing who she is as a person. Simply put, you need to look at your mate from the inside out and decide whether or not you actually "like" her, respect her ideals and beliefs. If you don't, the lust and love thing won't really matter in the long haul.

During our first phone conversation, my wife explained emphatically that her "divine purpose" was to teach Afrikans "prosperity consciousness." (She told me she was a dog lover, too!) The more we talked, the more I knew she and I were on the same page spiritually, which set the foundation for our union.

Want to know about your mate's beliefs and values? Just ask her.

✂ ✂ ✂

If and when you pass this class, you will graduate to many more. Currently, I'm enrolled in "Building a Fire: The Art of Keeping Passion Alive in a Relationship." This week's topic is "creativity," and we're learning new ways to start a fire in inclement weather.

Each day is a new lesson for my wife and me. With time comes a deeper understanding of what it takes to maintain peace and harmony in our marriage. Peace and harmony. Deep down, these were the two main reasons I strapped on my backpack and hiking boots in the first place.

I Don't Need No Man:
Does a New Kind of "Bling-Bling Feminism" Create a False Sense of Emotional Empowerment?

by Cheo Tyehimba

Recently, I conducted an informal poll. I asked single Black women if they felt they "needed a man" in their life. As suspected, about 90 percent happily testified "no." The other 10 percent confessed to needing a man only after requesting further clarification of the word "need," making me wonder about the legacy of the hip-hop era on the collective mindset of strong Black women everywhere. Of course, that Black women can survive and prosper without a man is no news flash. Life is anything but a crystal stair for most Black folks and sistas have been doing for self for a very long time.

But something has changed. There is a new generation of young single women—call them the "Lil' Kim Generation"—who seem to have supplanted the need for emotional intimacy in favor of material gratification. Traditionally, chasing "money, power, and respect" was the domain of men, and we prided ourselves on being hard, uncaring, workaholic egomaniacs who could equally be turned around by a shiny new convertible or a big butt and a smile. Yeah, back in the day you could count on us to be easy-to-read, shallow dogs more concerned with climbing the ladder to success than settling down. Now, I'm not saying we've changed much, but what I can't figure out is why a lot of women are trying to beat us at our own game, primarily, a game of power.

We all know power has been the playground of men for centuries. To us, our survival has always been determined by our ability to enforce our will over the world. We place a high premium on this ability and the physical representations of power that come with it. Of course, when your basic nature is to use external forces (read: money, machines, political influence) to achieve your goals, you rarely learn to empathize with the little people. But why would we want to anyway? Men have always been too preoccupied with causing pain to take the time to feel that of the next guy. Some would even argue that a certain take-charge detachment and shallowness is a prerequisite for manhood. This is the kind of power that every young brother ultimately thinks he must attain in order to survive among his peers. A large part of his self-worth and value is based not on how loving and supportive he can be, but rather how he can "hold his own" when other males are vying to take what he's got, be it lunch money, a job, or an NBA championship. This is nothing new. Black sociologists and feminists have written about it for many years. Blaxploitation flicks of the '70s celebrated it. The "Black macho" self-image is often based upon how much pain a brother can withstand or inflict, or how many women he can sleep with, or how many children he has. And whether myth or menace, it continues to be a factor in how many brothers navigate through our society.

Of course, the power that Black men have grasped at over the years is a hand-me-down version of the kind of patriarchy practiced by White men for centuries. As Black men, the kind of power we managed to eke out for ourselves has historically come at the expense of subordinating Black women—look no further than your neighborhood pimp for an example. Black women, all people for that matter, deserve to be in loving, whole relationships where a higher value is placed on intimacy than material gain. However, I think this long-held belief is being reconfigured by a new generation of women who, inspired by popular culture and music videos, have bought into the myth of material empowerment as a measure of womanhood.

The way I see it, the world is messed up enough now because of men. Our actions have probably caused more unnecessary wars, terrorism, homelessness, and political strife in the world than most women could ever dream of creating. However, some women are beginning to show signs of catching up. Go to any nightclub and you'll hear party anthems that blur the lines between a woman fulfilling her own sense of empowerment and a woman supplanting a man with money and objects. You've heard them: *All my independent ladies in the house. If you got your own ride, pay your own mortgage, pay your own way through school, and don't need a man for nothing, let me hear you scream!* And all the ladies go, "Owww!" Driven partly by our consumerist society and partly by their own desire to satisfy a deep loneliness through material gratification, some women have taken a walk on the shallow side of the pool. A world full of women behaving like men gives me chills. But a trend is afoot. Women have become the new men.

So now you suck your teeth and say, "Anyway, he ain't talking about *me*." Hold up. This is not a neo-conservative editorial to lament the breakdown of so-called traditional values or a sexist attempt to define gender roles. Just one man's observations about how women seem to be letting consumerism, well, consume their emotional lives. A brother can't step to some sistas nowadays unless he's prepared to match pay stubs. He best be ready to prove he's got at least as many baubles to offer as a professional athlete or a married suga daddy. Think I'm exaggerating? Just check out any NBA all-star weekend after-party. Whether it's in Atlanta, San Francisco, or New York, the mating power play is the same: Ballers and gold-diggers on the court, *while broke brothas sit on the bench.*

Although there are no simple conclusions to be drawn, we all know what's up. A tide of consumerist media "violence" has flooded our psyches. The staccato fire of a gangsta rapper's Uzi can't compare to the mind-shrapnel launched by some rap videos. Forget Sadaam's so-called weapons of mass destruction. Every time you click on shows like B.E.T.'s *106 and Park,* which perpetuates mostly bling-bling culture rather than old school hip-hop, you might as well hold the remote to your temple and fire. Whenever bling-bling videos are in rotation (which is always), America's "psychological weapons" reach their targets faster than a heat-seeking Scud.

What's all this have to do with women becoming more like men and connecting more with *Sex and the City* than with *Love Jones?* We've read the depressing statistics about the high level of unpartnered African Americans. Recent census figures show that 35 percent of Americans between twenty-four and thirty-four have never married; for African Americans in the same age range, it is 54 percent. Besides a growing trend by women to be less preoccupied by marriage (just as men have traditionally been), there is also evidence that many Black women can't find Black men who are on the same economic and professional playing field. Although some have opted for mixed marriages, either by race or class, many are just holding out, hoping that in time, brothers will step up their game a bit. Either way you look at it, some sistas, heavily influenced by bling-bling videos, may see men as disposable distractions, less and less available, and measurably less relevant than the opulent lifestyles extolled in these videos.

Of course, the effect these videos have on the desires of both young women and men could be measured along class lines. But even though a Harvard-educated, middle-class person may be more prepared intellectually to deal with the barrage of mindless exploitation in the media, a message still gets in. All hip-hop–loving Black women easily decode this message every time they see images of brothers as would-be prince charmings, gangsta-leanin' behind the wheel of a shiny SUV, yacht, or private jet while getting freaked by a bevy of gigglin' and jigglin' "models." Even if certain women do not see representative images of themselves in these videos or relate to them in any way, many connect with the hedonistic lifestyles the men (and women) flaunt. It becomes very easy to see why some women may find designer clothes, flat-screen TVs, cars, and an "MTV crib" in the Hamptons more important than having a loving relationship.

Personally, I have never been attracted to women who value these things in a relationship. Like most men, I view these women with a certain suspicion (when I'm looking for a friend or relative, since gold-digger types are usually not attracted to poverty-stricken writers!).

As a single Black man, the kind of women I've attracted are usually more vocal about the misrepresentation of Black women in videos than I am. As a writer and a thinker, I require more than eye-candy when it comes to women. Don't get me wrong, the women in these videos are amazing but after awhile, like their non-expressive, non-opinionated, non-evolving, glistening digital images, they become little more than guilty pleasures. And I know of nothing significant that ever came of a guilty pleasure.

The fact is, we all live in a society where the watermark of success has more to do with our zip codes and bank accounts than our willingness to bare it all in front of Dr. Phil. However, what I've learned is that for some women, "not needing a man" is closer to a defense mechanism than the truth. It's a human reaction to a very complicated situation. But ultimately, it's healthy to understand that we all need each other. Funny thing is, women have always known the power of their own vulnerability. They understood long before men that to be truly vulnerable was first to be vulnerable to oneself, to honor and nurture oneself, and to follow one's inner voice. Women have always done this infinitely better than men. Really, a lot of it depends on us brothers. And men are simple. What do we really think it takes to make a relationship work? We want honest, intelligent, nurturing women who value our manhood, stand by us, and respect our (often limited) emotional capacity.

One of the greatest compliments I ever received was from a sista who said I renewed her faith in Black men. We met while I was in grad school. From the start, I noticed that she was very guarded and I sensed that she wanted more but was unwilling to take any chances on love. My own past heartaches helped me easily identify with her "once burned, twice shy" disposition and I informed her that I was also in no rush to hop on the freeway of love. We became friends, which has somehow always been a requirement for me. Later, after gaining her trust, I found out that she had been in an abusive relationship and didn't think she'd learn to open up again. Looking back, the value of our relationship was one where power and material gain were less important than intangibles like walking across the Brooklyn Bridge on a Sunday at dawn or cooking breakfast together. I'm not sure how other guys figure it out, but besides being able to curl my socks in the bedroom, a sista has to be a really good friend to me. Believe it or not, most men really want to *like* the woman they are in love with. At the end of the day, all we really have are our common interests and our ability to grow together.

There are no easy solutions for a successful relationship, but I do think we play ourselves cheap when we don't enter a committed relationship with the same type of preparation and support that we'd have if we were, for example, entering medical school. Would you try to become a doctor without studying for the MCAT? Or try to complete the New York City marathon without so much as training one day? My suggestion is that Black folks entering a committed relationship *start out* with some help. Get a therapist, life-coach, or counselor at the beginning—when the sex is the bomb and you'd make soup with his dirty bath water—rather than later when issues surface. And they will surface. But understanding that love is a constant negotiation, rather than a power play, is the key.

In some small but very significant ways, back before the days of bling-bling videos, the power of Black love could wage a more united front against all the obstacles aligned against it. During slavery, loving bonds between Black men and women were a constant threat to White supremacy. In her book *Salvation: Black People and Love,* renowned scholar and feminist bell hooks sees the African-American male-female relationship as a union informed as much by our joint oppression as by our sexist socialization. "Reading accounts of heterosexual Black relationships during slavery reveals the extent to which desire to create longstanding domestic partnerships, whether through marriage or shacking, often served as the catalyst inspiring individuals to fiercely resist bondage and work for freedom." Clearly, there is something about loving and being loved in return that makes you want to be free, in every aspect of your life.

I agree with bell hooks: Black love is a revolutionary act. Although society is constantly conspiring to devalue the human experience and some women (and men) will continue to equate self-fulfillment with the external trappings of power, hope is out there. Perhaps, a lesson from the ancestors can still illuminate a purpose in our lives in the twenty-first century. Perhaps something as simple as renewing our understanding of our joint purpose (to simply be there for one another) is enough to convince some women that yes, they *need* men in their lives. Because forget what you've heard: We need you.

The World of Yes

By Lawrence C. Ross, Jr.

You may not realize this, but I am the designated marriage-relationship-what-does-it-take-to-find-a-good-man counselor for every single Black woman I know (and those that I meet), including my wife's friends, sisters in the grocery store, readers of my books, and my recently divorced mother.

The conversations can be light or deep, but they always occur. And there doesn't need to be a proper segue for the conversation to begin. Anything can start the conversation. Here's how a typical relationship conversation might start, say, at a party:

Me: Excuse me, sister, but could someone please pass me the chips?

Sister: Here's the chips, Lawrence. By the way, can you tell me why brothers have a chip on their shoulder when it comes to relationships?

See? Now it's not that I have any professional training on the subject or that I feel a need to seek out sisters in order to provide free relationship advice. If anything, I tend to shy away from questions, and when I do state an opinion, it's purely anecdotal and not academic in any way. I give my ideas on what's right and what's wrong with absolutely no quantitative analysis. I can't quote statistics, nor refer to sociological articles.

But that doesn't matter to most single sisters. I, my friends, am an expert because I hold a distinctive qualification: I have a ring on my finger. I'm a brother who made a commitment, and lo and behold, kept it! In the eyes of these single sisters, I am a member of a tribe rarely seen but dearly valued. I am the married African-American man. And these women want to know why those who look like me, talk like me, and think like me, won't commit like me. So they ask questions, and more questions, searching for the answers that have eluded them so far. And I, being the dutiful amateur relationship counselor, answer their queries the best I can.

But I know going into each relationship conversation that my specious answers are never going to be adequate. You see, I'm thirty-seven years old, and the sisters who ask me questions are my contemporaries. They related instantly to actress Marisa Tomei, when in the movie *My Cousin Vinnie,* her character stomps her foot and declares, "My clock is ticking!" You better believe these sisters *know* their clocks are ticking. In fact, those clocks have been ticking for a while and to these sisters, it's beginning to sound like the clock is attached to a relationship time-bomb.

For these single sisters, their lives are a perplexing conundrum. They've fulfilled most of their educational, career, and spiritual goals, but why can't they just close the deal and find that special someone? I mean, they've done *nothing* wrong.

They've listened to the relationship gurus who told them to broaden their pool. So instead of being picky about which type of brother to date, they're now going over those brothers they wouldn't have given the time of day during their younger years. Recently divorced? That's okay, I didn't know his former wife anyway. Never married? Well, what's wrong with him and can I fix him? He's not very attractive? Nothing a good wardrobe can't fix. Are his teeth crooked? Well, I got him covered with my health insurance.

Yes, the fact that their clocks are ticking is reinforced each time they read the covers of *Essence, Cosmopolitan, Newsweek,* and *Glamour.* These sisters know the statistics, there's no need to repeat them. *Out of the adult Black men, X percent (make up your own shocking percentage) are gay, in jail, or dead. The rest are dating White women.* Yet, these sisters still hope that that elusive, well-qualified brother is out there, waiting to be swooped up.

So I tell them that that brother *is* out there. He's just scared, waiting to find himself, getting his stuff together, a little intimidated, looking for the same thing, yada, yada, yada. And some of that is true. There are brothers looking for sisters to spend the rest of their lives with. Then again, a lot of brothers know that they really don't have to do anything because they are in a proverbial "buyer's market." These brothers know they really *can* have their cake and eat it too. And they are gorging on the cake.

Take for example, Sean. Sean's my frat brother, scromee, ace-boon-coon, best friend, and by any standard, a success. He's a handsome young lawyer, who likes to have fun. He owns his home, is learning how to cook, and makes women swoon when he gives them impromptu foot massages. A gentleman at all times, he has no vices, has never been to jail, and is, by any measure, a good catch for any sister. But when asked during a recent party, why he hadn't settled down, he had a simple, yet clear explanation for all of the sisters in the room.

"You see, what you are asking me to do is move from my world of yes, to your world of no," he said with a gentle smile. "Today, when I wake up, if I want to throw my clothes on the floor, am I allowed to do it?"

"Yes!" was the response from the men in the room.

"If I'm married, and I want to throw my clothes on the floor, am I allowed to do it?"

"No!" yelled the men.

"If I want to get drunk and fall out today, am I allowed to do it?" Sean asked.

"Yes!" screamed the men, with the married ones briefly ruing their loss of freedom.

"If I'm married, can I do it?"

"No!"

"I have my own money. Do I need you to spend or take half of it?"

"No!" laughed the men.

"And that," Sean said, handing a sister a flute filled with Champagne, "is why I stay single."

Everyone laughed, but the sisters laughed with only their mouths, not their eyes. Their eyes betrayed them, glazed over in a thousand-yard stare that only longtime veterans of the Black male and female relationship wars know. To them, Sean's "world of yes" is rough, ready, and raw, and the humor of his world escapes them.

Ah, but what Sean fails to tell you is that he'd quickly give up his "world of yes" for the easy laughter of a true soul mate. And all of the pimps, playas, mack, and other scared Black men are just as desperate as single sisters, yet they mask it through outward indifference and nonchalance.

Where does this disconnect begin?

Perhaps it begins at the informal coffee klatches Black women host at their homes? You know the place because if you're a woman, you've attended at least one. It's where sisters gather to fellowship, and the conversation quickly turns to how bad their past and present men are, with each woman being careful to not look at the other women's faces too closely, for it could betray the pain and desperation their defiant words don't convey? Perhaps it starts there?

Or maybe it is the idle conversation that masquerades as expert relationship advice in Black men's barbershops? Here, the men all try to save face from their own relationship failures by signifying that the women just didn't understand them. "Amen!" shouts the Greek choir in barber chairs. *If it wasn't for the Black women doin' this and doin' that, they* certainly *would have lived up to their responsibilities.* Yet these men too, through their laughs and smiles, stare a little too intently at the latest *Jet* beauty. No hurt and pain is going to seep onto their faces and threaten the mask of machismo. Perhaps it starts there?

Where does it come from, this modern disconnect that keeps Black men and women from coming together, loving together, and staying together? Why can't people, who are all desperate for the same things, put aside the malignancies of past relationships and walk hand in hand with that one special person?

I imagine we're all aware of the cosmic repercussions of slavery on Black men and women relationships. Black women raped at the whim and will of White men, with the resultant emasculation of the Black man. And we can also study the postslavery ramifications on the Black family and say that society actually encouraged the dissolution of the Black family.

Yes, I know and acknowledge this. And while the ramifications of the unjust past are deep and long lasting, it still doesn't answer the question that a lot of brothers and sisters today can't look into each other's eyes and just submit to each other, without the drama. It seems so simple, yet it has become so tragic.

In some ways, the seeds of our discontent are sown from the shards of destroyed relationships we've seen through our Black childhoods, and reinforced through the words of our loved ones. Destroyed marriages where each former spouse spouts to the children that the other spouse "ain't shit." Baby's-mama and daddy relationships denigrate the permanence or importance of a complete family unit, they all conspire to bring us to a point which leaves us confused about each other.

We as Black people think we know one another but we don't. Black men and Black women live secret and separate lives that only intersect when we talk *at* each other versus talking *to* each other. Those brothers and sisters at the barbershop and coffee klatch are there for a reason: They listen to reinforce the experiences in their lives, not to question their own culpability in their failure to succeed in those relationships.

Brothers and sisters are speaking the same language, but not the same words. It's only when the words begin to sound the same will the worlds come together.

So what are men looking for? Often, we are looking for those mythic visions of love that may not have existed in the first place, except within the recesses of our mind. We men imagine a life where his wife laughs at her husband's jokes, finds him endlessly fascinating and charming, while constantly praising him for his prowess in bed. Oh yes, most importantly, she never complains about him watching sports.

For other men, the goal is to find a wife who is a reasonable facsimile of his mother, for better or for worse. So ladies, get ready to prep those wonderfully delicious meals, keep the house clean, and cheerfully iron his clothes. In other words, welcome to the Madonna complex.

As author Michael Datcher eloquently states in his book *Raising Fences,* most brothers want the "white picket dreams" of home, hearth, and family. The bravado and bluster that tinges our views of relationships are just mere disguises for what we truly want. We want to be surrounded by love. And we as men also go around trying to chase this type of love down.

So by this time, you must be asking a simple question: What about you? Why have you been able to find love? Haven't you been afflicted with the same maladies that dog other brothers throughout their lives?

As Dave Matthew sings, "I am no superman . . ." and that accurately described me when it came to relationships. So don't think I walk the earth without the battle scars of relationships past. I too held the same misconceptions, the same issues, and the same problems. But I was lucky, extremely lucky.

When I met my wife, April, I wasn't looking for a wife. In fact I wasn't looking for a girlfriend. I'd just got out of a relationship and I was a poverty-stricken college student. Now, the previous relationship wasn't particularly bad or good, it just was there, just like all of the others. So I wasn't too keen on another "just there" relationship.

My frat brother and I had been invited to a small birthday party at Mills College, an all-women's college in Oakland. There was nothing special about the party; it was something to do before the Christmas break. Plus, we got to visit an all-women's school. That's always a plus. Going in, I was quite content to sip my beer, be funny, and roll out when it was all over.

I met April almost immediately after walking into the room. She was a pretty thing, but I thought for some reason that she was real young. Our initial conversation was pleasant. April talked, and I listened, which is pretty unusual since I talk nonstop. She was intelligent and obviously a go-getter. But still, I wasn't looking for someone, so I left the party without getting her phone number.

Then, about four weeks later, I received a phone call from Caterina, a mutual friend who'd invited me to the party.

"April would like to know if she could call you," Caterina said.

My first thought was, How refreshing! Here was a sister who didn't wait for the brother to make the first move. Well, of course she could call me. But I did have one reservation.

"Uh, Caterina, was she the cute one at the party?" I asked nervously, racking my brain to recover a memory of April.

"She's cute and you'll like her."

Caterina was right. April and I began dating and we hit it off instantly. We both loved a wide variety of music, a good laugh, and soon we were finishing each other's sentences. It was a natural match. And our relationship was easy, because we were young and in love, and when you are young and in love, nothing comes hard.

Our families met and they got along. And this was important, because for both of us, family, no matter how much they got on our nerves, or the secrets they kept, were important to us. My future father-in-law noted with amazement that April had picked someone that fit right in with the family.

Things were perfect, and after about two years, we finally decided to get married.

Now why did we get married? Well, there just comes a time where you say to yourself, this is the person I want to share things with. This is the person I want to stay in my house forever. This is the person I'd rather be with than my best friends.

But at our young ages, our early twenties, we were literally the first of our friends to get married. A lot of our friends laughed, and you could hear them silently predicting disaster for us. Why, you might ask?

Well, for one thing, we were dead broke. I mean, no furniture in the living room broke. Keep the bacon grease in a coffee can broke. Pay everything late broke. And of course, don't pick up the phone because the creditors are calling broke.

April had just graduated from school and I was trying to make my business a success. While everyone else was single and going to the clubs, we were scraping together change so we could buy a two-piece chicken dinner from the local restaurant. Our friends laughed at how we drove a fifth-hand truck we nicknamed Jethro, while they had the money to buy brand-new cars. They told us they'd get married when things were completely right in their lives, a sly dig at our wedded poverty.

Yet, we had something others didn't know. We had faith in each other. We happily grubbed on two-piece chicken meals, laughing at the absurdity of spending two hours to find enough change to pay for it. When the rent was a couple of months behind, and we had to have a *special* talk with the landlord for the umpteenth time, you still couldn't have told us that we weren't going to not only survive but thrive, just you see! We learned that if you stay true to each other, then good things come.

But this is not to say we didn't have our difficulties. Like all young married couples, we argued. But we had and have rules for our arguments. First, the argument has to be about an *issue* and not the person. Second, the argument must be resolved and can't linger. Third, and most importantly, the argument can't be used as a weapon in later arguments. And fourth, and probably *the* most important rule, April was always right. Okay, that was an unofficial rule, but a rule nonetheless.

We also had to deal with the power struggle that comes with defining gender roles within a marriage. And just like women have fairy-tale ideas of what their marriage is going to be like, men have the same dreams. Both dreams may be warped, but hey, that's human nature. The trouble comes when the married couple is unwilling to let go of preconceived notions of what the other should do within the marriage.

My belief is that no matter how equal the responsibilities within a marriage, at the end of the day, it is the husband's responsibility to provide home, money, and security for the family. If the bills aren't paid on time, and the lights go out, people look to *me* as not doing my job. If I don't properly save for our retirement, our son's college education, or for our health, then I am to blame. But instead of being a burden, I look at that as being a welcome responsibility.

Now I hear the cries of some Black women who will say, "I don't *need* anyone to provide for me, I can take care of myself!" Well, that's not the issue. I didn't say women weren't and aren't capable of providing for themselves. And my wife, a feminist graduate of an all-women's university *certainly* believes in providing for her own security.

However, within a marriage, each person can't be the be-all and end-all. It just doesn't work. You must be willing to acknowledge the needs and aspirations of each mate, and then make sacrifices in order to have a balanced marriage. April saw my need for this responsibility, and let me fulfill that role. But this didn't mean she couldn't still be the dynamic career woman she'd gone to school to be. In fact, I wanted her to be that. I had no desire to have a Stepford wife at home.

But on other things, couples need to compromise. I, like 95 percent of Black men everywhere, thought my wife should cook dinner every night. And not just a meal, but a delicious meal. A meal to make other brothers jealous. I wanted meals that I could look forward to with pride and relish. But I ignored one thing: April hates to cook. In fact, April avoided cooking like the plague. But I thought it was my *right* as a husband to have my wife cook for me, and therefore, needless arguments ensued as I tried to make my wife into something she was not. It was now time for *me* to compromise and realize that it was not her responsibility to fulfill a role *I'd* made for her. Marriage and relationships are about adapting and compromising

As our marriage and relationship grew, we learned to be caring to each other within, while not letting others from without influence our marriage. To us, we are a team, and others are the infidels, no matter how much we love them. They are infidels because they give so-called free advice when oftentimes, none is requested. They are infidels because that advice is almost always awful.

You see, when people see a happy relationship, they tend to probe and prod for weaknesses, even when they love you. They'll cut you with one thousand slights and suggestions, all done "because we love you," but often rooted in the same relationship dysfunction you've seen all of your life.

So when people gave us dumb advice, such as suggesting we have a baby before we could guarantee our fifty-dollar light bill was paid on time, we ignored them. When an aunt suggested that our public affection for one another was a sign we were insecure, we laughed. How insecure she'd like to be, we thought, particularly since she toiled in a loveless marriage year after year. No, we listened to ourselves and analyzed what we wanted to do. And then we went forward, no matter the opinion of others.

Which brings up another aspect of having a successful relationship: listening to each other. Men, myself included, tend to avoid long, serious conversations as much as possible. Women, April included, attempt to have these long, serious conversations as much as possible. How do you listen to each other when you are so different? Again, you compromise.

Men want to be right, and women want to be right. Well, there has to be honesty in all discussions, serious or not. Men have to give up their feeling, often reinforced by other insecure men, that in order to act truly like a man, the man must be obeyed, and obeyed blindly. Men must realize that there are no gods in a happy marriage.

I figured this out because for one, in most arguments, I've found that we're only arguing in the first place because I messed up somehow. Yes, I admit it, and this doesn't make me weak. I've honestly lost most of the arguments in my house because I was wrong in the first place. But here's where other men go wrong: They don't ultimately admit when they have been wrong. They continue to argue for the hell of arguing, hoping that with the anger created, the furor unleashed, and the force demonstrated, though the battle is lost, they can still win the war. But in reality, the only thing that results from this is resentment from your wife, and I guarantee you'll end up resenting it in the future.

As for wives, well, they tend to know they have the upper hand in arguments, and it is equally important for them to not constantly throw that knowledge back in their husbands' faces. What good does it do, besides erode the foundation of the relationship, to tell the husband about how wrong he is all of the time? And if the husband hears this enough, he will think that not only was he wrong on the arguments he constantly hears about, but perhaps he was wrong to get married in the first place. And he may be right.

To avoid these situations, you need what I like to call pre-emptive listening. From the beginning of the relationship, truly care about what the other is saying. Let the words roll into your head and when you don't understand the context or meaning, ask!

As the years went by, some of our friends got married. They'd waited until the time was "right" and entered marriage because both people were where they wanted to be. On paper, these marriages looked promising. Educated, professional, and good-looking, these couples walked down the aisle full of hope. But in less than five years, most had suffered divorces. Why did these marriages and relationships fail, especially when everything seemed so right?

Often, these men and women had become so invested in their own lives, they didn't see a reason to change for anyone. Also, the love was sometimes fleeting. After a few years, they figured out that instead of being in love with their mates, they'd just been in a state of intense like. And now, that wasn't good enough.

The men and women who left these relationships didn't leave unscathed. There were repercussions.

For the men, the disappointment had been that they didn't get what they wanted from the marriage, so they bailed as fast as they could. Who's to tell them to stick with the marriage for the long term? The idea of marriage had been a good one (Lawrence and April are doing great, they'd noted) but the reality of their own marriages didn't match those far-off dreams they'd built up over the years. The dreams were replaced by bitter memories, and they tended to walk around like wounded soldiers. They were damaged goods for the next relationship.

For the women, the disappointment seemed deeper. Those women who had children by their now-former husbands, moved from the secure status of wives to the unsecured status of "baby mamas." They faced an uncertain future that combined the pressures of single womanhood and the desire to still find Mr. Right.

And for the women who didn't have children and yet desired them, the knowledge that it would now take years to find a proper mate, marry, and then have children, was a daunting and depressing prospect. Each date, no matter how small or insignificant, tended to take on much more importance than it did when she was younger.

So, what is the reaction to this relationship desperation? Our friends, both men and women, tend to concentrate even more on something else. Almost obsessively, they search for something to give them a sense of fulfillment beyond the search for a relationship. This look inward has some element of self-deprivation. Some have given up meat and become vegetarians. Others have embraced celibacy, thinking sexual relationships have warped their judgment.

In reality, none of the above is probably true. Most likely, it only takes two people to look into each other's eyes and mean what they say and say what they mean. Can they trust each other enough to risk having a happy relationship in their lives? If they can't answer this affirmatively, they'll continue to search for something that doesn't exist: a happy and loving relationship without honesty and trust.

As for April and me, our marriage continues to thrive, and ten years later, we still make each other laugh, smile, and mad. We're no longer poverty stricken and have been fortunate enough to have reached most of our goals, and we did it together. We take nothing for granted because we know how hard it has been and the obstacles still left in our lives.

Each year, there's an article in a major magazine decrying the failure of Black male and female relationships. According to these articles, sisters are going to give up on Black men and begin marrying White men. And this makes me sad. I'm not sad because of interracial dating, but because Black men and women are so close to each other yet so far apart. And in reality, it doesn't have to be that way. We could fill the gap.

So where does the hope lie for successful Black male and female relationships? It lies in the simple human fact that Black men and Black women need each other. And like water, they find their own level. We need to keep looking for that level. We've survived the evils of slavery, Jim Crow, integration, and modern life, and if you hold out, eventually your prince or princess will come. Just relax, take what comes at you, and adjust accordingly. Most importantly, listen, listen, and listen some more. Listen to your heart and listen to your instincts.

And what is my last bit of information for sisters who want my much-sought-after expertise? Ignore people who give you relationship advice.

Acknowledgments

I have truly been blessed with one of life's greatest pleasures—friendship. The women in my life are like air. I depend on them, I cherish them, and I need them. I often yearn for the simple pleasures of gossip-filled brunches and after-work cups of tea. Thankfully, my girls are always nearby. This work was inspired by the hundreds of conversations I've had over the years about relationships and men. Thank you, Nikki, Vanessa, Rene, Rochelle, Tracy, Erica P., Neneh, Apryl, Katrina, Melissa, Nateena, Renina, Anika, Danette, LaVeta, Ia, Marina, and Vivia for sharing your life experiences, inspiring this collection of essays, and always being a phone call away. I am a better person because of each of you.

Vanessa, you're really the best friend a girl could ask for. I am so proud of the work you're doing. Duron, your friendship means more to me than you'll ever know. I hope that I can one day be as good a friend to you as you've been to me—I love you dearly. Audrey Edwards, thank you for being a role model and mentor. Your guidance, advice (on everything!), and insight on life means so much. I must acknowledge my grandmother, Ethel Molina, a stone-cold fox who still turned heads at seventy-nine years old. Grandma, hopefully you're up in heaven frying chicken wings for the angels. Mom, thank you for being a tremendous source of inspiration and, Dad, thank you for being my biggest supporter and most vocal fan. I love you both. To my Granny and Grandaddy for being the best grandparents in the world. I am so thankful for both of you. Kevin Powell, thank you, thank you, thank you. Your willingness to help me every step of the way made this book what it is today. Jon Berry, you listened to me talk about this book for almost a year and never once did you turn a deaf ear. Thank you for all of your input, advice, and wisdom. Todd Johnson, thank you for throwing the hottest parties in Brooklyn and sending out the world's best e-mails. You really make Brooklyn a better place. Danyel Smith, thank you for being an inspiration to me. You didn't have to meet with me in that Brooklyn coffee shop last year, but you did, and for that, I am grateful. Your words of encouragement and support gave me the courage I needed to move forward with *Sometimes Rhythm, Sometimes Blues.* A special thanks goes out to Susan Zirinsky and Linda Mason at CBS NEWS for being relentless supporters and true mentors. Harold Wilson, the world is a funnier place because you're in it. To my extended family in the Mission—I love you all. Hey Bahama Mamas! Dexter and Phillip Ashby of NYCWEBS.com, thank you for the constant technical support and free Internet access. You two are reminders that there are good brothers everywhere.

Leslie Miller, you are the most supportive editor an editor could ever ask for. Thank you for giving me the freedom and opportunity to bring this idea to life. Do you realize that during the course of this project we've talked on the phone from more than ten different states? You didn't let my hectic travel schedule, multiple e-mail addresses, or ability to procrastinate get in the way of doing this book. You got tough when you needed to be tough, kept me on the straight and narrow, and allowed me to compile a collection of essays that are gutsy, opinionated, and hard-hitting. Personally, you have been a tremendous supporter of my essays over the years, and there's no one else I would have trusted with the production and publication of this book. Thank you for helping me make sense of it all.

Kenyatta, what can I say? You read every single one of these essays over and over and over again. You lived and breathed them alongside me and, although I know you grew tired of listening to me talk about this book, you never stopped being supportive or helping me realize this dream. You sat next to me night after night as I struggled to bring this book to life, and you made me stay awake at night to work on this book after I put in twelve-hour days at the office. Thank you for walking Moxie, making the coffee, and being patient. Even when I was on the road shooting stories, you never let me lose sight of my deadlines or my goals. I am so blessed to have you in my life. I love you.

Most importantly, I must thank each of the writers brave enough to share their stories with the world. You took a chance with me, someone many of you didn't even know. You allowed me to peek and pry into the most private parts of your lives, and ask questions about your relationships that were sometimes uncomfortable, but you never gave up. Instead, you dug deeper and deeper, and through the process of writing and rewriting, you produced essays that will forever be etched into the minds of those who read them. I am so proud of each of you and so grateful to have gotten to know you. Words cannot express how excited I am to present your works to the world.

About the Contributors

Keisha-Gaye Anderson is a diasporic medley, reverberating for you. I am no one new, just spirit rearranged and played in tune to guide you through this new reality and remind you of your humanity. I leave my words with you and hope that you will learn to live your truth. *Circle Unbroken* is my new poetry book. Order a copy at www.keishagaye.com. I've also contributed poetry to *Poems on the Road to Peace*, a Yale University Press anthology. As a journalist for the past nine years, I have worked on cultural and historical documentaries for CBS, PBS, and Japanese TV, and contributed feature articles to magazines such as *Honey, Black Enterprise,* and *Upscale.*

asha bandele is the features editor at *Essence* Magazine. She lives in New York and is the author of several books, including *The Prisoner's Wife.* She is also a poet.

I am **Misumbo Byrd**, an only child, privatized activist, mother of one, hardcore superwoman on the road to spiritual enlightenment. I currently reside in Central Harlem and pray every night for a swift relocation to the lush countryside. Passionate about my parenting, partnering, and political ideas, I currently head Columbia University's Office of Sexual Misconduct Prevention and Education, and I still wonder how it happened that I became a "nine-to-fiver." On a good day, I am bright and sunny. My spiritual goal? To manifest that warmth and clarity each and every day.

Corrie Claiborne is originally from Columbia, South Carolina, and is currently an English professor at Claflin University in Orangeburg, South Carolina. She holds a B.A. from Syracuse University, an M.A. from the University of South Carolina, and a Ph.D. from Ohio State University. Corrie has written and lectured throughout her academic career on the topic of Black women and culture. She was accepted into the 2002 Hurston/Wright Writer's Workshop at Howard University, an invaluable experience that encouraged her to share her voice. Corrie is currently completing her first novel, entitled "Work."

I am a butterfly, flitting from one experience to another, breathing in the nectar, learning from the bitter moondrops of my past. I am eternally smiling because of all the raspberry kisses and spiritually blessed love my Jashed gives to me. I love our child more than my heart can hold, feeling the beauty of each moment as my universe unfolds. Thanking Stenovia and Sweet Charlie Brown for the seed and ovaries, creating a warm, safe womb for me to grow freely. I am **Tina Fakhrid-Deen**—Mother, Wife, Birkenstock Diva, Slacker, Friend, Wench, Sunshine, and Hope for the Flowers. My work has been published in *Venus Magazine, Melanin Magazine, DykeMamasGrrrl Zine,* and *Families Like Mine: Children of Gay Parents Tell It Like It Is.* I am a writer, activist, and performer, currently working on a collection of essays from African-American children with Lesbian/Gay/Bisexual/Transgender parents and on a book, "How to Unlock your Dreadlocks" (yes, it can be done!). Peace.

Leah P. Hollis is from Kenlock, Pennsylvania, a small blue-collar town outside greater Pittsburgh and was born in the late 1960s. My determined parents forged me from an alloy of steel workers, coal mining, World War II, education, and those Southern histories so common to many who migrated North during industrialization. The eldest child of Levi and Clea, I have written several scholarly and creative works over the years with missions and struggles in mind. Just as the Pennsylvania confluence of three rivers flows to the major Mississippi vein which nourishes a nation, the confluence of writings flows rhythmically, vigorously even, to edify and nourish a national consciousness. My contribution to this consciousness includes a series of national conferences and workshops on diversity and student issues. Publications and creative works include pieces with the *Journal of College Student Retention: Research, Theory & Practice, Athletic/Academic Journal,* and the 1998 edition of *The Official Handbook of the National Association of Academic Advisors for Athletes.* Also, I have written two full-length stage plays which progressed to a pre-production level, and, lastly, a full text which chronicles some of my father's professional history, *Echoes from the Halls: Saga of the Johnstown City Schools,* which was released summer, 2002.

My name is **Kimberly Virginia Hoskins**. During the nine years before my birth, my mother vibed on the name Kimberly. Three weeks into the ninth winter of her vibing, and on the ninth day, I answered her call. I am Saturn born; Saturn squares my sun, so the lessons that come my way are hard. Daddy says a hard lesson is a lesson well learned. Spirit inspires me to spin words into silk as I sit in a chrysalis fluttering into butterfly. Heart boomslapslapbooms me to share what I've learned. Desire, weighty, insistent, asks: Can you feel God? Enraptured, I write. Enraptured, I live. First, there was a word, and it took on flesh. Take care the words—watch them manifest. As Y. A. Folayan, I have published poetry in *Catalyst, Nommo 2, Nommo 3,* and an essay in *Black-Eyed Peas for the Soul.*

shani jamila is a traveler, writer, scholar-activist, and cultural worker who first came to voice while an undergrad at Spelman. Since then she has been studying the souls of Black folk in the diaspora through fellowships like the Fulbright, New Voices, and the Graduate Opportunity that afforded her a master's from UCLA in Africana Cultural Studies. A Scorpio who can trace her family back seven generations on both sides, shani is a founding member of the Trinidad & Tobago Ten Sisters poetry collective. She also co-founded a school library in Gabon, Central Africa. Her publications include contributions to *Colonize This! Young Women of Color on Today's Feminism; Race, Class, and Gender: An Anthology;* and *The Encyclopedia of Sociology.* Perpetually in motion, she's visited more than twenty countries and has read from her work on four continents and counting. Currently she's doing international human rights work in D.C. & rockin' waistbeads that jingle lullabies for brown babies yet to be flamenco dancin' through this world with a rose held in her teeth. Posture Proud. Dimples Deep.

Victor LaValle was raised in Flushing and Rosedale, Queens. He graduated from Cornell University with a degree in English and received his M.F.A. in Fiction from Columbia University. He has been a fellow at the Fine Arts Work Center in Provincetown. He lives in Brooklyn, but teaches writing at Mills College. He is the author of two books: *Slapboxing with Jesus,* which was the winner of the Pen Open Book Award, and *The Ecstatic.* LaValle's work has appeared in *Step into a World: An Anthology of the New Black Literature.* LaValle was also profiled in the *Washington Post.*

I, **Danielle K. Little**, write because I am fascinated by lies: the collective ones we live by and the secret ones that haunt and make us who we are. I also write in an attempt to make peace with what is true and I struggle with not letting anything—tribalism, fear of not being beautiful, the literal truth (which as all lawyers know is there for the twisting)—silence me. I see God in the earth (which I've been told makes me a sinner), and I firmly believe that people who don't believe in love at first sight are the true tyrants of the world. My guardian angels are James Baldwin, Nina Simone, and Marilyn Monroe (who, like many of us, was maligned for reasons she did not deserve). My creative work has been published in *Oxford Magazine, Touchstone,* and *Potpourri.* I have also been published in the *New York Law Journal, QBR: The Black Book Review,* and *Black Issues Book Review.* I currently live in California.

Thembisa S. Mshaka is hard at work fulfilling her dream of being an author. Her first book, *Handle Your [music] Business: Her Guide to Entering, Navigating, and Exiting the Record Industry,* is a much-needed career guide for women in music. She pens a music business column of the same name for *Emixshow* magazine. Currently an award-winning senior advertising writer for Sony Music, Thembisa holds the distinction of being the only African-American female rap editor for the renowned music trade *Gavin,* where she introduced D'Angelo, Timbaland, and many other stars to the music world. Her often searing, always insightful writings on women, hip-hop, and urban culture have been published in *Honey,* Launch.com, Essence.com, and The Hotness.com, where she is an editor-at-large. Her work will also appear in "Chicken Soup for the Hip-Hop Soul", slated for a 2005 release. She welcomes feedback on her essay in this volume at handleyourmusicbusiness.com.

The legendary and world-famous poet Nikki Giovanni has said "**Kevin Powell** is pushing to bring, as he has so brilliantly done before, the voices of his generation: the concerns, the cares, the fears, and the fearlessness." A poet, journalist, essayist, editor, cultural curator, hip-hop historian, public speaker, political consultant and fundraiser, and community activist, Kevin Powell is also known for his stint as a cast member on the first season of MTV's *The Real World*. A native of Jersey City, New Jersey, Kevin Powell is now a resident of Brooklyn, New York. It is from his base in New York City that Kevin Powell has published six books, including his most recent, *Who's Gonna Take the Weight? Manhood, Race, and Power in America*. Additionally, Kevin has written numerous essays, articles, and reviews over the past seventeen years for publications such as *Newsweek,* the *Washington Post, Essence, Code, Rolling Stone,* and *Vibe,* where he was a founding staff member and worked as a senior writer.

Shawn E. Rhea is a journalist, essayist, fiction writer, and native of Detroit, Michigan. Her work has appeared in *The Source, Essence, Savoy,* and *YES* magazines; the anthologies *Black Women's Erotica 2* and *When Race Becomes Real: Black and White Writers Confront Their Personal Histories*; the literary journal *Anansi*; and the *New Orleans Times-Picayune* newspaper. Shawn is currently the health reporter for the *Post-Crescent,* a Wisconsin-based Gannett newspaper. She received her bachelor's degree from Howard University and her master's from Columbia University's Graduate School of Journalism.

Lawrence C. Ross, Jr., a.k.a. "L" to his boys, was born, raised, and came back to buy a house in Inglewood, Cali (don't call it "The Wood" cause no one from here does that. It's kinda like callin' Brooklyn "The Lyn.") He is the son of Eveline, husband of April, and father of Langston. Ross has lectured at over one hundred and fifty universities, as he is universally recognized as an expert in the field of African-American fraternities and sororities. He has appeared on National Public Radio, "Good Morning Atlanta," and has been interviewed in *Ebony, Savoy,* and *Essence* magazines, the *Los Angeles Times,* Africana.com, and the *London Times,* among others. A graduate of UCLA, where he received a degree in history, Ross will be studying for a Ph.D. in history beginning in the fall of 2004. He has written two books, including *The Divine Nine: The History of African American Fraternities and Sororities* and *The Ways of Black Folks: A Year in the Life of a People. The Divine Nine* is a multiple *Los Angeles Times, Essence,* and *Blackboard* magazine bestseller.

I first found my voice on July 30, 1968, at Metropolitan hospital, where I was born. To some, it was a shrill cry, but to Rebecca Ruffin, it was music. Since early childhood, I've loved writing, and the rhythms and hues of my home in the Bronx have inspired my words over the years. From the corner bodegas, to the sweet smell of the world's best Italian bakeries, my life has been laced with flavor. My pieces were born between rhymes I sang while jumping double-dutch at age four. My words found their rhythm in the fresh, def jams at the Skate Key roller rink in my teens. Just like my father, Ronald Ruffin, Uptown gave me style. Words are art. I channel that energy when I write. I'm just like the finest graffiti: Many may argue over our value and artistic merit, but no matter what they feel, the words can't be ignored. The BX isn't my only love or source of inspiration. A bad-ass cat named Elmo sits perched atop my computer as protector and writing companion. I have a passion for writing erotic poetry and have started an Internet forum called the Ebony Erotic Lounge. I am currently putting together an anthology by the same title. I've been twice published in the *Nubian Chronicles,* and will keep drawing from the deep well of my surrounding culture, so that I may continue to write and publish. In time, my works will stand as record that **Tracy LaRae Ruffin** indeed has a voice.

Kiini Ibura Salaam is a realistic woman. She likes the feel of a warm bed and understands the necessity of food, so she works. At her day job, she corrects inconsequential errors while remembering mornings spent wrestling with words and sucking meaning from images. She frets, knowing her 9-to-5 threatens her fragile relationship with writing. Yet, she always manages to coax writing back into her graces. She begs writing's absolution with essays published in *Colonize This!, When Race Becomes Real, Roll Call, Men We Cherish, Utne Reader, Essence,* and *Ms.* magazine. She prostrates herself obediently with fiction published in *Mojo: Conjure Stories, Black Silk, When Butterflies Kiss, Dark Matter,* and *Dark Eros.* She tithes her art form with the KIS.list, a monthly e-report on life as a writer. She produces a website—kiiniibura.com—as an altar, an offering of words. Writing, expansive and forgiving, responds with a flood of inspired embraces. Whether she be in her native New Orleans, her adopted Brooklyn, or her beloved Bahia, the writer unabashedly bares herself to the caress of words. She writes with holy gratitude, forever in love with her craft.

Shrona Foreman Sheppard is a journalist whose publishing credits include *USA Today*, the *Washington Times, Navy Times,* and Knight-Ridder newspapers. She lives in Jacksonville, North Carolina, with her husband and their two children. Her first novel, "Roots and Rhythms," will feature a series of vignettes based upon the family narratives she collected as part of her graduate studies at Georgetown University. Ms. Sheppard hopes to publish the work in 2005.

A couple of years ago, I was seriously broke and sleeping on the couches of various friends who lived in various parts of the city when I heard that Lucille Clifton and Sonia Sanchez were giving a reading at the New School. I was exhausted and hungry from weeks of barely eating, but I took my last little bit of money and headed downtown. Maybe it was because it was so soon after September 11, but when I got there, the entire audience was a little bit sleepy, a little bit sad. Yet the moment these two energetic poets entered the room, a glow spread over the room, and it only grew brighter as they read the most beautiful, life-affirming poems that I'd ever heard. During that moment, I, **Rochelle Nicole Spencer**, felt stronger and refreshed. What's more is that I also felt a sense of pride, because I realized at that moment that art was as important to me as food. And guess what? When I left the reading, I wasn't even hungry anymore.

I am **Denise Burrell-Stinson**, thirty years old and a native New Yorker, although my genealogy reaches far beyond these hectic city limits into places like South Carolina and Barbados. Through writing I hope to salute my foremothers and forefathers by exceeding their accomplishments while living up to the lofty expectations that many lifetimes of interminable hard work and unshakable faith have set before me. I am equally inspired and intimidated by the power of writing to give matter form and form function, to reinvent the mundane as exceptional. It is my hope that my own contributions to the craft will properly salute the legacy of those I have adopted as my creative ancestors (Ralph Ellison, Flannery O'Connor, Jamaica Kincaid, etc.) and those who I have had the good fortune to give to me as blood ancestors (Victoria, Sharon, Sherwood, Sr. and Jr., Tom). To others who are doing the same, keep up the hard work! I have a B.A. in politics from Princeton University and my work has appeared in *Elle* (South Africa edition), *Heart & Soul, Latin Girl,* Fashion-WireDaily.com, and OnlyReal.com.

I am **Richard Anthony Symister**, a.k.a. Imhotep. I am the product of Jamaican heritage, strict parents (one of whom died when I was fairly young) and a Gemini mind usually at war with itself. Since I was a child, I have always written to escape, to reach a catharsis and release any demons that still haunt my mind's catacombs. My tortuous (or "winding" since some may confuse "tortuous" with "torturous") literary path has taken me to university journals, state representative headquarters, homeless shelters, and finally, back to myself where I've discovered that to maintain my passion and vigor, I must write about people, places, and things that make my heart race and my stomach twist. I must write about things that I hate as well as love. My latest venture, "The Melanin Project," is my first full-length novel involving a little sci-fi, a little love, a little mystery, and a lot of dual Gemini influence. Hetepu (much peace and tranquility).

Cheo Tyehimba writes to rearrange worlds. He is an award-winning journalist, an editor, author, and college writing instructor. His writing has been published in *Savoy, Entertainment Weekly,* the *Washington Post,* and *O, The Oprah Magazine,* among other publications. He is currently writing "When It Is," a slightly supernatural story collection about the mystery and power of Black love.

My name is **Amontaine Aurore Woods**. I am the youngest of four girls born to Charles and Ophelia. I come from a strong people. We are fighters. We are doers. We are "overcomers." I sometimes see myself in my mother's slanted eyes, in my father's high, worried forehead, in the tight lips of my aunt. I hear myself in the honey voices of my three sisters. Their straight backs and large hands are like my mirrors.

I am fortunate, for often there is a beautiful and defiant thing that bites me on my shoulder, pulls my hair, kicks me in my groin, for it will not be ignored. It demands that I pay heed to the hidden self, to the ball of life within, crying to be seen and heard, like crazy or impassioned women banished to the attic. And so it is through writing that I bring it forth, giving birth to what could have been forever stifled, if not for the urgency of art. The words, whether painfully constipated or fast and furious do, by the grace of God, get onto the page. And lo and behold, there I am. A "me" not palpable until that moment. And then I sit back, stroke my chin in deep thought and trip on what else, who else could be trapped inside, fighting to be born. My articles and essays have been published in *The Raven Chronicles, Aim* magazine,

Colors NW, Midwest Express magazine, and others. I am the recipient of several literary grants. I am completing my first novel.

Kristal Brent Zook is a New York–based writer and adjunct professor at Columbia University's Graduate School of Journalism. Her work has appeared in *Essence, Savoy,* the *Village Voice, L.A. Weekly,* the *Washington Post,* the *New York Times Magazine,* and many other outlets. She is author of *Color by Fox: The Fox Network and the Revolution in Black Television.* Kristal Brent Zook can be reached at www.kristalbrentzook.com.

I am **Taigi Smith,** the only child of Debbie, born in 1972, and granddaughter of women named Ethel and Marion. I am a child of San Francisco, a descendant of Pennsylvania Blacks and Indians, an offspring of women with calloused hands, strong backs, and hardened feet. There are stories in my head that plague me when they are ignored; words in my mind, vivid pictures that beg to be validated. I write because as a network news producer, I have seen more, heard more, and been more places than I ever thought possible. The need to write these stories overwhelms me, and more than anything else, I fear that I will forget these things when I grow old. Just as Debbie, and Marion, and Ethel have verbally immortalized themselves through me, I must eternalize myself through words. I am haunted by the need to be remembered, driven by the desire not to forget.

About the Editor

 Taigi Smith is a network news producer and freelance writer living in Brooklyn, New York. Her work has been published in the *San Francisco Chronicle, New York Newsday, Honey, OneWorld Magazine,* and several literary anthologies including *Step into a World, Colonize This!, Listen Up,* and *Testimony.* Smith is a graduate of Mills College and grew up in San Francisco.

Selected Titles from Seal Press

Colonize This!: Young Women of Color on Today's Feminism
edited by Daisy Hernández and Bushra Rehman. $16.95, 1-58005-067-0.
It has been decades since women of color first turned feminism upside
down. Now a new generation of brilliant, outspoken women of color is
speaking to the concerns of a new feminism, and their place in it.

Listen Up: Voices from the Next Feminist Generation edited by
Barbara Findlen. $16.95, 1-58005-054-9. A revised and expanded edi-
tion of the Seal Press classic, featuring the voices of a new generation of
women expressing the vibrancy and vitality of today's feminist movement.

Body Outlaws: Rewriting the Rules of Beauty and Body Image edited
by Ophira Edut, foreword by Rebecca Walker. $15.95, 1-58005-108-1.
Filled with honesty and humor, this groundbreaking anthology offers stories by those who have chosen to ignore, subvert, or redefine the dominant beauty standard in order to feel at home in their bodies.

***Without a Net: The Female Experience of Growing Up Working
Class*** edited by Michelle Tea. $14.95, 1-58005-103-0. The first anthology
in which women with working-class backgrounds explore how growing
up poor impacts identity.

Seal Press publishes many books of fiction and nonfiction by women
writers. Please visit our Web site at **www.sealpress.com**.